State, power and politics in the making of the modern Middle East

This book is a comprehensive introduction to the politics of the Middle East for all those wishing to understand contemporary developments in the region. It covers the Arab countries, plus Turkey, Israel and Iran, providing unique comparative treatment of such central topics as the growth of the state and the political response of Middle Eastern governments to the economic crises of the 1970s and 1980s.

In Part I Roger Owen traces the political history of the Middle East since the creation of the state system at the end of the First World War. In Part II he looks in detail at a number of key themes in the recent development of the region: the role of the military, the role of religious organizations, the politics of economic restructuring, the dynamics of one party rule and the return to greater democracy. The book provides an analysis of the extent to which the Middle East has changed since the creation of the state system and it looks at the possibility of further democratization in the region.

Roger Owen is a leading authority on Middle Eastern politics and has taught at St Antony's College, Oxford for the past twenty-five years. He has lectured widely on the Middle East and is a regular contributor to a variety of newspapers and journals, including *The Times* and *The Los Angeles Times*. He is also the author of numerous books about the Middle East and the series editor of the *Making of the Modern Middle East* series.

D0377484

State, power and politics in the making of the modern Middle East

Roger Owen

London and New York

First published 1992
by Routledge
11 New Fetter Lane, London EC4P 4EE

Simultaneously published in the USA and Canada
by Routledge
29 West 35th Street, New York, NY 10001

Reprinted 1993

© 1992 Roger Owen

Typeset in 10/12pt Times by
Falcon Typographic Art Ltd, Fife, Scotland
Printed and bound in Great Britain by
Biddles Ltd, Guildford and King's Lynn

*A catalogue reference for this title is available from the
British Library*

ISBN 0–415–07590–4
     0–415–07591–2

Library of Congress Cataloging in Publication Data
   Owen, Roger, 1935–
   State, power, and politics in the making of the modern
   Middle East / Roger Owen.
   Includes bibliographical references and index.
   1. Middle East – Politics and government. 2. Africa,
   North – Politics and government. I. Title.
   DS63.094   1992
   320.956 – dc20   91–41501   CIP

ISBN 0–415–07590–4
     0–415–07591–2

About thirty years ago there was much talk that geology ought only to observe and not theorize: and I well remember someone saying that at this rate a man might as well go into a gravel pit and count the pebbles and describe the colours. How odd it is that anyone should not see that all observation must be for or against some view if it is to be of any service.

Charles Darwin to Henry Fawcett, 1861

For Ben

Contents

List of tables

Preface

This book is the first of a series which aims at providing a good, general introduction to the individual countries of the Middle East and to some of the major processes that have dominated its recent political and social history. For our purposes the region has been defined in large terms to include the 20 member states of the Arab League in West Asia and North Africa (less Mauritania and Somalia), as well as Israel, Iran and Turkey. This is more or less the area known in Britain as the Near and Middle East until the Second World War, when reference to the Near East was dropped in most official documents, following a lead from Winston Churchill. As for its history, we have decided to confine ourselves almost exclusively to the 20th century, limiting reference to earlier periods to those events and processes which we feel are necessary for a proper understanding of the present. Lastly, we have included Turkey as a Middle Eastern state on the grounds of its long historical connection with the region, even though we are well aware that many Turks (as well as the editors of *Le Monde* and the *Financial Times*) now regard it as part of Europe.

It is also important to say something about our intended audience. The series is aimed at the non-specialist, or 'first-time', western reader who wants to understand more about a part of the world which, although constantly in the news, continues to be presented as mysterious, unpredictable and subject to its own, usually violent, laws of motion. In trying to present a deeper, more realistic, more rounded, account we run all the usual risks encountered by those who set themselves up as cultural middlemen and who attempt to explain one set of political practices to people who live and work in terms of quite another. This is a project with many pitfalls, as Edward Said and others have forcefully pointed out. But there are also ways of trying to minimize such dangers.

One is to choose authors who have lived many years in the region itself and who are in a position to use their own experiences as a check on the knowledge they have gained from the printed page. Another is to ask whether the picture they present is one that will be recognized as true, or mostly true, by the people who live in the Middle East itself. This, after all, is how we tend to judge the work of any outsider writing about ourselves.

To turn to this present volume, here my aim is to provide a general introduction to the recent political history of the Middle East. The first major theme is the emergence of the individual states, the creation of their particular national institutions and the interaction between them. This is treated in historical fashion in Part I, with particular emphasis on the construction of the Middle East state system following the break-up of the Ottoman Empire at the end of the First World War, the influence of British and French colonialism, the enormous increase in centralized administrative and political power in the early independence period and, finally, the particular pattern of inter-state relations that came to dominate the area from the 1930s onwards. There is also a chapter dealing briefly with historical developments in Iran, Israel and Turkey which took a somewhat different course from those in the majority of Arab states.

Some of the major themes arising from this analysis are then treated in greater detail in Part II. These include the expanding role of the military within the political system; the politics of economic restructuring; the character of Middle Eastern political parties; the various attempts to define (and to re-define) democratic practice; and the changing relationship between religion and politics in a number of Muslim countries.

There are various reasons for adopting this particular type of approach. The first is that the region contains too many major states to allow the conventional, country-by-country, treatment. Second, it is my belief that there are a number of significant issues; for example, such questions as: What is a party? How are elections conducted? Where are the boundaries between the public and the private, the religious and the secular, the military and the civil? which are very much better analysed on a comparative basis, with examples from a variety of different countries.

A third, and much more important, reason stems from the attempt to tackle one of the most vexatious questions involved in analysing the politics of any particular region of the world: What is it that the various states and societies and systems have in common? As far as the Middle East itself is concerned, this problem is usually treated in an essentialist and reductionist fashion, which sees the key to the whole region in terms of a shared element of religion, geography and race. From such a perspective – and to parody it only slightly – what unites the Middle East, as well as providing an explanation for almost everything that happens there, is the fact that the majority of its people are Arabs and Muslims who lived (at least until very recently) in deserts. This view is then very often combined with a second, equally unhelpful, notion of the unchanging East, in which, underneath the hectic pace of superficial change, things remain for ever the same, whether in terms of tribalism, dictatorial rule or the desire of people to kill each other in the name of religion.

For my own part, views of this kind are simplistic, say nothing about historical change and explain very little. Nevertheless, they are so deeply embedded in so much of the work on the Middle East – by Middle Easterners themselves, as well as outsiders – that they require a major effort to counter them. In my opinion this is best done by beginning from a perspective that sees the Middle East first and foremost as part of the Third, or non-European, World, and subject to most of the same universal historical processes, from colonial rule, through the era of planning and development to the present era of a much more eclectic pattern of political and economic management. Such an approach has many advantages. It opens up the Middle East to international comparison, and draws on a much larger body of useful economic and political analysis. It suggests a number of important themes for closer examination, such as single party rule or the introduction of various types of managed democracy. It gets away from the idea of the region as a special type of area with its own distinctive form of society, of political behaviour and of cultural expression. And it provides a check against those kinds of explanations that rely on the notion of Middle Eastern exclusivity; for example, the idea that it is Islam that encourages a tendency towards military rule, when, in fact, the politically ambitious soldier, like so much else in the region, is essentially a Third World phenomenon.

A final note: as this series is intended primarily for readers of English, I have tried to cite the majority of references in that

Acknowledgements

This book relies not only on the usual printed and documentary sources but also, more importantly, on the people I have met since my first visits to Israel, Jordan, Lebanon and Egypt in 1956. I also owe a particular debt of gratitude to Mark Cohen who masterminded the creation of the series of which this is the introduction, and to my many friends and colleagues with whom I have discussed the study of Middle Eastern politics over the years, whether at St Antony's College, at the MERIP offices in Washington, or during the regular meetings of the Middle East Discussion Group in Britain and the Joint Near and Middle East Committee of the Social Science Research Council in New York and elsewhere. The book could not have been written without them.

In addition, I would like to give special thanks to Joel Beinin, Caglar Keyder and Charles Tripp for helpful comments on particular chapters; to Michael Shalev, Elizabeth Picard and Nazih Ayubi for lending me some of their ideas; and to Talal Asad, Huri Islamoglu, Ghassan Salamé, Tim Mitchell and Sami Zubaida for their influence on my thinking throughout the book.

List of abbreviations

ACC	Arab Co-operation Council
ANAP	Motherland Party (Turkey)
ASU	Arab Socialist Union (Egypt)
CIA	Central Intelligence Agency (USA)
CU	Constitutionalists' Union (Morocco)
DMC	Democratic Movement for Change (Israel)
DISK	Confederation of Revolutionary Workers' Unions (Turkey)
DP	Democrat Party (Turkey)
FDIC	Front pour la Défense des Institutions Constitutionelles (Morocco)
FIS	Islamic Salvation Front (Algeria)
FLN	National Liberation Front (Algeria)
GCC	Gulf Co-operation Council
IDF	Israeli Defence Force
IBRD	International Bank for Reconstruction and Development (World Bank)
IMF	International Monetary Fund
IRP	Islamic Republic Party (Iran)
JP	Justice Party (Turkey)
MP	Mouvement Populaire (Morocco)
MTI	Mouvement de Tendance Islamique (Tunisia)
MAN	Movement of Arab Nationalists
NAP	National Action Party (Turkey)
NDP	National Democratic Party (Egypt)
NIF	National Islamic Front (Sudan)
NRP	National Religious Party (Israel)
NSP	National Salvation Party (Turkey)
NUC	National Unity Committee (Turkey)
OYAK	Armed Forces Assistance Fund (Turkey)

PDRY	People's Democratic Republic of Yemen (former South Yemen)
PLO	Palestine Liberation Organization
PSD	Parti Socialiste Destourien (Tunisia)
RCD	Rassemblement Constitutionnel Democratique (Tunisia) Rally for Culture and Democracy (Algeria)
RNI	National Independents' Rally (Morocco)
RPP	Republican People's Party (Turkey)
PSP	Progressive Socialist Party (Lebanon)
SHP	Socialist Democratic Populist Party (Turkey)
SODEP	Social Democratic Party (Turkey)
SSNP	Syrian Socialist Nationalist Party
SSU	Sudan Socialist Union (Sudan)
TUSAID	Turkish Industrialists' and Businessmen's Association
UAE	United Arab Emirates
UC	Union Constitutionnel (Morocco)
UGTT	Union Générale des Travailleurs Tunisiens
UMT	Union Marocaine du Travail (Morocco)
UNFP	Union Nationale des Forces Populaires (Morocco)
UNTT	Union Nationale des Travailleurs Tunisiens (Tunisia)
USAID	United States Aid Agency
USFP	Union Socialiste des Forces Populaires (Morocco)

Part I

States and state building

Introduction

The five chapters of Part I are concerned with the establishment and consolidation of the various modern Middle Eastern states which emerged out of the Ottoman and Persian empires at the end of the 19th and the beginning of the 20th centuries. My approach to the concept of 'state' employed here requires some explanation.

As has often been pointed out, ideas about the state – or the nation state – come straight from western historical experience. They were, as Sami Zubaida points out, part of the 'compulsory model' when it came to establishing new political units in the non-European world, if only for the lack of any viable alternative.[1] In these circumstances it seems possible to analyse the Middle East using definitions of the word 'state' that also come from western political thought, provided this is done with care and by paying attention to local differences. In Zubaida's succinct phrase, Middle Eastern states are not western states but they are 'like western states'.[2] They are also 'modern' states, in the sense that they employ distinctive practices and distinctive ways of organizing the societies they control which are only to be found in the modern world.[3]

A second point to note is that there are a number of different definitions of the word 'state' to be found in the literature, many with their own associated vocabularies and theoretical perspectives. In what follows I will make use of two such definitions: the notion of the state as a sovereign political entity with international recognition, its own boundaries, its own flag, and so on; and the notion of the state as the supreme coercive and rule-making body. However, it seems to me that neither of these definitions is without its problems, and that they require amplification and elaboration in a number of ways which need specification.

A useful starting place is the observation that both of the

above definitions consist, in essence, of claims to sovereignty and authority, which first have to be established and then constantly re-justified. How this is done depends, in part, on the resources available to those who control the central administration, whether in terms of finance, of power, of bureaucratic capacities or of ideological appeal. But it is also a question of presentation, in the sense that rulers, typically, attempt to reinforce their claims by the use of discourses and practices that stress the coherence of the state apparatus and its separateness and distinctiveness from the rest of society. Such a project is perhaps most easily attempted in a colonial situation where the state – in terms of both of the above definitions – is very obviously a foreign construct, run largely by foreign personnel and based on power derived from sources that exist quite outside the country in question. However, the rulers of many post-independent states were also able to produce much the same type of effect via the creation of authoritarian systems of government or, in the case of republican Turkey, by building on the statist bureaucratic practices of the late Ottoman period. Once achieved, the advantages of being able to present the state as a single, coherent, abstract enterprise are numerous. It maximizes the rulers' own power. It encourages fear and respect, as well as the undivided loyalty of the people. It helps the government to control its own officials. And it makes it more difficult for any internal divisions within the administration to be used against it.

The next point to underline is that a discussion of the claims made on behalf of any particular state does not, in fact, tell you a great deal about what it really is. As Philip Abrams has argued, states are not single things – however much those who control them may wish us to believe that they are – but, rather, a bundle of structures, institutions, arenas, practices and claims.[4] I would also like to suggest that the reality of any particular bundle is best examined in concrete historical situations, and at various levels. An especially useful starting point is an examination of those moments when the process of classifying the different parts of a state system, of defining their interrelationship and then of drawing a boundary round them is at its most open, for example, at the beginning of the colonial, or of the immediate post-independence, period.

A last introductory point concerns the extremely difficult question of how to analyse the relationship between state and society. Here, it seems to me, the challenge is one of being able to illustrate the complexity of this relationship without being forced into the position of characterizing the state as autonomous, that is, as something that simply acts upon society from a position quite outside it. As to how this might be done, I have only enough space to offer a few notes.[5] First, the modern Middle Eastern state was being created at a time when Middle Eastern society was itself subject to many of the same processes of transformation to be found at work throughout the non-European world. These would include, par excellence, a type of capitalist development in which, in very general terms, expanding international trade, increasing agricultural specialization and the beginnings of modern industry act to dissolve the old solidarities and to replace them with others based on the emergence of the individual citizen as peasant, or farmer or worker, and so to the possibility of the formation of new forms of association based on class.

Second, relations between state and society have to be seen as being constructed over time in a way that is, again, particularly characteristic of the modern world. The very notion of society itself as something to be organized, arranged, separated into discrete components, is itself a relatively recent formulation. So too are most of the methods by which this is described, for example, the conceptual division into the public (the sphere of the state) and the private (the sphere of society), or the idea of the people as a group of persons with legally defined and circumscribed identities such as man and woman, parent and child, property owner, and so on. It should be noted here that the process of establishing these new categories is always a lengthy one, which is always contested and can never be complete; boundaries between categories remain ambiguous and fuzzy, attempts to enclose people are subject to continual challenge.

Third, the construction of the relationship between state and society takes place at the same time as, and is always strongly influenced by, the establishment of what Zubaida has called a 'national political field', within which almost all significant political activities are then focused.[6] The hardening of the external boundaries at the frontier acts to inhibit cross-border interactions and to re-direct all assertions of local power or interests towards the new centre. Meanwhile, the majority of what seem at first sight to be simply atavistic responses to the new order have to be interpreted as attempts to influence the government in some way. A good illustration of this is the *fatwa* issued by the Shi'i *ulama* (clergy) of Najaf and Karbala in November 1922 protesting against the proposal to hold elections for a new Iraqi constituent assembly, something that is often described as a 'traditional' or non-modern act but which is better viewed as an attempt to protect their role as unelected leaders of their community within the framework of the developing Iraqi political system.[7] For the rest, more and more of the political process tends to take place in terms of the arenas, the institutions and the vocabularies that are nurtured and promoted by the state.

Fourth, and finally, the modern state has a special and problematic relationship with another constructed entity, the nation. In the Middle East, as elsewhere, state formation took place during a period when peoples were being invited to imagine themselves, and often to act, as members of a variety of different communities, some tribal and local or narrowly religious, others larger, such as pan-Arab, pan-Turkish, Zionist or Pan-Islamic. Different regimes then attempted both to accommodate and to control this process in terms of the practices they developed towards frontiers, passports, legal systems and so forth, although all the time being pushed in the direction of establishing one fixed and singular identity for their citizens. To understand the way this process played out in Middle Eastern terms requires that the relationship between state, nation and religious community be examined not only at the cultural and imaginative level but also in terms of particular types of political and administrative forms.

Turning at last to the way I want to approach the history of the various Middle Eastern states, it seems useful to divide them into three – the colonial state, the immediate post-independent state and the authoritarian state – each with its own particular politics and practices and policies. Chapter 1 looks at the first two of these phases as far as the major Arab countries are concerned and Chapters 2 and 3 the third. This is then followed by a chapter (4) that examines the interaction between the many Arab states in terms of the various solidarities that their people shared, and the contradictions between their desire for greater political unity and their fear of many of its consequences.

The 20th-century histories of the three major non-Arab states are dealt with in Chapters 1 and 5. These followed a somewhat different trajectory. All three were influenced by their experience of foreign intervention and control. But in each case the actual creation of the states themselves was the work of powerful groups within their own national societies, often drawing on a considerable history of organizational and political development. This at once provided them with a greater continuity with what had gone before, and a greater latitude when it came to their efforts at institutionalizing state/society relations.

Notes

1 Sami Zubaida, *Islam, the People and the State* (London and New York: Routledge, 1989), p. 121.
2 Ibid., p. 145.
3 Talal Asad, 'Conscripts of Western civilization', in Christine Gailey (ed.), *Essays in Honor of Stanley Diamond* (forthcoming).
4 'Notes on the difficulty of studying the state', *The Journal of Historical Sociology*, 1/1 (March, 1988), pp. 58–89.
5 This train of thought is amplified in Timothy Mitchell and Roger Owen, 'Defining the state in the Middle East: Report on a workshop', *Bulletin of the Middle East Studies Association of North America*, 24/2 (1990). See also, Timothy Mitchell, 'The limits of the state: beyond statist approaches and their critics', *American Political Science Review*, 85/1 (1991).
6 Zubaida, *Islam, the People and the State*, pp. 126, 162.
7 Described in Peter Sluglett, *Britain in Iraq 1914–1932* (London: Ithaca Press, 1976), pp. 82–3.

1 The end of empires: the emergence of the modern Middle Eastern states

The end of The Ottoman Empire

At the beginning of this century the Middle East was still dominated by the Ottoman Empire, a world empire that had existed for some 400 years. Although its main strength derived from its provinces in Europe, it also controlled extensive territories in the Arab lands of the eastern end of the Mediterranean including what are now known as Syria, Iraq, Lebanon, Jordan, North Yemen and Israel/Palestine. Furthermore, it maintained a foothold in North Africa round Tripoli and Benghazi in Libya, although it had lost control of the rest of its possessions along the African coast, either to the British (Egypt) or the French (Algeria and Tunisia). Only the lands on the very frontiers of the region, Persia and the central Arabian peninsula in the east and Morocco in the west, had managed to resist the exercise of direct Ottoman power. Everywhere else in the Middle East, centuries of rule by governors who owed their ultimate allegiance to Istanbul had produced a legacy of Ottoman administrative practice and Ottoman culture which continued to affect political life in countless important ways.

Nevertheless, for all its size and importance, the rulers of the empire had spent the last hundred years trying to confront the growing power of a Europe driven on by the influence of the two great revolutions that it had experienced at the end of the 18th century: the political revolution in France from 1789 onwards; and the industrial revolution in Britain. One result was the nibbling away of the frontiers of the empire in Africa and West Asia, marked by the establishment of European colonies and spheres of influence. Another was the repeated attempts to reform and to revive the Ottoman imperial structure as a way of defending itself against foreign domination. By the beginning of the 20th century these reforms had done much to transform the legal and administrative practices throughout the empire but only at the expense of allowing Europe an increasing economic and cultural presence, and of stirring up incipient nationalist movements among many of its subject peoples, like the Armenians of Anatolia and the Maronite Christians of Mount Lebanon.

The effect of these processes intensified greatly in the years just before 1914. A series of Balkan wars led to the loss of most of the empire's remaining possessions in Europe, while the Italians took advantage of Ottoman weakness to make a sustained attack on the region around Tripoli in North Africa. Meanwhile, the Young Turk Revolution of 1908 had brought to power a group of officers and officials dedicated not only to the accelerated reform of Ottoman institutions but also to an incipient Turkish nationalism which threatened to drive a wedge between the Turks who controlled the empire and the Arabs who had previously been regarded as their main partners. This placed something of a strain on the loyalties of many Arab army officers and civil servants, although very few of them went so far as to argue the need for a state, or states, of their own. It was difficult for them to imagine a world without the Ottoman sultan as their political and (if they were Muslims) their religious leader. It was equally obvious that the Ottoman state – with its army, its flag and its embassies in Europe – was their only protector against further European encroachment. Nowhere was this better understood than in Palestine, where Arab concern that the Ottomans were not doing enough to contain Jewish immigration and Zionist colonization was tempered by the realization that turning away from the Ottomans to a great power like the British or the French for support would be like jumping from a familiar frying-pan into a still more dangerous fire.

The Ottoman military defeat by the British and French during the First World War produced a radical change throughout the whole Middle East. As a result of treaties negotiated during the war itself, the Arab provinces of the empire were carved up into a number of successor states, each of them under the control of one or other of the victorious powers: the new Syria and Lebanon under the French; the new Iraq, Palestine and Trans-Jordan under the British. However, there was also a half-hearted attempt by Britain and France to bring the Arabs themselves into the picture. This was partly because some Arabs, notably the Hashemite

rulers of the Hijaz, had become their military allies against
the Ottomans during the war; and partly as a concession to
what the British sometimes referred to as 'the spirit of the
age', a phrase that suggested the need to come to terms with
the emphasis that the Americans and some of the founders of
the new League of Nations were now giving to such powerful
notions as freedom and self-determination. The result was the
invention of a new instrument of political control, the mandate,
which was used to legitimize British and French government of
their Middle Eastern possessions. This had many of the features of
an old-fashioned colony but it also required the mandate holders
to submit to certain internationally sanctioned guidelines, notably
the need to establish constitutional governments in the new states
as a way of preparing their peoples for eventual independence.
One of the most important set of guidelines was in Mandatory
Palestine, where Britain was required, by treaty, to implement the
provisions of the Balfour Declaration of November 1917 calling for
the establishment of a Jewish national home.

The new order in the Middle East was not accepted tamely by
many of its inhabitants. There was a serious revolt against Britain in
Iraq in 1920, and anti-British, as well as anti-Jewish, disturbances in
Palestine in the same year. Meanwhile, France's attempt to take up
its mandate in Syria was challenged, first by the Arab government
that had established itself in Damascus after the Turkish retreat, then
by a series of rural revolts culminating in the country-wide uprising
of 1925–7. All such challenges were contained in the mandated
territories. But in Egypt, where Britain had declared a protectorate
in 1914, the rebuff given to nationalist attempts to send a delegation
– or *wafd* – to the Paris Peace Conference stimulated a widespread
revolt in 1919 that was serious enough to cause a major change in
British policy and a unilateral grant of qualified independence in 1922.
There was even stronger resistance in Anatolia, where efforts by a
number of European powers to create military spheres of influence
led to a rallying of Turkish forces behind General Mustafa Kemal
(later Ataturk) and the creation of the Turkish Republic in 1922.
Much the same happened in Persia, where Reza Khan (later Reza
Shah) used his army to regain control of the whole country from the
British, the Russians and the tribal forces that established themselves
in many of its provinces during and after the war.

Nevertheless, in spite of all local resistance, there is no doubt
that by the mid-1920s the British and the French were the masters

of the Middle East. It was they who determined almost all of the new boundaries; they who decided who should rule, and what form of governments should be established; and it was also they, in association with the Americans, who had a major say in how access to the region's natural resources should be allocated, particularly the oil fields that were just beginning to be discovered along the Persian Gulf and in the Mosul district of northern Iraq. Such was Britain's and France's strength that even the rulers of nominally independent countries like Turkey, Egypt and Persia (renamed Iran in 1925) were forced to recognize the new boundaries and the new order, while those like Abd al-Aziz Ibn Saud, who aspired to create a new state in Arabia after his defeat of the Hashemites, knew that he could only achieve this goal with British assistance and support. Writing in the early 1960s, Elizabeth Monroe could refer to the period 1914 to 1956 as Britain's 'moment' in the Middle East.[1] But short as this period now seems, it was then that the framework for Middle Eastern political life was firmly laid – together with many of its still unsolved problems involving disputed boundaries, inappropriate political institutions or the existence of many national minorities which either failed to obtain a state of their own, like the Kurds, or were prevented from doing so by *force majeure*, like the Palestinians.

The political practices of a colonial state

Strictly speaking there were only a handful of real colonies in the Middle East in the 20th century: Aden (British), Libya (Italian) and Algeria (French). For the rest, imperial power was exercised under a variety of different names, most notably mandates and protectorates but also by treaty (as in Trucial Oman) and in one case by condominium (the Anglo-Egyptian Sudan) – see map. There were important differences, too, in types of government: for example, monarchical or republican; in the degree of direct and indirect rule; and in the political importance of local European settler communities, whether of the same nationality as the ruling power, like the French in Algeria, or another, like the Jews in Palestine.

Nevertheless, for the purpose of analysing the Middle Eastern political systems of the post-First World War period, a useful starting point is provided by the observation that there existed a particular pattern of control known as the 'colonial state'.[2] This

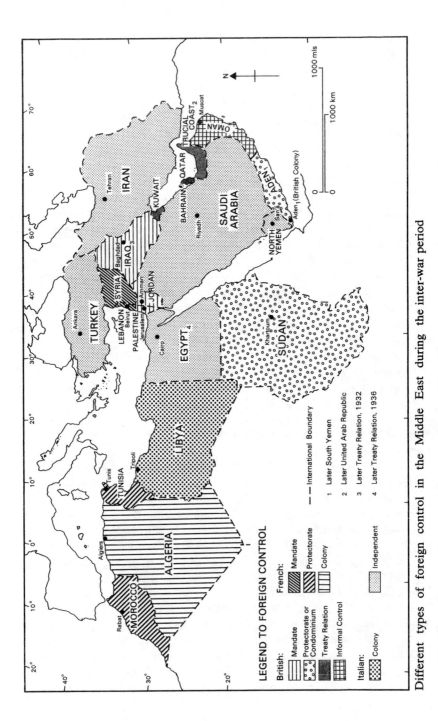

LEGEND TO FOREIGN CONTROL

British:
- Mandate
- Protectorate or Condominium
- Treaty Relation
- Informal Control

French:
- Mandate
- Protectorate
- Colony

Italian:
- Colony

- Independent

— International Boundary

1 Later South Yemen
2 Later United Arab Republic
3 Later Treaty Relation, 1932
4 Later Treaty Relation, 1936

Different types of foreign control in the Middle East during the inter-war period can then be used to highlight a number of general features that shaped the exercise of power and defined the political arena in most of the countries created or dominated by the Europeans. I will group these features under three headings: central administration; the policies of the colonial power; and colonialism as a conduit for external influences.

Central administration

As far as the Middle East was concerned, it was generally the dominant colonial power that first created the essential features of a state, by giving it a capital, a legal system, a flag and internationally recognized boundaries. In some cases this was done on the basis of some pre-existing administrative entity, as in Algeria; in others it involved either detaching some part of a former Ottoman province (for example, Trans-Jordan) or, more usually, adding several provinces together (for example, Syria and Iraq). This gave many of the new states a somewhat artificial appearance, with their new names, their new capitals, their lack of social homogeneity and their dead-straight boundaries that were so obviously the work of a British or French colonial official using a ruler. However, this point can be pushed too far. Very often there was an administrative logic which defined, if not the boundaries, then at least the area to be controlled from one central location like Tunis or Jerusalem. Very often, too, some of the vital processes thought essential to state building were already under way in the late Ottoman period, for example, the creation of bureaucracies, regional markets and the beginnings of the breakdown of what are usually called 'traditional' social units like the tribe or the extended family. However, this is a hotly debated point, particularly among Arab nationalists, for whom the notion of 'artificiality' is a key argument in favour of Arab unity, and many orientalist historians, who continue to see religious and ethnic communities as more basic forms of political organization and reference than citizenship or local nationality. I will return to this important argument many times in this and later chapters.

Once a specific territorial state was established, other things quickly followed. One was the attempt to enumerate, control and define the people who lived there. This involved, among other things, the organization of a census and the passage of a law laying down the principles upon which the nationality of citizens was usually to be based. In the case of the new Arab states, the latter was usually based on a combination of the notion of territory (that is, all people living within the new boundaries at a certain point in time) and family (that is, people descended from someone born in the country before a certain date), as in the Trans-Jordanian nationality law of the late 1920s. A second consequence was the need to control and police the new borders in order to prevent incursions, smuggling and illegal migration. And a third was the conclusion of treaties with neighbouring states involving rights of passage and the extradition of persons wanted for certain kinds of illegal activity. Naturally, few of the early efforts in any of these directions were particularly effective, and tribes and nomads continued to wander across borders and in and out of the new states as if none of the new controls existed. Nevertheless, they had an important part to play in consolidating the role of the political centre, and paved the way for the emergence of the much stronger and more powerful regimes of the post-Second World War period.

The new states were also given new bureaucracies and a new emphasis on homogeneity and equality. There was now to be one centre of authority, issuing standard rules and regulations which were supposed to be applied equally to all those who lived within its boundaries as citizens. However, as in many other aspects of state building, this ideal took many years to establish, the more so as the colonial regimes and their successors had their own security to think of, as well as a number of obvious constraints such as the existence of white settlers with entrenched privileges, the commitment given to the League of Nations to protect religious minorities, and so on. One important instance of this concerned religious identity. In theory, at least, a modern state is implicitly secular, in the sense that laws are made by the civil, not the religious, authorities, and are supposed to apply equally to all, whether members of a dominant religious community or not. In the Middle Eastern context, however, the effect of such principles was considerably diluted as groups defined in religious terms were not only given special rights of self-management but were also allocated a place within the political system on a communal rather than an individual basis. Hence seats were reserved for minorities in most colonial legislatures, a process that was taken to its extreme in Lebanon, where representation in parliament and appointment to the bureaucracy were based almost entirely on being assigned membership in one of the specified religious communities to which all Lebanese, by definition, had to belong.

Table 1.1 Expenditure of colonial governments in the 1920s by purpose (per cent)

	India 1921–30	Cyprus 1923–38[a]	Iraq 1921–30	Trans-Jordan 1924–31	Syria 1923–40	Avg[b]
General administration	19.7	32.0	34.6	20.8	35.4	28.5
Defence and public safety	33.8	17.5	34.4	45.8	28.1	31.9
Economic and environmental services	20.1	16.5	14.5	7.7	7.2	13.2
Public works (development)		13.9	7.0	8.6	15.1	11.2
Social welfare services	7.2	20.1	9.5	10.3	8.9	11.2
Domestic debt service and un- specified expenditure	19.2	n.a.	n.a.	6.8	5.4	10.5
Total domestic expenditure	*100.0*	*100.0*	*100.0*	*100.0*	*100.0*	
Administration and safety	53.5	49.5	69.0	66.0	63.5	60.4
Economic, environmental and development	20.1	30.4	21.5	16.3	22.3	24.4

Notes: [a]   Average of the years 1923, 1924, 1934, 1935, 1973, 1938.
   [b]   Arithmetic mean of each line; last two lines are summations.
Source: Nachum T. Gress and Jacob Metzer, 'Public finance in the Jewish economy in interwar Palestine', Table 18, *Research in Economic History*, 3 (1978), pp. 87–59.

A last important feature of the administrative systems established in the colonial period was their particular emphasis on police and security. No doubt this is a feature of all new states. But in the case of the colonial powers it was, for obvious reasons, considered to be the key to continued political control. This can easily be seen by an examination of the budgets of the period in which, typically, some two-thirds of total expenditure was security related (see Table 1.1). Most of this was spent on creating and developing a police force and, perhaps also, a rural gendarmerie. Less importance was attached to a local army, partly for financial reasons, partly because the colonial power itself accepted the major responsibility for external defence. Nevertheless, small military formations of a few thousand men or so were organized in all colonial states, and even though they were given few heavy weapons and were used mainly for internal security, patterns of recruitment and politicization were established which were to play a significant role in the immediate post-independence period (see Chapter 8).

Such emphasis on security left little money for education, public health and welfare, although enough was still spent on secondary schools and technical institutes to produce a growing number of activist youths who were willing recruits into the first anti-colonial movements of the 1920s and 1930s (see Table 1.2).

Table 1.2 The growth in the numbers of schoolchildren and students in certain selected Arab countries, 1920–50

Country	Educational establishment		Numbers (1921/2)	Numbers(1948/9)
Egypt[a]	Elementary		342,820	1,069,383
	Preparatory/Primary		126,066	321,315
	Secondary		15,442	90,353
	University		2,282	26,740
			Numbers (1920/1)	Numbers (1939/40)
Iraq[b]	Elementary		8,001	89,482
	Secondary		110	13,959
	College		99	1,218 (1940/1)
			Numbers (1945/6)	
Syria[c]	Primary	state	99,703	
		private	50,431	
	Intermediary	state	8,276	
	Secondary	private	4,385	
	University		1,058	

Sources[a]   Donald C. Mead, *Growth and Structural Change in the Egyptian Economy* (Homewood, Illinois: Richard D. Irwin, 1967), p. 299.

[b] Hanna Batatu, *The Old Social Classes and the Revolutionary Movements of Iraq* (Princeton, NJ: Princeton UP, 1978), p. 25n.

[c] International Bank for Reconstruction and Development, *The Economic Development of Syria* (Baltimore: The Johns Hopkins Press, 1955), p. 457.

Colonial policy

If there were certain principles underlying the creation of the colonial state, there were also a number of typical colonial practices. One was the attempt to create an alliance, implicit or explicit, with the large landowners and, in some cases, the tribal shaikhs who controlled much of the rural areas. Such men were soon identified as a conservative social force which could be won over to support the colonial position, even when, as in Syria and Iraq, many of their number had participated in the rebellions against the British and the French just after the First World War. Their importance was seen as twofold. First, they could be used to maintain rural security at a time when the government had neither the money nor the administrative resources to maintain a comprehensive police coverage. Second, in those states where constitutional government and general elections – based on some type of manhood suffrage – had been introduced in the 1920s, the large landowners could be relied upon both to manage the rural vote and, in many cases, to put themselves forward as candidates for the new parliaments. This could be made even safer when, in countries like Syria and Iraq, a system of two-tier elections was introduced, by which the male electors voted for members of a local electoral college who, in turn, chose one of their number as the district's representative. To seal this alliance, large landowners were given a host of special privileges like tax exemptions and legal powers over their peasant tenants, as well as being allowed to benefit from certain aspects of colonial policy such as land registration and improved irrigation.

A second, equally important, feature of colonial politics was the attention paid to sectarian, ethnic and tribal divisions, generally for the purpose of some strategy of 'divide and rule'. This was as true of the French in Morocco, with their special emphasis on the distinction between Arabs and Berbers, as it was in the mandated territories in the east. Such policies could take many forms. They could find expression in different legal systems, as in Morocco or the tribal courts in Trans-Jordan; or in actual geographic separation, for example, the French division of Syria into, among other things, a mini-state for the Alawis along the Mediterranean coast and another for the Druze. Inevitably this did much to counter the centralizing, homogenizing processes emanating from other parts of the colonial system.

Last, but by no means least, was the particular pattern of colonial economic management. Even if colonies did not pay, they were supposed to balance their books and to be able to get along without loans from the centre in all but very special circumstances. This constraint, together with the emphasis placed on security, left little money for development other than the small amounts spent on public works projects like roads, railways, ports and improved irrigation. Colonies were also subject to a particular type of fiscal and monetary regime, with their currency tied to that of the colonial power and managed by a currency board in the metropolis. To make matters more difficult, they were not allowed a central bank which could have regulated the money supply or moved the rate of interest in such a way as to expand or dampen local demand. Meanwhile, throughout most of the Middle East, the new states remained subject to 19th-century commercial treaties, which, until they ran out round about 1930, prevented them from setting their own tariffs. The result was the creation of a more or less open economy, subject to influences stemming from the metropolis and the world at large, over which the states had little or no control. Criticism of what was seen as this unsatisfactory state of affairs formed an essential component of the anti-colonial, nationalist argument, the more so as the colonial powers themselves often attempted to legitimize their rule by an appeal to the many economic benefits that it was supposed to have introduced.

External influences

Another essential component of the colonial state was the way in which it acted as a conduit for powerful forces from outside. This was most obvious in the political field, where British and French policies were made in London and Paris and were usually the direct reflection of the balance between the various metropolitan parties and pressure groups there. As far as the colony, or dominated country, itself was concerned, it meant that its own political life was greatly affected by events like changes of government in Britain and France, or even defeats in wars, over which it had no control. It also meant that it was subject to a variety of often quite contradictory influences and examples, for instance, the ambiguous lessons to be learned from the practice of pluralism and democracy at the centre combined with the day-to-day experience of dictatorial and arbitrary government in the colony itself. In these circumstances, local politicians cannot be blamed for learning as much about how to fix elections as they did about the virtues of pluralism or judicial independence. And, of course, both types of lessons proved useful to those who became leaders of movements of national opposition or ministers in any cabinets formed by the colonial power.

The role of the colonial state in mediating between the colony and the international economy was just as important. By and large, the British and French attempted to manage affairs in such a way that they monopolized these relations, awarding contracts and concessions to their own nationals, looking after the interests of their own merchants and, in general, attempting to keep the colony as their own economic preserve. Once again, there were often international constraints that made this more difficult, for example, the fact that what were known as 'A' mandates, that is, Syria, Iraq and Palestine, were technically independent countries and could not be included in any scheme designed to promote imperial preference at the expense of third parties. Nevertheless, this was far outweighed by the benefits to be obtained in terms of control over the Middle East's oil resources or access to its reserves of hard currency placed securely in the Bank of England and the National Bank of France.

The colonial state as a framework for a new type of politics

The boundaries of a colonial state and its administrative structures defined the arena in which most of the political life now took place, as well as doing much to give it its own particular dynamic.[3] Both points require elaboration. As far as the new arena was concerned, it was largely defined by the drive to obtain influence or, better still, paramountcy over the institutions created at the new political centre, that is, the capital city. It was also provided with new rules and new possibilities as a result of the day-to-day realities of colonial practice. To this end, existing forms of associations and solidarities were generally reorganized, the better to be able to exert direct pressure on government, or new ones created. Furthermore, just as there was a change in organization and in focus, there was also a change in the political vocabulary, with words that had their origin in more traditional discourse now having their meaning stretched or altered to meet the challenge of the new situation. One good example of this is the slide in the definition of the Arabic word, *umma*, from meaning the whole religious community to meaning the Arab nation in general, and then just a part of it, for instance, Egypt or Syria. Meanwhile, good use could be made of the opportunities presented by a process of accelerated economic and social change, which, via the stimulus it gave to mobility, to the creation of new jobs and so on, detached people from their old communities and old loyalties and allowed them to participate as individuals in new types of, mainly urban-based, political activity.

Once again, the point is a controversial one. In many analyses of Middle East politics, the so-called 'traditional' categories of tribe, sect or clan remain fixed and unchanging, giving them a timeless quality in which the same struggles over differences of community or religion are endlessly repeated in patterns that have little to do with national boundaries or national politics. Or, if the creation of new and larger loyalties is allowed, these are supposed to transcend the new boundaries so as to create pan-Islamic or pan-Arab aims and forms of organization. From this follows the still influential observation that politics in the Arab world continue to be a struggle between groups that are concerned with issues that are either smaller than those to be found at the state level or larger. In this view, tribes are always competing with tribes, even if the word itself now has to embrace units as widely different as a sect like the Alawites or men from a particular provincial town like Takrit, the home of many of the leaders of Ba'thi Iraq, while slogans and identities continue to be seen as examples of what remains a fundamentally unchanged religious or 'traditional' vocabulary.

Against this I would like to argue the counter proposition, that methods of political organization and styles of political rhetoric are largely defined by the context and that, from the colonial period on, this context was created by the territorial state. Certainly it took time for its effect to be felt throughout the whole of a particular society; certainly there were groups that continued to act as though they were still fighting their neighbours or some distant government to which they owed nothing. But, for the most part, those who wanted power, access to resources or simply self-aggrandizement had to organize themselves in a way that made sense in terms of the new realities, while those who did not, for example, the military raiders from Arabia known as the Ikhwan, or the Arab nationalist politicians who tried to use Trans-Jordan as a basis for anti-French agitation inside Syria, were soon marginalized or destroyed.

Three other points about the nature of this new arena are important. First, once the initial rural, anti-colonial, revolts had been put down, the main focus for the new politics became largely urban and, in many cases, was confined almost exclusively to the capital city. As a result it came to be dominated by members of a small elite who provided leadership for the growing number of educated town dwellers who were drawn into national political life. In Egypt, for example, the activists were drawn largely from the

53,000 or so people who had been identified as professionals in 1937, the vast majority of them schoolteachers.[4] But there was also a tendency to try to increase the strength of any political movement by seeking recruits among organizable groups elsewhere in the city, such as workers or students, who could be used in the orchestrated series of strikes, demonstrations and boycotts that came to be seen as an essential feature of the politics of this period.[5]

A second important feature was the difference between a monarchical and a republican system of government. As far as Britain was concerned it was the former that was much preferred. This was because a king, constrained by a constitution, was seen as a vital support for the British position, since he provided an important element of continuity and could always be used to dismiss any popularly elected government of nationalists that threatened to tear up or amend the arrangements – usually summed up in a treaty – defining Britain's rights. Such a case clearly existed in Egypt, where King Fuad (1922–36) repeatedly dismissed governments based on huge majorities obtained by the Wafd Party in the preceding elections. Paradoxically, his son, King Farouk (1936–52), had to be coerced into appointing the same party to power in 1942, when new conditions demanded a different strategy of allowing the nationalists to keep a neutral Egypt quiet for the duration of the Second World War.

But, whatever the British interest, such a system inevitably turned the monarch into an important political actor with some powers of veto and, at the very least, great influence over the local politicians and their competition for domestic resources. Later, as independence approached, a great deal depended on whether a king managed the difficult transformation of putting himself at the head of the local nationalist movement – something achieved by the kings of Morocco and King Hussein of Jordan (1953–) – or whether they became so closely associated with the structures of colonialism that they did not long outlast them, for example, in Tunisia, Libya, Egypt and Iraq. The French, for their part, were more willing to countenance republican forms of government, as in Lebanon and Syria, and to forgo the sometimes uncertain advantages of monarchy for the much easier to manage system led by a docile president.

A last significant feature affecting the politics of the colonial period was the presence of a white settler community in Palestine and all of North Africa. Its role can be seen in its classic form in the French colonies and protectorates, where, having strong connections with the mother country, the settlers were able to obtain a privileged position, with their own political advisory bodies, an extra-market system for obtaining control of the best land and, for a long time, their own exclusive trade unions to which, for example, native-born Algerians and others were not admitted. In these circumstances, a major part of the settlers' efforts were directed towards preserving and expanding these privileges against both metropolitan and local nationalist pressures, something that inevitably brought them into conflict with the colonized population at both the political and the economic level. Much the same was true of Libya, although there the period of Italian control was much shorter; not more than two decades in Tripolitania, and only one in Cyrenaica, where fighting against the Senussi order and the tribes continued well into the 1930s.

In Egypt, however, the major component in the European population was provided by Greeks and Italians who, although protected by the capitulatory treaties until the 1930s, and by the special mixed courts for trying foreigners, never received sufficient support from the country's British occupiers to obtain privileged access to land or the power to institutionalize a split-labour market with higher wages for themselves. Perhaps because of this, their relations with the Egyptian nationalists were relatively harmonious and they played only a marginal role in the political life of the colonial period. Palestine was different again. Although the Zionist settlers received initial support from the British, it was later realized that their project of establishing a national home ran counter to the interests of the native Palestinians. Thereafter, the mandatory authorities tried to play a more balancing role between the two communities, incurring the increasing hostility of both sides. In these circumstances there was little chance of introducing any common political institutions, leaving the Jews and Arabs to develop their own organizations, forged largely in direct conflict with one another.

Apart from the creation of a political arena, a second way in which the colonial state engendered a new type of political practice was by providing a fresh focus for political struggle. What it did, essentially, was to give birth to the familiar dialectic by which imperial rulers are forced to generate the nationalist forces that will eventually drive them out. In the Middle Eastern context this meant that, throughout most of the area, the colonial powers provided both a sufficient challenge and a sufficient opportunity for a local political movement to develop, until such time that it was easier to give way to it than to try to resist it for ever. However, to make matters more complicated, by offering posts to local politicians and officials, and by providing new resources to compete for, via control over an expanding bureaucracy, the colonial state also encouraged another type of struggle, this time among different local groups or factions themselves. Just how the political activity conducted within each of these two spheres was interrelated poses difficult problems of analysis, the more so as the second, domestic, sphere usually contained men engaged in the anti-colonial struggle as well.

Independence and after

Just as the First World War had created the conditions that led to the grant of formal independence of Egypt in 1922, so too did the Second World War pave the way for the end of colonial domination in many parts of the Middle East. Expectations of freedom were raised. The defeats suffered by France and Italy, and the emergence of the United States and Soviet Russia as world superpowers, severely damaged the prestige of the old imperial countries. And in Palestine the growth of Jewish economic activity during the war, and then the revelations about the Nazi extermination camps, made the drive for Jewish statehood virtually unstoppable. The result was that Syria and Lebanon obtained their formal independence in 1943 and Trans-Jordan (re-named Jordan) in 1946. Next, Israel emerged out of the military partition of Mandatory Palestine after the British withdrawal in 1948, leaving most of the areas assigned by the United Nations to an Arab entity to be taken over by the Jordanians. And, in 1951, Libya was established as an amalgamation of the former Italian colonies of Tripoli, Cyrenaica and the Fezzan.

There was then a brief interval while Britain and France tried to renegotiate their position in Egypt and Iraq (which had been virtually re-conquered by British troops during the war) and in North Africa. But the Free Officers' coup of 1952 soon opened up the way for the 1954 agreement on the final withdrawal of the British forces from Egypt, and the independence of Sudan in 1956. At the same time, efforts to contain the Algerian revolt that broke out in 1954 led the French to cut their losses and to grant freedom to Tunisia and Morocco, also in 1956. Hence, just over a decade after the end of the Second World War, all the states in the region had obtained their independence, with the exception of Algeria, which had to wait until 1962, and the British colonies and protectorates round the southern and eastern coasts of Arabia.

Patterns of transfer of power differed enormously. In some cases there was a year or so of preparation, capped by an election to decide which political group was to form the first post-independence government. In others, like Syria and Lebanon, French troops lingered on, and it was only in 1946 that they were finally persuaded to leave. Another even messier route was followed in Palestine, where the British made no effort to hand over power to anyone, leaving the Palestinian Arabs in confusion and allowing the Jews to proclaim a state of their own because they had developed significant para-statal institutions well beforehand.

Nevertheless, whatever the conditions in which they had obtained power, the rulers of the newly independent Middle Eastern states faced many of the same problems. It was one thing to create a nationalist coalition against the retreating imperial power, quite another to obtain the allegiance of all of its new citizens. There were also huge problems posed by poverty, illiteracy, religious and social division and the need to find money for development. As a rule, nationalist parties had elaborated quite a powerful critique of the economic policies of their colonial masters before independence, in terms of their failures to support industry, to spend money on education and to allow the creation of certain key institutions like national banks. Now, having achieved power themselves, this critique was generally recycled as a programme for immediate action. But this had to be carried out at a time when state structures, deprived of the cohesion provided by the colonial presence, were relatively amorphous and fluid, with fragmented and highly politicized bureaucratic structures. Meanwhile, it was also necessary to find funds for expanding and re-equipping the colonial armies that were now needed not just for internal policing but also for external defence, for example, during the Palestine War of 1948.

In these difficult circumstances it was perhaps inevitable that there was a great deal of initial instability leading, in a number of cases, to military coups. In Syria, Iraq and Egypt, the first governments, consisting, essentially, of an alliance of city notables and professionals supported, in the rural areas, by the large land-owners, were dominated by well-to-do men who had been closely associated with the British and the French. In Sudan the major politicians were the leaders of the country's three main religious sects. All found it difficult to meet the political challenge of running relatively poor states. They were also open to accusations that their class position made them particularly unreceptive to questions of income redistribution and social justice. In return, they defended themselves against attack by manipulating the electoral system to their advantage, in such a way that their radical critics could be reasonably sure that they would never obtain enough seats in parliament to form a government. Given such barriers, it made obvious sense for the opposition to turn to the military for help. Frustrated army officers were only too willing to oblige, although usually on their own terms. This happened first in Iraq in 1936, and was repeated in Syria in 1949, in Egypt in 1952, in Iraq again in 1958 and in Sudan in the same year.

The regimes that managed to tide themselves over the early independence period problems do not seem to have had a great deal in common. In some cases a royal family was able to mobilize just sufficient resources to beat off, or outwit, the inevitable military plotters, for example, in Jordan in the 1950s and Morocco in the 1960s and early 1970s. In another, Tunisia, the Neo-Destour and its leader, Bourguiba, were skilful enough to use the years immediately before and after independence to build up a one-party monopoly over the state and all the co-opted groups and associations within the society, sufficient to pre-empt early opposition. Lebanon presents the example of a third route forwards, its pluralist, confessional system lurching uneasily from crisis to crisis but only finally coming unstuck as a result of the accumulation of external as well as internal challenges in the early 1970s.

Many political analysts of the Middle East seem to have had little difficulty in accounting for the early instability of the independent Arab states in terms of explanations derived from a combination of religious and historical factors supposedly specific to the region. One example would be the role of Islam, which, in some arguments, makes all regimes illegitimate, either because they are secular or because they destroy the vital religious promise of the creation of a community that embraces all believers. Another is Arabism, which is often supposed to play much the same role.

But although religious or trans-national allegiances always have to be taken into account, the difficulties experienced in the first post-independent decades do not seem markedly different from those to be observed elsewhere in the Third World, where ambivalent commitments to pluralism and parliamentarianism also tended to give way to military or one-party rule. It also has to be pointed out that in the Middle East, as in many other regions, political instability was overcome largely as a result of the general process of the expansion of the power of the central bureaucracy and of the security forces. This development will form the main subject of Chapter 2.

The creation of centralized state systems in Turkey and Iran

The creation of centralized state systems in Turkey and Iran had a number of important features in common. Both were based on the ruins of dynastic empires which had been challenged by constitutional and reformist groups in the early 20th century, occupied by foreign troops and finally overthrown by regimes led by military officers who had seized power in alliance with nationalist forces in the early 1920s. Both were then refashioned through the creation of national armies, centralized bureaucracies and secular legal systems, according to models based very largely on Western European experience. Both were then the site for statist development projects in which reforms were imposed on society with very little discussion or debate.

Nevertheless, as far as their political histories and types of political practice were concerned, there were also many significant differences between the two. I will deal with these in the light of four of the most significant variables: foreign influence and foreign domination; the role of the bureaucracy; the role of the local bourgeoisie; and the presence or absence of a ruling party.

The main institutions of the Turkish Republic were created in two stages.[6] The first of these was in the period when Mustafa Kemal was organizing his resistance to foreign invasion in Ankara, when it was necessary to persuade leading politicians, officials and others to transfer their loyalties away from the British-dominated rump of the old Ottoman government still ruling in Istanbul. To this end Mustafa Kemal created what he called the Grand National Assembly, with a council of state drawn from among its own members to exercise government on a day-to-day basis. The fact that it represented a wide spectrum of political and social beliefs meant that its authority was accepted throughout most of Turkey, and it became an ideal vehicle for the creation of a new order based on the transfer of government from Istanbul to Ankara and the abolition of the Ottoman sultan's temporal power in 1922. Nevertheless, from Mustafa Kemal's point of view it possessed certain drawbacks, not the least being that it contained a majority of members who still saw the sultan as the ideal religious leader of an Islamic constitutional state. This led him to take measures to dominate the assembly, first through the creation of a new party (the People's Party), then through his intervention to ensure that it was well represented in the 1923 elections. As a result he was able to force through the abolition of the caliphate in 1924 and, more generally, to use the new party – soon re-named the Republican People's Party (RPP) – to isolate his major opponents and then push through a series of radical reforms aimed at laying the foundations for a modern, secular nation state. One important step taken at this time was to insist that military officers could only take part in political life if they resigned their commissions, thus isolating those who chose to remain in the army from participation in the decision-making process.

The second stage involved the establishment of the RPP at the centre of what was, essentially, a one-party system. This was greatly assisted by the law for the maintenance of order passed at the beginning of the Kurdish and religious revolt of 1925, which was used to put down all political activity outside the party itself. It was followed, in the early 1930s, by more positive steps to turn the RPP into a national organization with an elite membership and an ideology. The former allowed the party to dominate the two-stage election system so as to ensure that it always had huge majorities in the Assembly. As for the ideology, this was provided by the six principles of Kemalism introduced in May 1931 – republicanism, nationalism, populism, statism, secularism and something that can be translated as either revolutionism or reformism.[7] These moves were not only supposed to define the basic character of the state but were also part of an attempt to create a political consensus around 'unchanging' guidelines which were beyond criticism and to which all political actors had to owe allegiance. From then on there was little practical difference between party and administration, even when, as after 1939, there were rules preventing party officials from holding state office. The hold of the party was further demonstrated by the way in which its nominee, Ismet Inonu, was so quickly elected as president, and then as chairman of the RPP, following Ataturk's death in November 1938.

A last ingredient of the new system was the statist tradition inherited from the Ottoman period and eagerly continued by Turkey's civilian bureaucratic elite. In these circumstances there was no great problem in presenting the state as a single, coherent, autonomous enterprise, the more so as rival social forces, like the large landowners, remained relatively weak. In these circumstances the beginnings of the growing challenge to the RPP's monopoly of power represented by the creation of the Democrat Party in 1946 is best explained in terms of intra-élite rivalry.[8]

Nevertheless, there were also powerful factors at work that ensured that the opposition received widening popular support all the way up to its overwhelming victory in the 1950 general election. One of these was a growing dissatisfaction with RPP rule, particularly its heavy-handed management of the economy during the Second World War and, in the rural areas, its challenge to Islamic religious practice. A second was the mounting American pressure for political change once Turkey had become reliant on its economic and military assistance after the Second World War. Finally, there was the impact of the RPP's policy of encouraging the enlargement of a native Turkish bourgeoisie, something begun on purely nationalist grounds but which received an important fillip from the statist development plans of the 1930s with their emphasis on joint public/private ventures as a way of building an industrial base. Certain members of this class within the RPP developed into vocal critics of those definitions of the Kemalist principle of 'statism' that emphasized the need for government control over all major aspects of economic life and, in the years after 1945, they became spokesmen for the many entrepreneurs who were anxious for more freedom to run their own affairs, large numbers of whom defected to the Democrats.

The RPP's willingness to surrender the government to the victorious Democrats in 1950 marked the start of a new era of multi-party activity in Turkish politics. But, as elsewhere in the non-European world, the long period of single-party rule had produced structures that made life difficult for its successors, notably the close association between the RPP and its supporters in both the army and the bureaucracy. I will return to this point in Chapter 5.

Resistance to foreign occupation and the establishment of a new order in Persia also owed much to the efforts of one man, this time Colonel Reza Khan, who took advantage of the political crisis of the early 1920s to manoeuvre himself into such a position of personal dominance that he was able to have a constituent assembly depose the previous Kajar ruler and offer him the imperial throne in December 1925. Thereafter, however, his method of rule showed significant differences from that of Ataturk. For one thing, Iran possessed only a weak bureaucratic tradition, while the central government remained heavily dependent on the support of the large landowners and tribal shaikhs who dominated the rural areas. For another, Reza Shah chose to browbeat and control a captive parliament (the Majles) by means of personal domination rather than the creation of a single party. To this end he employed all the powers and the patronage that accrued to him as ruler. The result was a species of dictatorship which he used to push through some of the same reforms as Ataturk, although never with the same degree of administrative and organizational single-mindedness. Hence, although he too attacked the powers of the religious establishment by expanding the sphere of the secular educational and legal system, he still left the mullahs and the ayatullahs in possession of both large endowments and an influential system of religious education which ensured that much of their basic power remained intact.

Another very important way in which the history of Iranian politics differed from that of Turkey stemmed from the re-occupation of the country by British and Soviet forces in 1941 and the deposition of Reza Shah in favour of his son, Mohamed. This at once paved the way for an incoherent period of political pluralism in which Persian politicians vied with each other for power in an arena heavily dominated by the representatives of the occupying powers and by the young shah, stripped of much of his father's power but still able to count on the loyalty of much of the army. To make the situation more complicated, the practice of politics had also to come to terms with the effects of an upsurge in tribal and provincial separatism, industrialization and a huge expansion of education; these had all produced a variety of social forces, none strong enough to dominate the centre like the Turkish bourgeoisie but all demanding some kind of parliamentary representation.

In these circumstances, politicians were grouped together in loosely co-ordinated factions rather than parties, and the resulting instability produced an enormously rapid turnover of cabinets, with an average of a new prime minister every eight months between 1941 and 1953.[9] Meanwhile, the best that the few skilled political leaders could manage was to create short-lived coalitions based on a temporary coincidence of interest. But a sustained effort to dominate the system long enough to build up a permanent political force which could change the balance of power was impossible. The most obvious example was that of the prime minister, Muhammad Mossadeq, who was unable to take advantage of the explosion of popular nationalism following the Iranian takeover of the Anglo-Persian Oil Company in 1951 to establish a constitutional regime dominated by his own political alliance, the National Front. Instead, he himself was undermined by a combination of royalist, religious and foreign opposition, paving the way for the dramatic return of the Shah from his temporary exile, and the creation of a new imperial dictatorship based on what Abrahamian has styled a 'military monarchy'.[10]

Notes

1 Elizabeth Monroe, *Britain's Moment in the Middle East 1914–1956* (London: Chatto & Windus, 1963).
2 For useful discussions of the political and economic practices of the colonial state see Hamza Alavi, 'The state in post-colonial societies: Pakistan and Bangladesh', *New Left Review*, 74 (July/Aug., 1972); and A. G. Hopkins, *An Economic History of West Africa* (London: Longman, 1973), Ch. 5.
3 The arguments in this section draw heavily on those in Sami Zubaida, *Islam, The People and the State* (London and New York: Routledge, 1989), pp. 145–52.
4 Figures from Jean-Jacques Waardenburg, *Les universités dans la monde Arabe*, quoted in Ahmed Abdalla, *The Student Movement and National Politics in Egypt 1923–1973* (London: Al-Saqi Books, 1985), p. 19.
5 For example, Philip Khoury, *Syria and the French Mandate: The Politics of Arab Nationalism 1920–1945* (London: I. B. Tauris, 1987), especially Part V; or his 'Syrian urban politics in transition: The quarters of Damascus during the French Mandate', *International Journal of Middle East Studies*, 16 (Nov., 1984), pp. 507–40.
6 Feroz Ahmad, *The Making of Modern Turkey* (London: Routledge, 1992).

7 Ibid.
8 Metin Heper, 'Transitions to democracy reconsidered: A historical perspective', in Dankwart A. Rustow and Kenneth Paul Erickson (eds), *Comparative Political Dynamics: Global Research Perspectives* (New York: Harper & Row, 1990).
9 Fahkreddin Azimi, *Iran: The Crisis of Democracy* (London: I. B. Tauris, 1989), Ch. 1.
10 Ervand Abrahamian, *Iran Between Two Revolutions* (Princeton, NJ: Princeton University Press, 1982), p. 441.

2 The growth of state power in the Arab world: the single-party regimes

Introduction

A huge expansion in the power and pervasiveness of the state apparatus is a common feature of the post-independence Middle East. This was largely a result of growth in the size of the bureaucracy, the police and the army, as well as, in many cases, the number of public enterprises. Similar types of expansion took place in many other parts of the Third World at the same time, and for many of the same reasons. These included the need to maintain security after the departure of the colonial power; the drive to establish control over the whole of the new national territory; and the desire to use the state to promote large programmes of economic development and social welfare. Once started, such processes were given further stimulus by foreign aid, by bureaucratic empire building and by the natural predilection of nationalist politicians for technological rather than political solutions to the problems of rapid modernization.

There were specific Middle Eastern reasons for administrative expansion as well. These included: the implementation of programmes of land reform in a number of Arab countries in the 1950s; the apparent failure of the private sector to meet the challenge of development in the early independence period; and the sudden exodus of many hundreds of thousands of foreign officials, businessmen and agriculturalists that took place in Egypt during the Suez crisis of 1956 and in French North Africa immediately after the end of colonialism. The drive for Arab unity was another locally specific feature, with the Egyptian regime speeding up the process of state expansion in Syria during the three years of union between the two countries, 1958–61, and then encouraging the same process in Iraq in 1963/4, which it demanded as a necessary precondition for any possible union between Cairo and Baghdad. Oil wealth, too, played its part, financing the development plans of populous countries like Algeria and Iraq and forcing the rulers of the smaller desert states like Libya, Saudi Arabia and the Gulf shaikhdoms to begin to create modern systems of administration and to spend part of their new wealth on systems of welfare for their own citizens.

In this chapter I will deal with the process of administrative expansion and control as it affected those five, well-populated, Arab countries that passed into the control of one-party regimes dedicated to state-led development under the banner of some form of Arab socialism – Algeria, Egypt, Iraq, Syria and Tunisia. All shared many features, whether the increase in state power or the type of politics that this produced. However, some of the same processes were also at work in Sudan, with its Arab Socialist Union created in the early 1970s, and in the two Yemens. Chapter 3 will then examine the same topic in the context of a number of the less populated countries ruled by monarchs and royal families, like Jordan and the desert oil producers, as well as of the somewhat anomalous case of Libya.

As for the period under examination in this chapter, what is said about Egypt, Syria and Tunisia will relate mainly to the years of 'socialist' management up to 1969/70, when all three experienced what was variously described as a 'correction' or 'rectification' which introduced important new features into their economic and political systems. But in Algeria and Iraq, where the process started later and could be sustained for longer as a result of increasing oil revenues, examples will be drawn from the 1970s as well.

Expansion in the size of the state apparatus and of its ability to regulate and control

From a chronological point of view, the first country to experience a process of large-scale bureaucratic expansion was Egypt. This followed closely on the military coup of 1952 that brought Colonel Gamal Abdel-Nasser and his fellow officers to power. Immediate attention was paid to increasing the strength of the police and public security while, as soon as British agreement had been obtained to evacuate its troops from the Suez Canal in 1954, the new rulers began to enlarge the armed forces and to re-equip them with more modern weapons, a process that continued through the Anglo-French and Israeli invasion of 1956, the Egyptian intervention in Yemen in the early 1960s and the disastrous Middle East war of 1967. The new regime also took immediate steps to institute measures of economic development based on ideas that had been elaborated by some of the more radical civilian politicians in the last years of King Farouk's monarchy. These included the land reform of 1952, the decision to build the Aswan High Dam and the inauguration of the Helwan Iron and Steel Complex in 1954. The nationalizations of foreign property during the Suez invasion then produced a further stimulus to state-led development, culminating in the first five year plan, 1960–5, and the nationalizations of Egyptian private banks, factories and other enterprises in 1960/1.

The effect of this on the size and the role of the state apparatus can best be demonstrated by looking at a variety of key indices. As far as the numbers of those employed in the bureaucracy and the public enterprises were concerned, these rose from some 350,000 persons in 1951/2 to over 1,000,000 in 1965/6, an expansion far in excess of general employment, production or the population as a whole. Meanwhile, the number of government ministries had nearly doubled, from 15 to 29, during the same period.[1] This meant that, at the time of the 1960 census, the government employed about a third of Egypt's non-agricultural labour force.[2] As for the armed forces, the number of soldiers, sailors and airmen increased from 80,000 in 1955/6 to some 180,000 in 1966 plus about 90,000 paramilitary police (see Table 8.2 on page 207). A final index is that of government expenditure as a proportion of Egypt's gross national product; this increased from 18.3 per cent in 1954/5 to 55.7 per cent in 1970 (including defence).[3]

In Syria the main period of expansion took place in the 1960s as the result, first, of the export of Egyptian systems of economic and political management during the brief period of the United Arab Republic, then of the statist policies of the Ba'th Party as part of its drive to establish itself in power from 1963 onwards. As a result the number of state employees rose from 34,000 in 1960 to some 170,000 civil servants in 1975 plus 81,000 in the public sector.[4] If we add that there were also 180,000 men in the armed forces in this latter year, it means that about a quarter of the total labour force, and about half of those in urban employment, were then on the state payroll.[5]

Table 2.1 The increase in the expenditure of central government and public enterprise as a proportion of GDP in certain Arab countries during the 1960s

	1960 (%)	1970 (%)
Algeria	25.3 (1963)	42.8 (1969)
Egypt	29.7	55.7
Iraq	28.4	44.2
Syria	23.5	37.9
Tunisia	20.7	40.7

Source: C.H. Moore, 'The consolidation and dissipation of power in unincorporated societies: Egypt and Tunisia', mimeo.

Much the same process took place in Iraq after the revolution of 1958; in Tunisia, where the number of local Muslim employees jumped from 12,000 to 80,000 between 1956 and 1960; and in Algeria after independence in 1962.[6] Figures in Table 2.1 provide an illustration of this expansion in terms of huge increases in the proportion of government expenditure to gross national product during the 1960s. The only significant difference between the countries concerned spending on defence, where the Tunisian regime of Habib Bourguiba made a determined effort to limit the size of the army as a way of preventing possible coups. No such option was open to the Algerians, with their border dispute with Morocco, nor to the Iraqi military regimes of the 1960s, which were forced to confront the revival of Kurdish militancy in the north after the return of the exiled leader, Mustafa Barzani, in 1958. The result was a growth in the size of Algeria's armed forces from 40,000 in 1962 to 65,000 in 1965, and of Iraq's from 40,000 in 1955 to some 80,000 at the end of the 1960s (see Table 2.2).

An important component in state expansion was the increased spending on education and welfare. Both are very labour intensive in terms of the numbers of doctors, teachers and health workers who have to be employed to provide comprehensive national programmes. And, in the case of education, it was the huge increase in the size of the school population that first helped to staff the growing civil service and then encouraged the creation of more and more posts for unemployed school leavers. The fact that promotion and rank were dependent on educational qualifications provided a further link between the two processes. As far as Egypt was concerned, the number of young people in all types of education rose from 1,900,000 in 1953/4 to 4,500,000 in 1965/6 and 5,900,000 in 1972/3. Of these, 54,000 were in universities at the beginning of the period and 195,000 at the end.[7] Figures in the World Bank's annual *World Development Report* show the same process at work in Syria, where the proportion of school-age children enrolled in secondary education rose from 16 to 48 per cent between 1960 and 1975, and in Iraq from 19 to 35 per cent. Progress was initially slower in North Africa but then accelerated dramatically. To look only at Algeria, the numbers of children in secondary schools there jumped from 164,000 in 1966/7 to 742,000 a decade later.[8]

The process of expanding administrative control can also be seen at work in policies towards agriculture and industry. As far as agriculture was concerned, the regimes in all five Arab countries took quite considerable amounts of rural land into public ownership, usually as part of a programme of expropriating the larger estates for redistribution to small proprietors and landless peasants. In the Egyptian reforms of 1952 and 1961 a seventh of the total cultivated land was expropriated in this way; in Syria in 1958, and then from 1963 onwards, about a fifth; and in Iraq after 1958 almost half.[9] As it turned out, only in Egypt did the bulk of this land pass directly into peasant hands. But even where only a part of it was redistributed, as in Syria and Iraq, the rest remained under state control and provided the occasion for the central government to extend its power into most of the rural areas, reducing the role of the old landed class and replacing it with a system of direct administration by the police, the ministries and the party.

Events followed a slightly different course in Tunisia and Algeria, where the first extension of state ownership was mainly as a result of the seizure of lands left by the departing French *colons*. But in Algeria this was then followed in the early 1970s by the expropriation of 1,300,000 hectares owned by absentee landlords, some 16 per cent of the total cultivated area.[10] As elsewhere, this allowed the state to play a much closer role in rural affairs, usually through the establishment of various types of supervised co-operatives.

Programmes of nationalization and of large-scale industrialization provided the state with further opportunities for expansion and control. As elsewhere in the Third World, the creation of an industrial base was seen as the essential component of economic modernity. And as elsewhere, a process of import substitution, beginning with relatively simple consumer durables and ending up, hopefully, with the production of iron and steel and then machines, seemed to offer an easy way forward. The result was what Albert Hirschman has referred to in the Latin American context as the 'exuberant phase' of industrialization, when Arab politicians and planners were extravagantly encouraged by the way in which local demand for many products was so quickly met by an increase in local production.[11] Only later, in Egypt and Tunisia in the late 1960s, and in Iraq and Algeria in the late 1970s, did the problems inherent in such a strategy – the drain on scarce foreign currency reserves to buy foreign machinery and raw materials, the lack of attention to agriculture and exports, the problems of managing huge industrial plant – begin to demand serious attention (see Chapter 6). Meanwhile, there was a large increase in the numbers of new factories and in the size of the industrial labour force, providing new jobs and new opportunities for profit and placing the state right at the centre of the drive for economic advance.

A last point of note is that the whole process of expanding state involvement in the economy was justified by the need for rapid development and for a more equitable distribution of a rising national income. This provided an important source of legitimation for the regimes, as well as allowing them to bolster their authority and to reduce the possibility of challenge by an appeal to the expertize of the scientist or the planner. Such notions could be expressed in fine-sounding technological language or in the more idealistic language of Arab socialism. Speeches by the leaders of all five countries leaned heavily on both vocabularies, although they were always careful to make it quite clear that, in a Middle Eastern context, socialism had nothing to do with the dangerous notion of social division and class struggle. Only very rarely was it suggested that any local class or group was no longer to be considered as part of the national community. And even then, as in the occasional references to feudalists or parasitic capitalists, the impression was usually given that such persons were either foreigners or else so closely allied with the forces of reactionary imperialism as to have lost the right to be called citizens. In this way the emphasis on socialist planning provided an essential ingredient for the public ideology of regimes heavily embarked on statist, integrative programmes of national development and control.

Control over so large an apparatus with such extensive commitments gave the small numbers of individuals at the apex of each regime enormous power. The result was a type of system best classified as authoritarian.[12] This is one in which power is highly centralized, pluralism is suspect and where the regime seeks to exercise a monopoly over all legitimate political activity. Something of its logic in an Egyptian context can be seen from the vehemence with which President Nasser and his supporters denounced the emergence of what they termed 'an alternative centre of power' around Field Marshall Abd al-Hakim Amer, the Chief of the General Staff, in the years just before the 1967 war. On the evidence of their speeches and declarations, it was enough simply to draw attention to the enormity of such a development without, for a moment, having to explain why a multiplication of such centres was actually wrong.

Authoritarian systems are different from totalitarian ones, however, as they lack the powerful institutions that would be needed to control or to transform society by means of bureaucratic methods alone. As a result, people have to be mobilized, different groups integrated, opposition contained, by a variety of methods which range from terror and brute force (the stick) to economic inducement (the carrot), and from the use of personal, ethnic or group affiliations to the compulsory membership of carefully constructed unions and professional associations designed to keep all those at work in the modern sector strictly in their place. In these circumstances it is only possible to describe some of the major strategies employed in these five Arab states.

When it comes to organized groups within the society, the ideal strategy for an authoritarian regime is to destroy those that it cannot control, and to re-make and re-order those that it can. This in fact was the policy first employed in Egypt and Tunisia, where society was relatively homogeneous and where bureaucratic structures were already well developed at the time when the Nasser and Bourguiba regimes came to power. Independent political parties were soon suppressed or forced to disband, while existing unions and associations were either banned or driven to reorganize themselves according to new sets of rules and regulations. The result was a monopoly of political activity for the regime's single party or national rally: the Neo-Destour in Tunisia; the Liberation Rally, followed by the National Union and then the Arab Socialist Union in Egypt. At the same time, a tightly controlled trade union structure was created under the UGTT and the Confederation of Egyptian Workers. This was paralleled by the establishment of a number of associations for students, women, peasants and others, while the existing professional associations for doctors, lawyers, journalists and the like were brought under state control, new leaders installed and, in Egypt, membership in one or other of them made compulsory for all university graduates.

Once in place, such a structure was used not only to ensure the controlled collaboration of the groups in question but also to define the way in which the different groups presented their demands and were represented politically at the national level. In the case of trade unions, for instance, industrial disputes or negotiations about pay and conditions could not be pursued by strike action and were subject to rigid processes of arbitration. More generally, the division of so much of the population into unions and associations allowed the regime to define the role that their members were expected to play in the general process of modernization and national integration. Where women were concerned, for example, this would usually stress the need for them to go out to work, an appeal tempered, as the occasion demanded, by reference to their other role as wives and mothers.

At a rural level, state control was initially represented by such centrally appointed persons as the village policeman and the village schoolteacher. But all the regimes then used the mechanism of the land reform and the co-operative to create new institutions at a local level. These could include a village council, a branch of the party and, in Iraq and Syria, a branch of the Peasants' Union as well. In addition, the government was usually represented directly by officials of the ministry of agriculture or agrarian reform who were responsible for providing instructions about the type of crops to be grown, the methods to be employed and the way they should be marketed. In such circumstances, the balance between local initiative and central guidance varied greatly according to the degree of village-level input that was either tolerated or actively encouraged. To speak very generally, whereas the Syrian Ba'thi regime seems to have made the most strenuous efforts to encourage the recruitment of active party cadres, perhaps because of its strong rural base, this strategy was only employed briefly in Egypt in the

1960s and hardly at all in Iraq, where the party approached the agricultural sector in a very much more heavy-handed way based on fixed ideas about how it ought properly to be managed.[13] The Algerian case is different again. There the production and service co-operatives created to assist the beneficiaries of the 1971 land reform were granted a great deal of autonomy in theory but found themselves heavily circumscribed by the fact that the peasants were required to cultivate their land according to the country's national plan, as well as by their need to rely on certain state monopolies to supply agricultural inputs and to market certain of their crops.[14]

A second type of strategy was used to extend state control over the educational and legal systems, as well as over the religious establishment. In all three cases the main incentive was to combine control over the space that the school and university, the court and the mosque might offer to political opponents, with an attempt to appropriate their ideas and practices to serve regime purposes. In the case of the educational system, this was effected quite simply by establishing a national curriculum and by either forbidding student political activity entirely or steering it into the safer channels provided by the party and by government-controlled youth organizations. As for the law, the courts were brought under control by a dual process of coercing or replacing the existing judges and then drastically limiting the scope of the system by delegating responsibility for adjudicating and enforcement to a host of extra-legal authorities, for example, the military, the internal security forces, the managers of state enterprises or the village-level councils. The shrinkage of the legal system was pushed still further in certain countries by the development of the notion that there existed a higher socialist, or revolutionary, legality, which, when applied, superseded the ordinary laws of the land.

Religion seemed to prove no more of an obstacle to state control, at least during the period of bureaucratic consolidation. No regime felt able to abandon Islam entirely, for this would have been to cut the most important single ideological and cultural link between it and the bulk of its population. Nevertheless, all of them explicitly or implicitly asserted the primacy of the political over the religious. And all relied heavily on two important legacies from the Middle East's 19th-century past. One was the Ottoman practice of bringing the religious establishment under state control by paying the *ulama* (the clergy) official salaries, by creating a government ministry to manage its property, and by building up a secular educational and legal system to challenge its previous monopoly over these two important areas. The other was the use of the dominant modernist strand in Sunni Islam to obtain official legitimation for state policy. Algeria's establishment of a ministry of traditional education and religious affairs would be an example of the first type of policy; President Nasser's ability to obtain a *fatwa* (religious proclamation) justifying many of his major policy decisions is a good example of the second. This structure of control was further reinforced by rules making membership of independent religious parties and associations, like Egypt's Muslim Brothers, illegal. Such policies seemed to work smoothly for a while but came under increasing attack in the new political atmosphere of the 1970s (see Chapter 7).

Control over the educational system and the religious establishment, as well as over the press, radio and television, gave the regimes one further advantage, and that was the capacity to establish an ideological hegemony in terms of a statist, universalistic, discourse based on notions of nationalism, socialism and populism, which drove out or subdued alternative political vocabularies. This gave them the power to set the terms of any debate, to direct discussion and, in general, to make it absolutely clear what could and could not be said. It is only necessary to read through the accounts of the meeting of any national assembly or any party congress to see what a powerful weapon this could be.

The bottom line as far as state control was concerned was the presence of the army and the police, backed up by the many intelligence services, the secret courts, the torture chambers and the prisons.[15] This is not to say that some of the regimes were not popular to begin with, even if they themselves then proceeded to destroy all the methods that would have made it possible to test such an opinion. President Nasser, President Bourguiba and the National Liberation Front (FLN) in Algeria won real battles in their struggles against the old colonial powers; in addition, the enforced retreat of the foreign business communities offered great advantages to local entrepreneurs, while the land reforms and the expansion of the educational systems provided obvious opportunities for a better life for millions of people. Nevertheless, no regime was prepared to share power with more than a limited number of chosen collaborators; organized opposition was ferociously crushed; and all rulers were careful to cultivate an atmosphere of arbitrariness and fear. As in the political system described by the Hungarian novelist, Georg Konrad, the system itself required political prisoners.[16] And whereas some, like the Egyptians, the Tunisians and the Algerians, were able, in Konrad's words, to 'create great order with little terror', others, like the Ba'thi regime that came to power in Iraq in 1968, used violence and threats of violence as a basic instrument for maintaining itself in power.[17]

Given the existence of these types of large, powerful, durable, authoritarian structures, it was inevitable that the ordinary citizen encountered the state at every turn, whether in the Mugamma, the huge building in central Cairo where it was necessary to go for passports, identity cards, export visas and the like, or out in the villages, where the local co-operative had replaced the old landlords as a provider of seeds, fertilizer and credit. Meanwhile, regime policies were shaping people's lives by opening up new possibilities, providing new resources, forcing them into new organizations and creating new relationships – between employers and employees, owners and tenants, parents and children, and even men and women. A few chose to confront the state; others tried to ignore it or to imagine that it could be made to go away. But for the vast majority it was there to be used, manipulated or exploited where possible. For them, access to the channels of influence that led to a job or a loan or a licence was all.

Politics in an authoritarian state

Authoritarian states pose particular problems for political analysis. One of the ways in which the regimes that control them try to give an impression of coherence and of concentrated power and might is to cloak themselves in secrecy. Decisions are generally made behind closed doors. Divisions are hidden away in the interests of presenting a united front. Everything seems to be locked up inside a vast, opaque, bureaucratic apparatus. Meanwhile, on the outside, there are few spaces for independent political activity, and it is only on rare occasions that a university, factory or mosque escapes from state control long enough to create its own leadership and its own rival political platform. Any other type of organized opposition is forced into an underground existence. There are no polls, and the various controlled elections or referenda provide only fragmentary evidence about what a public might be thinking.

The search for a way of locating the politics within this particular type of system has generally taken one of two forms. Perhaps the most influential has been to focus on the activities of rival factions among the political élite.[18] A second is to concentrate on the way in which the struggle for access to state resources is structured in terms of groups based on ties of region or sect rather than of class.[19] Both approaches are said to be justified on the basis that the authoritarian systems to be found in the Middle East possess four major, and related, characteristics. One, they cannot tolerate organized groups within their own structures. Two, they tend to deal with the people not as individuals but as members of some larger regional, ethnic or religious collectivity. Three, they systematically inhibit the development of an active class consciousness, for example, by preventing the development of free trade unions. Four, they subordinate economic policies to measures of political control.

However, it is easy to quarrel both with the restricted nature of such approaches and with the premises on which they are based. The criticism that has been levelled against studies that focus simply on a narrow political élite is well known: they allow the political leaders too much freedom to make decisions without constraint; they reduce politics to a battle for power; they neglect the economic interests of those involved. In addition, factions are not a single type of unit, they do not remain the same over time and, most important of all, they cannot be said to constitute a system of political activity, being embedded in a structure of institutions, classes and interests that is very much wider than themselves.[20] Focus on the role of groups is open to many of the same challenges. They certainly exist but in such a bewildering variety of forms – tribes, regional affiliations, sects and so on – that they resist simple classification, while their role in the political life of the Middle East is equally various and very much more obvious in countries like Algeria and Syria than it is in Tunisia or Egypt. Furthermore, there are many more ways of access to state power and to state resources than by means of the use of collectivities, for example, through institutions like the party or the army, or through formal economic or professional associations like chambers of commerce.

Lastly, the characterization of Middle Eastern political systems upon which such theories are based is equally over-simplified, and leaves out much too much. Classes do exist as political actors, whether in an active manner, where a sense of common consciousness is present, as in the case of many large groups of workers; or in a more passive way, as when a whole élite chooses policies based clearly and obviously on the defence of private property, for instance, the Egyptian and Syrian land reforms, and to the exclusion of other possible types of arrangement, for instance, collectivization. Another example would be the common decision to establish plants making cars, which are an individual form of transport, rather than buses, which are of use only to the masses. It follows that the point about the primacy of political over economic considerations also requires further elaboration. Viewed simply from the angle of the immediate decision, it obviously exists, just as it does everywhere else in the world. But there is another sense in which policies involving rapid industrialization or the attempt to earn scarce foreign currency through the development of tourism have their own logic and a dynamic that often goes on to affect huge areas of economic life, regardless of political attempts at control.

In these circumstances it is better to start afresh by focusing on two general questions: What is politics? And where does the process of political activity take place? This has the major virtue of encouraging us to take a large view of the subject and then forcing us to have to specify the different types of actors and different types of arenas involved, as well as their different orders of importance. In the case of the former, this will involve consideration of individuals, of unofficial as well as of organized groups, of classes, and so on. In the latter it necessitates a discussion of the various locations – bureaucratic, institutional, provincial, local – in which political activity takes place. Viewed from this perspective, there cannot be any one answer to the initial set of questions, and the analysis will have to take account of many different levels, arenas and types of situation. I will begin by looking at the state apparatus itself.

Given the concentration of power in an authoritarian, one-party, state, the most important political actor is clearly the president. As a rule he is not only head of state but also commander-in-chief of the armed forces and party chairman as well. Typically he makes most key decisions on his own in the light of his own version of the public interest. He does not have to seek advice, and takes good care to ensure that no one else within the system can accumulate sufficient power to challenge his authority. Further power comes from his ability to stand above the various institutions of state, and the various factions they contain, and to adjudicate between them. Once the five Arab regimes had managed to consolidate themselves, only one president, Ben Bella of Algeria, was ousted by his colleagues, and only two others, Ahmed Hassan al-Bakr of Iraq and Habib Bourguiba of Tunisia, were eased out towards the end of their lives by ambitious younger men. On the evidence so far, death is the only certain way in which a president's rule can be brought to an end.

Nevertheless, presidents cannot do exactly what they want, and their power is subject to significant constraints. On the whole, they have the least freedom in certain areas of domestic policy; none of them has had a strong enough political or social base simply to impose his ideas on the rest of the country, and all have had to make concessions to important groups of supporters, like the Alawi notables in Syria or the landowners from the Sahel region in Tunisia who were so close to President Bourguiba. It has also been necessary to delegate enough power to certain individuals and groups simply to get things done. Presidents may prefer cabinets full of technocrats with no power base of their own, or a system of institutional balances in which one ministry or one agency is set up to check another, but, when faced with a major crisis, all of them have generally realized that this is a recipe for impotence and immobilism.

The president presides over a state apparatus that consists, in the first instance, of its major component institutions: the military, the party, the security services, the bureaucracy and the economic enterprises. All have their own organizational reasons for obtaining resources, influencing policy and preserving as much as possible of their autonomy. Examples abound of major institutional rivalries in which, for example, a party may try to seek to extend its influence into an army and be strongly resisted. More examples will be given in later chapters. In addition, certain ministries will tend to represent certain major economic and social interests, which they will seek to protect and extend; for instance, the link between the ministry of labour and the unions or the ministry of agriculture and the various groups of land-owning peasants.

The state itself then provides the major arena for the politics of the centre. It contains all the major institutional actors involved in national issues and the distribution of national resources. Here too are the major individual actors; the men (and a few women) who control these large institutions or who represent significant interests inside and outside the state apparatus. As a rule the most significant of them will come from the group of colleagues who established the regime in the first place, the Free Officers in Egypt or the so-called Oujda group of close military associates of President Boumedienne of Algeria. It is they who will be given control over the key posts like the Ministry of Defence and the ministry of the interior. But, over time, their numbers will tend to dwindle and they will be replaced by others who have worked their way into senior positions in the party, the army and intelligence. On the whole, the politicians who are invited to run the domestic side of the economy are much less powerful, control less important ministries and are subject to a very much higher rate of turnover. A last source of power is identification with, and possible support from, some major outside actor, perhaps the embassy of a superpower, like the USSR or the United States, or perhaps a high-placed Saudi prince with enough influence to direct large sums of money towards the regime.

The more durable of the major regime politicians will usually be patrons of quite large networks of clients. As a rule these will consist simply of people who have attached themselves to them for reasons of ambition or in order to use them to protect or extend some particular interest. But it may be that the network is also held together by some kind of shared political or ideological position. Important patrons will try to ensure that their clients obtain high-level posts, perhaps as ministers or chairmen of economic enterprises, in exchange for their co-operation in helping them with policies or schemes of their own. This is a reminder that patronage can be a two-way process – patron and client both need each other – and that it is also something that has to be worked at, attended to, over time. There are scarcely any analyses of network building in the Arab world written from this particular perspective. One of the few people who have examined the process in detail in its Algerian context, Bruno Etienne, suggests that a possible dynamic is one that leads a patron whose position in national politics depends initially on the support of a particularly important interest group to try to reduce this dependence over time.[21] Another of Etienne's important insights concerns the way in which different networks may coalesce for a while to form factions when important interests coincide.[22]

The political role of classes and other social groups in homogeneous and divided societies

An analysis of the role of classes and other social groups within authoritarian systems presents particular problems. Some of these arise from the usual difficulty in locating and defining each particular class, especially in a situation in which the rapid increase in educational opportunity and state employment is bound to make for considerable mobility and general fluidity. In addition, the authoritarian state itself often plays an active role in shaping or denying expressions of class interest. In some cases, particular classes are either destroyed or very much reduced in economic and social power (for example, the large landowners in Egypt, Iraq and Syria). In others, parties, associations and unions that might otherwise act as vehicles for class politics are either banned or reorganized as part of the apparatus of state control. As Ahmed Ben Saleh, the Tunisian labour leader, noted after his dismissal from government office in 1969, 'My behaviour is to be explained by my dual membership in party and trade union', a divided loyalty which inhibited him from being able to represent working class interests when they clashed with those of the regime.[23] For all these reasons, class conflict, the main motor force for developing class consciousness, is permitted only muted expression.

Nevertheless, the expression of class interests cannot be made to disappear entirely. As far as the private sector is concerned, whether in industry, trade or agriculture, an essential component of the ownership of property, and of the employment of workers, is an implicit conflict between capital and labour. It also follows that both sides are likely to organize themselves, if they can, either for the purposes of direct confrontation or, more usually, in order to obtain the intervention of the state on their own side.

Working class activity in the state sector has sometimes been more difficult to discern. But in Egypt, as elsewhere, groups of workers were often able to obtain sufficient independence from official control to organize strikes and sit-ins or to develop a local leadership which was independent of the official union structure. Workers' representatives were also able to use their presence at the numerous official economic conferences called by government or party to defend their interests in job security, a minimum wage and participation on the board of state enterprises against management efforts to curtail their privileges. On other occasions they found champions among senior regime politicians, aware of their strategic position within the economy and the vital role they had been given in government development programmes. Lastly, there were a few instances of overt opposition at the national level, for example, the leading role played by the workers at the huge Helwan Iron and Steel complex just outside Cairo in triggering the wave of popular dissatisfaction with the Nasser regime in February 1968 that forced the major change of political tack represented by the 30 March Declaration with its tentative moves towards economic liberalization and greater democracy within the Arab Socialist Union.

An identification of the political role of the middle class is more complicated, and depends on being able to establish a link between the continued existence of private property and the political practices of senior officers, high-level bureaucrats and others aspiring to a bourgeois lifestyle within the regime.[24] Such a link is seen most clearly in the case of rural land, where ownership of quite substantial holdings, often in defiance of the government's reforms, constituted a common bond between important figures within many regimes, affecting both their policy towards the agricultural sector and, more generally, making them keen defenders of their country's rural elite.

More generally, writers like Roberts and Leca have argued for the existence of a fundamental link between state officials and private property based on the desire of significant numbers of the former to augment their own, and their family's, resources, as an insurance against the possible loss of a job that gives them regular access to state resources.[25] This encourages them to establish links with the private sector, a task made easier, according to Roberts, by the fact that the boundary between public and private is so fluid and allows all kinds of profitable arrangements between bureaucrats, managers of public enterprises and private companies and individuals.[26] Rules governing such transactions are usually not well enforced, and the major risk that their exponents run is the malevolence of their political enemies or the occasional official campaign against an ill-defined notion of 'corruption'. It is the existence of such links, based on shared interest and aspirations to a common lifestyle, that played an important role in skewing public policy in directions favourable to private accumulation, whether in the area of income tax (kept low), support for local companies against foreign competition, or access to scarce foreign exchange.

Another aspect of state policy that has received considerable attention is the way in which regimes inhibit the development of class solidarities by structuring their system of access to political power, and of distributing resources in such a way that people benefit from it 'not on the bases of class affiliation but as individuals, families, particular communities, villages or regions'.[27] In the case of the five states in question, this would seem to be truer of Syria, Iraq and, to some extent, Algeria than it is of Egypt and Tunisia. One obvious difference is that the former are much less homogeneous, more socially divided, societies with regimes that are based very obviously on support from particular regions and, in the case of Syria since 1966, from one particular sect, the Alawis. This can easily be demonstrated by looking at the social composition of the leading political institutions of such states. In Iraq just after the Ba'th seizure of power in 1968, for example, all the members of both the Revolutionary Command Council and the Regional Command of the party were from the small, predominantly Sunni, region between Baghdad and Takrit.[28] And, although efforts were later made to widen the circle of leadership to include Shi'is and Kurds, as well as persons from the rural areas, the fact that so many of the top personnel have continued to come from the same small region has given some of its inhabitants great privileges, as can be seen from the fact that so many of the country's leading public works contractors now come from Takrit.[29] By the same token, major acts of resistance have been launched by groups from regions or sects that have felt themselves systematically disadvantaged by the new regimes, for example, the Sunni inhabitants of Hama in Syria who provided major support for the Muslim Brothers' revolt in 1982, or the Berber leaders of the strikes and demonstrations that broke out in the Kabyle region of Algeria in 1980.[30]

It is probably also significant that the development of different classes had proceeded much further in Egypt and Tunisia before the creation of the authoritarian state than it had in Algeria, Syria and Iraq. As Joel Beinin notes of the Egyptian case, there was an underlying continuity in the workers' movement before and after

1952, even though it has often been concealed in the literature by books which treat labour history as simply the institutional history of the official trade unions.[31] The same is true of the Tunisian working class, whose power and organization continued to assert itself well after independence and in spite of all Bourguiba's efforts to bring it under control. Industry and commerce were less well developed in Syria and Iraq, with few large concerns to take into public ownership and a much smaller number of well-organized workers. In the case of Iraq the political consequences of its situation were masked for a while by the ability of the local Communist Party to mobilize large numbers of followers in street demonstrations in the 1950s. But its lack of a solid class base in Iraqi society was soon revealed when it quickly succumbed to the assaults of its enemies from 1959 onwards. And if it was invited to join the Ba'th-dominated National Progressive Front for a few years in the mid-1970s, this was mainly because it was still better represented among certain rural communities than its Ba'thi rival. As for Algeria, here local industrialization was deliberately held up by the French so that regionalism, rather than class identity, remained the major basis of solidarity.

Against the reification of the state

For many writers, the huge size of the bureaucracy in most Middle East – and Third World – countries has been taken as a sign of a very strong state. And this, in turn, has led them to wonder how anything so strong could have achieved so little success when it came to pushing through much-heralded programmes of economic development and social transformation.[32] But this is to ask the wrong question, and then to look for answers in the wrong place.

Arguments that seek to explain the apparent paradox of a strong state with weak powers rest on two misleading assumptions. One is that the state is a coherent entity with a single intent. The other is that this same entity tries to penetrate and transform a second entity called 'society'. However, as already argued in the introduction to Part I, the state's apparent coherence is more a matter of presentation than reality. This is how most regimes would wish things to be. They base much of their legitimacy on their role as the masters of a well-defined path towards modernization, a claim that not only reinforces the appearance of single-mindedness but also justifies whatever interferences and interventions in existing social structures and relations they may choose to make.

However, when it comes to an analysis of how policies are actually made and executed, what is revealed is a whole range of often contradictory aims and conflicting interests which intersect with those of the wider society in such a way as to blur boundaries and to call into question the whole notion of one distinct entity acting upon another. One good example among many is that of the Egyptian land reform programme. This is usually presented as a major instrument of rural social transformation but in reality it proved to be something much more various and complex.[33] To begin with, the first reform law was passed only six weeks after the Free Officers came to power in 1952, and cannot be regarded as a well thought out piece of social legislation. Further negative evidence comes from the fact that so little effort was subsequently made to monitor the effects of the reform on the agrarian economy, as well as the fact that, for most of the 1950s, the main focus of administrative attention was directed towards solving the problems of over-population and landlessness not by redistribution but by bringing large quantities of new land into cultivation, for example, in the so-called 'Liberation' Province between Cairo and Alexandria, later to be provided with water by the construction of the High Dam at Aswan.

Looked at from this perspective, even the more thorough-going 1961 agrarian reform law is best seen as just another rather limited attack on landlord power, passed hurriedly as a response to the alleged role of Syrian feudalists and capitalists in the break-up of the union of the two countries in the United Arab Republic. Hence, when the Nasser regime took up the matter of the persistence of 'feudalism' in Egypt itself, as revealed by the investigations following the killing of a peasant activist at the village of Kamshish in 1966, it experienced the greatest difficulty in reaching a consensus about what, if anything, had gone wrong and so what ought to be done.[34] It did not help matters that in such a case the boundaries between what were defined as state and private interests were clearly very blurred, and that allegations of corruption and other wrongdoing could be backed up not only by appeals to a bewildering variety of different notions of legality and of interpretations of public policy but also by sheer political expediency.

In all this the idea of the supposed coherence of the state as a single actor with a systematic programme of social transformation is impossible to sustain. What we have instead is the various bits and pieces of the Egyptian version of Hobbes' great *Leviathan*, acting and reacting in ways that can only be understood through a process of disaggregation which challenges the conventional dichotomies of state versus society, legal versus illegal, or scientific planning versus private self-interest. This then is not a question of testing the strength of a supposed single entity – the state – or of its ability to mould another – society. Rather, it is a question of how to interpret a significant moment, when the veil of omnipotence created around itself by an authoritarian regime slips to reveal the bundle of competing, and often contradictory, interests that have always lain just beneath.

Notes

1 Nazih N. M. Ayubi, *Bureaucracy and Politics in Contemporary Egypt* (London: Ithaca, 1980), p. 189.

2 Clement H. Moore, 'Authoritarian politics in unincorporated society: The case of Nasser's Egypt', *Comparative Politics*, IV/2 (Jan., 1974), p. 199.

3 Ibid., Table 2, p. 199; and C. H. Moore, 'The consolidation and dissipation of power in unincorporated societies: Egypt and Tunisia, mimeo.

4 Hanna Batatu, 'Political power and social structure', in Samih K. Farsoun (ed.), *Arab Society: Continuity and Change* (London: Croom Helm, 1985), p. 39.

5 Nazih Ayubi, 'Arab bureaucracies: Expanding size, changing roles', in Adeed Dawisha and I. William Zartman (eds), *Beyond Coercion: The Durability of the Arab State* (London: Croom Helm, 1988), p. 19.

6 Lisa Anderson, *The State and Social Transformation in Tunisia and Libya 1830–1980* (Princeton: Princeton University Press, 1985), pp. 235–6.

7 Ahmed Abdalla, *The Student Movement and National Politics in Egypt* (London: Al-Saqi, 1985), Tables 6.1 and 6.2, p. 102.

8 Mahfoud Bennoune, *The Making of Contemporary Algeria 1830–1987* (Cambridge: Cambridge University Press, 1988), Table 9.3, p. 225.

9 E. R. J. Owen, 'Economic aspects of revolution in the Middle East', in P. J. Vatikiotis (ed.), *Revolution in the Middle East and Other Case Studies* (London: George Allen & Unwin, 1972), Table 1, p. 53; Elisabeth Longuenesse gives a different proportion for the

Syrian expropriation (1/4) in her 'Structures sociales et rapports de classe dans les sociétés du Proche-Orient', *Peuples Mediterranéens*, 20 (July/Sept., 1982), pp. 169–70.

10 Bennoune, *The Making of Contemporary Algeria*, p. 176.

11 A. O. Hirschman, 'The political economy of import-substituting industrialisation in Latin America', *The Quarterly Journal of Economics*, 82/1 (Feb., 1968), pp. 11–12.

12 A key work is Samuel P. Huntington and Clement H. Moore (eds), *Authoritarian Politics in Modern Societies: The Dynamics of Established One Party Systems* (New York: Basic Books, 1970). See also Guillermo O'Donnell, *Modernization and Bureaucratic Authoritarianism* (Berkeley, California: Institute of International Studies, 1973); and, in a Middle Eastern context, Moore, 'Authoritarian politics in unincorporated society', pp. 193–218.

13 Compare Raymond H. Hinnebusch, 'Local politics in Syria: organization and mobilization in four village cases', *Middle East Journal*, XXX/1 (Winter, 1976), pp. 1–24; Ilya Harik, *The Political Mobilization of Peasants: A Study of an Egyptian Peasant Community* (Bloomington, Indiana, and London: University of Indiana Press, 1974); and Robert Sprinborg, 'Baathism in practice: agriculture, politics and political culture in Syria and Iraq', *Middle Eastern Studies*, 15 (1981), pp. 191–206.

14 Gauthier de Villers, *Problèmes de l'emploi rural en Algérie* (Geneva: ILO Programme Mondiale d'Emploi, December, 1978), pp. 17–19.

15 The best sources are the many Amnesty International Reports on the Middle East: see, for example, *Iraq: Report of an Amnesty International Mission* (London, 1983); *Syria: Report to the Government* (London, 1983); and *Syria: Torture by the Security Forces* (London, 1987).

16 Georg Konrad, *The Loser* (London: Penguin, 1984), p. 205.

17 Idem. Also Samir Al-Khalil, *The Republic of Fear: The Politics of Modern Iraq* (London: Radius, 1989), Chs 1 and 2.

18 For example, R. Springborg, *Family, Power and Politics in Egypt* (Philadelphia, Pennsylvania: Pennsylvania University Press, 1982), p. 83; and William Zartman, 'L'élite algérienne sous le President Chadli Benjadid', *Maghreb/Machrek*, 106 (Oct./Nov./Dec., 1984), p. 39.

19 For example, Bruno Etienne, *L'Algérie, Cultures et révolution* (Paris: Editions du Seuil, 1977); and Jean Leca, 'Social structure and political stability: Comparative evidence from the Algerian, Syrian and Iraqi cases', in Dawisha and Zartman (eds), *Beyond Coercion*, p. 165.

20 This point is clearly acknowledged by Zartman, 'L'élite algérienne', p. 39; and Leca, 'Social structure and political stability', pp. 164–83.

21 Etienne, *L'Algérie*, pp. 92–106.

22 Ibid., pp. 40–45.

23 Quoted in Bassam Tibi, 'Trade unions as an organizational form of political opposition in Afro-Arab states – The case of Tunisia', *Orient*, 24/4 (Dec., 1979), p. 88.

54   *I: States and state building*

24 This topic is analysed by John Waterbury, *The Egypt of Nasser and Sadat: The Political Economy of Two Regimes* (Princeton, N.J: Princeton University Press, 1983), pp. 247–60; and by Hugh Roberts, *Political Development in Algeria: The Regime of Greater Kabylia*, D. Phil. Oxford 1980, pp. 69–74.
25 This analysis draws heavily on ideas put forward in Roberts, *Political Development in Algeria*, pp. 73–5.
26 Ibid., p. 84; Leca, 'Social structure and political stability', pp. 166–9.
27 Zubaida, *Islam, the People and the State*, p. 165.
28 Amatzia Baram, 'The ruling political elite in Ba'thi Iraq, 1968–1986: The changing features of a collective profile', *International Journal of Middle Eastern Studies*, 21/4 (Nov., 1989), pp. 450–2.
29 Marion Farouk-Sluglett, 'Iraq's transition to capitalism', *MERIP*, 125/126 (July–Sept., 1984), p. 52.
30 Raymond A. Hinnebusch, *Authoritarian Power and State Formation in Ba'thist Syria: Army, Party, and Peasant* (Boulder, Colorado: Westview Press, 1990), pp. 286–90; Hugh Roberts, 'The unforeseen development of the Kabyle question in Algeria', *Government and Opposition*, 17/3 (Summer, 1982), pp. 312–34.
31 Joel Beinin, 'Labor, capital, and the state in Nasserist Egypt, 1952–1961', *International Journal of Middle Eastern Studies*, 21/1 (Feb., 1989), p. 72.
32 For example, Ayubi, *Bureaucracy and Politics*, Ch. 2. But see also Joel Migdal, *Strong Societies, Weak States: State-Society Relations and State Capabilities in the Third World* (Princeton, NJ: Princeton University Press, 1988).
33 For example, Hamied Ansari, *Egypt, The Stalled Society* (Albany, NY: The State University of New York Press, 1986), particularly Chs 1 and 3; and Leonard Binder, *In a Moment of Enthusiasm: Political Power and the Second Stratum in Egypt* (Chicago and London: University of Chicago Press, 1978), Ch. 14.
34 Ansari, *Stalled Society*, pp. 34–8, 42, 102, 137–8. See also Waterbury's description of the 'revisionist' account of events at Khamshish, *The Egypt of Nasser and Sadat*, p. 340n.

3 The growth of state power in the Arab world under family rule, and the Libyan alternative

Introduction

The growth in the size and pervasiveness of the central government apparatus was not confined to those states with single-party regimes but took place under a variety of other systems as well, most notably those subject to monarchical or family rule in Morocco, Jordan and throughout most of the Arabian peninsula. The most dramatic example of this is to be found in the tiny Gulf shaikhdoms, where oil was found either just before or just after the Second World War, and which used their new-found wealth to create large bureaucracies and comprehensive welfare facilities for their growing populations. In Kuwait, for instance, the number of government employees increased from 22,073 in 1966 to 113,274 in 1976 and 145,000 in 1980 – nearly a quarter of the total labour force.[1] Growth was just as rapid in Saudi Arabia, where the civil service grew from a few hundreds in the 1950s to about 37,000 in 1962/3, 85,000 in 1970/1 and 245,000 in 1979/80.[2] As elsewhere, the expansion of educational opportunities was an important component of this growth; by 1980 there were 1,280,000 pupils in Saudi primary and secondary schools and 42,000 in the new universities.[3] Oil revenues were not the only encouragement to bureaucratic expansion, however. In the Hashemite Kingdom of Jordan, the ruling family had access to large external subsidies, first from the British, then from the richer Arab states, which they used to develop both their army and their central administration. By 1982 there were 59,000 persons in regular government employment, or just under 15 per cent of the labour force, with another 70,000–100,000 in the armed forces.[4]

Bureaucratic expansion of this size placed great power in the hands of each ruling family but also subjected them to great press-ure. Both King Hussein of Jordan and King Hassan II of Morocco narrowly avoided military coups against them on a number of occasions, while many of the regimes of the Arabian peninsula experienced considerable difficulty in coping with intra-family rivalries exacerbated by their new-found wealth and competition for high office. Nevertheless, even where individual rulers were deposed, as in Saudi Arabia in 1964, Abu Dhabi in 1966 or Oman in 1970, the families themselves survived to establish an unusual form of palace politics characterized by a great concentration of highly personalized power, a marked reluctance to permit the existence of political parties, trade unions or similar organizations (except in Morocco), limited social mobilization and a basic commitment to private economic enterprise. Only in Kuwait was a whole ruling family removed by *force majeure* as a result of the Iraqi invasion of August 1990.

A discussion of the various types of family rule will form the major theme of the present chapter. In addition, I will look at a particular state which passed from the monarchical type to one in which there was a deliberate attempt to create a new species of political and administrative structure – Libya.

The politics of family rule: some general observations

At the end of the colonial period 19 Arab states or statelets had as their head of state a king, amir, shaikh, sultan, bey or imam drawn from a family that had either established or been given hereditary right to rule. Five of these were then deposed in the 1950s and 1960s – in Egypt, Tunisia, Iraq, Libya and North Yemen – leaving 14 to survive until the present day – in Morocco, Jordan, Saudi Arabia, Kuwait, Bahrain, Qatar, Oman and the seven members of the United Arab Emirates.[5] At first sight this may seem something of an anachronism. Nevertheless, on closer inspection there are many reasons why these particular families have managed to survive, most notably their ability to concentrate power in their own hands, to contain their own internal rivalries and to resist demands to share the process of decision making with more than a small elite of loyal politicians. In doing this they have shown that family rule in the Middle East possesses certain functional advantages which were not so apparent to earlier writers, who relied overmuch on Samuel Huntington's notion of what he termed the 'king's dilemma', that is, his observation that 'the centralization of power necessary for promoting social, cultural and economic reform [would make] it difficult or impossible for the traditional monarchy to broaden its base and assimilate new groups produced by modernization'.[6] But in actual practice this has proved much less of a problem than was once thought. On the one hand, power sharing was rarely attempted, on the grounds that it might pose too many possible challenges to family authority. On the other, as Huntington himself pointed out, monarchs had a possible way out of the dilemma, by taking on the role of chief modernizers themselves and then by slowing down the process in such a way as to keep dislocation, as well as demands for participation, to a minimum.[7]

What were these advantages? And how could they be realized? Certainly the first point to make is that in a Middle Eastern context monarchy conferred none of the legitimacy that had once stemmed from the European notion of the divine right of kings. Indeed, only three of the rulers called themselves kings at all – in Jordan, Morocco and Saudi Arabia – and for reasons that had more to do with their determination to obtain the respect of the former great powers like Britain and France than it had to do with impressing their own people. Indeed, all three of them habitually used other titles, for example, 'shaikh', 'amir' or 'imam', which possessed much more resonance in terms of local custom. Meanwhile, in Saudi Arabia at least, the employment of the vocabulary of monarchy continued to provide a residual sense of embarrassment because, for some Sunni Muslims, and many Shi'is, it suggested a language that ought rigorously to have been confined to Allah himself. As King Faisal is reported to have told other members of his family in 1964, 'I beg of you, brothers, to look upon me as both brother and servant. "Majesty" is reserved to God alone and "the throne" is the throne of the Heavens and Earth.'[8] The Ayatullah Khomeini made the same point more forcefully in his polemics against the Saudi monarchy in the 1980s.

In Middle Eastern circumstances the right to rule resided not in the institution of kingship itself but in a combination of individual and family virtues, including noble lineage, noble deeds, qualities of leadership and, in the case of the kings of Jordan and Morocco, descent from the Prophet Muhammad himself. Indeed, one of the strengths of the system was the fact that legitimacy was based on such a bundle of factors, any one of which could be brought into play on the proper occasion and all of which could be used in various permutations to create powerful myths of origin that connected the family, its past achievements and its present strengths to the territory over which it now ruled. It had the further advantage of not tying a ruler to one particular source of legitimation, which might, in certain circumstances, prove embarrassing or act as a major constraint. A good example of this would be the anxiety of certain Saudi rulers, notably King Abd al-Aziz Ibn Saud himself, not to identify themselves too closely with the religious establishment, even though it was this that provided a fundamental pillar of their family's right to rule.

Another type of flexibility stemmed from the interplay between the family as a whole and the individual ruler, a relationship that allowed an aggregation of the traditional virtues represented by the one and the more modern qualities required to be successful as the other. It is probably no accident that the states where family rule survived were those where the leading families of nomadic tribes had played a prominent role in the recent past. But this did not absolve contemporary monarchs from developing the skills required to master large bureaucracies or to conduct complex international diplomacy. If the right balance could be found, the position of the family was correspondingly strengthened.

It would be wrong to suggest, however, that the maintenance of family rule was not without its problems. One of the most obvious and the most difficult has been the need to keep the family itself united. This has involved finding ways of dealing with the question of succession, as well as other potential sources of rivalry such as access to power, position and wealth. In large families where the founder, or founders, had many sons by many different wives, there was the additional problem of defining who was, and who was not, to be considered royal, and who was to be considered as a candidate for high office. In Saudi Arabia, where there may be anything up to 4,000 males with a claim to be called 'prince', the question was first tackled by King Abd al-Aziz himself in 1932 when he decreed that only his own offspring and those of his brothers and of families related to his common history and marriage were to be considered 'royal' and given a stipend. Later the list was twice pruned by King Faisal after 1958 and a number of names removed.[9] As for the Gulf states, by the 1980s many of them had written constitutions which defined who was a member and so who was a possible candidate for the succession.

Succession itself can be by primogeniture or by some version of the formula of the ruler's eldest, 'capable', male relative. Both methods possess advantages and disadvantages. Primogeniture is easy to apply and centralizes power and decision making in one single family line. However, it can also produce a monarch who is still a minor or unfit to rule. In addition, it automatically cuts out all the other lines, something that may well increase tensions, particularly in large families. The alternative, that of the eldest capable relative, is more or less bound to produce rulers who are old enough to have had considerable administrative experience. It also encourages family solidarity by allowing more lines to participate in rulership – or, at least, in the anticipation of rulership. The reverse of this is that it generally leads to short reigns and, as in the case of Saudi Arabia, where there were still 31 sons of King Abd al-Aziz alive in the mid-1970s, a long list of brothers and half-brothers to go through before it is possible to move on to the next generation.[10] A final point concerns the question of assessing the competence of any potential ruler. Not only is this a highly subjective matter but it is also something that is bound to change over time, depending on the degree of economic development and on the problems that the country faces.

In actual practice, different ruling families have applied different rules, as well as, on occasions, switching from one method to another. Among those that had institutionalized primogeniture by the 1980s were Morocco, Bahrain, Qatar, Abu Dhabi and Dubai.[11] Elsewhere different versions of the formula of the eldest competent male relative were in place, almost always supplemented by the nomination of a crown prince so as to reduce the possibility of a family quarrel breaking out immediately after the existing ruler's death. And in Saudi Arabia a mechanism had been developed for indicating who was to be considered next in line after the crown prince, the person in question being appointed as second deputy chairman of the Council of Ministers. Nevertheless, all such systems can be subject to change and to family bargaining. Jordan has had three crown princes during the reign of King Hussein – two of his (younger) brothers and his son by a marriage to a non-Muslim who was later cut out of the succession – while in Sharjah in the United Arab Emirates the 1987 dispute between the ruler and his brother was settled by changing the order of succession to make the latter the heir apparent.

If intra-family disputes could be kept to a minimum, a ruler possessed a pool of loyal personnel for use as advisers and in manning the higher offices of state. Where familes were large, as in Saudi Arabia and the Gulf, it remains usual for the ruler or his designated successor to be the prime minister and for the major positions in his cabinet – the ministers of defence, foreign affairs and the interior – to be held by other close relatives. Even where families are smaller, as in Jordan and Morocco, the king's uncles and cousins hold, or have held, important posts like commander-in-chief of the army or have been delegated important areas of policymaking like planning and development. Indeed, one of the advantages of family rule is that such appointments do not carry the stigma of nepotism as they must do in a republic. Against this, it is often difficult to remove or transfer a close relative from a position of power, so that senior family members tend to remain in the same post for long periods of time.

A second problem that faced the Arab monarch or family ruler in the past was how to obtain sufficient resources to avoid over-much dependence on important social groups and to build up support for themselves by the distribution of largesse. This was especially the case in the poorer Arabian states before the oil era, and in those like Jordan and Morocco where the monarch was kept on a tight financial leash by the colonial power, with only a small civil list and limited opportunities for accumulating land or other valuable assets. Independence or oil revenues or both provided almost all rulers with a way out. Those with oil now had an expanding income, part of which they could distribute to their own family in various ways, part of which they used to develop the infrastructure and the social services for the benefit of their own citizens. Meanwhile, growing economic activity gave them the option either of permitting their own relatives to go into business or, as in Kuwait, of striking a deal with the powerful merchant community, by which the latter was persuaded to limit its demands for political participation in exchange for a free hand to make money. As for those without oil, independence freed them from dependence on colonial subsidies, while allowing them to find alternative sources of financial support from outside (for example, aid from other Arab states) or, like Hassan II of Morocco, to go into business on his own account.[12] In either case, the tacit association of family rule with private enterprise allowed the rulers to build up a significant business clientele.

A third problem faced by family rulers was their relationship with the army. With the exception of the Bey of Tunis, who was eased out by President Bourguiba just after independence, the other four Arab monarchs who lost their thrones in the 1950s and 1960s were all deposed by military coups. And the same fate could well have overtaken the kings of Jordan, Morocco and Saudi Arabia if they had not been lucky or skilful enough to survive plots organized among their own armed forces. When confronting this problem, family rulers had only two possible options. The first, open for several decades to those in the Arabian peninsula, was to have only a very small army, often with a high proportion of foreign mercenaries, and placed under the direct supervision of loyal relatives. The other, forced upon those like the Moroccans and Jordanians who needed a large army for their own defence was for the king to play an active role as commander-in-chief, often wearing military uniform and constantly attending parades and manoeuvres. This strategy is particularly apparent in Jordan, where King Hussein showed great skill in obtaining the loyalty of his army after he had dismissed its British commander, General Glubb, early in 1956 and where, a decade later, he was said to address his soldiers by their first name 'as if he knows them all'.[13] More generally, it can well be argued that the institution of monarchy provides a better mechanism for maintaining the allegiance of an army, on the grounds that it makes more sense for a soldier to pledge himself to a person than to something abstract like a flag or a state.

A last problem, specific to ruling families that obtain part of their legitimacy from their close identification with religion, was how to benefit from this connection without being too constrained by it. By and large this involved many of the same techniques as those used in the Arab republics: government control over religious appointments and funds; the close monitoring of the Friday sermon; and so on. Another option was what might be called the 'management of tradition', for example, the introduction of certain practices that carried with them the aura of the past, such as the enforcement of what was considered proper Islamic conduct by the specially created Saudi religious police, the Mutawa.

The existence of the ruling families and their courts produced a type of politics that differed in a number of significant aspects from that in other types of system. For one thing, it involved the relationship between the family members themselves, a process of interaction in which questions of personality, ambition, state policy and the control of state institutions were inevitably mixed together. What made matters still more complicated was the fact that, in many cases, the senior princes or amirs were also in charge of the most important government ministries, which they could exploit as their own particular fiefs or power bases in support of their own particular interests. In these circumstances, the maintenance of family harmony was bound to be more important than a willingness to take difficult decisions. However, the situation may not have been quite as unsatisfactory as many commentators have argued. Ruling families were able to cover their activities with a discreet veil of secrecy and were rarely required to explain what their policies were or how decisions had been reached. Furthermore, the existence of rival points of view is not necessarily evidence of a struggle for power. Indeed, rather than being a weakness, it is probably better seen as a source of strength as long as it is kept within reasonable bounds. Certainly a situation in which all the members of a ruling family habitually shared the same approach towards major issues of policy would have ensured that issues were not properly aired and, in general, would have been a recipe for disaster.

Another special feature of family rule is the existence of the royal court, with its own particular atmosphere and its own particular dynamic. Some of its features seem timeless and are just as easily illustrated in the works of Machiavelli or Shakespeare as they are in the books of contemporary political scientists. There is the advice offered to the medieval courtier, to find out what a ruler wanted and then to go to him with suggestions as to how it might be carried out. There is King Lear's understanding of the importance of gossip, when he says that he desires to 'talk of court news . . . who loses and who wins; who's in, who's out'. All this in its modern Moroccan context is well described by Waterbury, with his observation that access to the king is the be-all and end-all of political manoeuvring, that palace watching and second guessing becomes an élite obsession, that evidence of royal favour is sought in the length of a meeting or the sight of a smile.[14] But court life is not just the stuff of a rarefied political drama; its pattern is structured by the dictates of a system in which rulers need political servants to advise them and to carry out their orders, and find it easier to draw them from a small, loyal, continuously circulating, élite.

For the public at large, courts or open councils also provide a stage for a continuous performance of what might be called the theatre of legitimacy, in which every event provides an occasion for some highly charged ritual designed to remind the people of their ruler's power and justice as well as of his noble lineage, his generosity and his devotion to his religion. 'To be invisible is to be forgotten' as Bagehot wrote of the 19th-century British royal family.[15] Once again Waterbury provides a good example of this aspect of royal behaviour, with an extract from a speech given by King Hassan II of Morocco on the occasion of his release of some prisoners.

> This clemency is proof of the innate nature of our family characterized by its profound wisdom, its great nobility and the solid communion which unites us ultimately with our people. Moreover, if we have adopted this attitude impregnated with wisdom and clemency, it is because we have answered to the humanitarian mission handed to us by the saviour of our nation and the liberator of our citizens, our late Father, Muhammad V, may God bless his memory.[16]

A final feature of note is the natural alliance between ruling families and the more conservative elements within a society, both of which see themselves as beneficiaries of a system under threat from certain movements and ideologies associated with modernity and rapid economic development. Both tend to admire tribal and rural values. Both tend to be suspicious of political parties and trade unions. One result is that royal courts contain a disproportionate number of members of the older, notable families. Another is that royal policies have a tendency to favour private property and private enterprise, as against nationalization, land reform or other collectivist solutions to economic problems. I will give illustrations of all these features of family rule in the next two sections of this chapter.

The politics of royal family rule in Jordan and Morocco

The political histories of Jordan and Morocco since independence have much in common. Both countries experienced a short period when their kings attempted to rule as constitutional monarchs before engineering a showdown with the nationalist parties and concentrating power in their own hands. Both had moments of serious military unrest. Both possessed monarchs who deliberately set themselves up as leaders of their respective national movements and as managers of their country's modernization. Nevertheless, the contexts in which these developments took place were very different. The modern history of Jordan has been dominated by its involvement with Palestine and the incorporation of a large Palestinian population, and by its close proximity to Israel; while King Hassan II of Morocco has focused nationalist attention on the incorporation of the former Spanish Sahara into his domain and made loyalty to this policy a touchstone for participation in the political process. Again, Morocco has always been a much more economically diversified country than resource-poor Jordan and, perhaps because of this, has always contained a greater diversity of political and trade union organizations, which the king has been able to use but has never quite been able to bring under control.

The turning point in King Hussein of Jordan's centralization of power came in April 1957, with his dismissal of Sulaiman Nabulsi's cabinet dominated by members of parties opposed to many basic features of Hashemite rule. This was immediately followed by the establishment of his authority over the army after the threatened military coup a few days later, and the arrival of the first American aid and then of the financial subsidies sent by a number of Arab states as a replacement for the money previously provided by the British. From then on political parties were outlawed, and the lower house of the Jordanian parliament was rarely in session (it met only once between 1974 and 1984); the king perfected a system that allowed him to make all the major decisions affecting foreign affairs and external security while leaving the execution of policy in other areas to a small group of loyal politicians who circulated between his own royal Hashemite *diwan* (or royal cabinet) and the ministers in charge of day-to-day administration.[17]

As laid down in the constitution, the King of Jordan is head of state and supreme commander of the armed forces. He also appoints the prime minister and, in consultation with him, the cabinet. Historically, both prime ministers and their cabinets were rotated rapidly, lasting an average of only seven months between 1947 and 1974 and for two years from then to the mid-1980s.[18] On appointment, each one received a public letter from the king setting out the main guidelines it would be expected to follow. Its role was essentially executive. Key decisions were taken in consultation with a small group of advisers in the royal cabinet; notably the chief of the royal *diwan*, the minister of the royal *diwan*, the commander-in-chief of the army and the prime minister – whose main allegiance was to the king rather than the cabinet. Particular prime ministers were often chosen for specific short-term political tasks, one being known for his ability to establish good relations with the Syrians, another for his willingness to take a tough stand against the Palestinians.

Members of the political élite who staffed the two cabinets came from a small group of several hundred families.[19] Before independence this élite was composed largely of persons who had been brought into Trans-Jordan (as it then was) by the British or who had moved there from Palestine. It was then expanded after the annexation of the West Bank to include representatives of the major Palestinian families that were not tainted by their connection with King Abdullah's arch rival, the Mufti. Later it was expanded further to include members of important Jordanian families, notably those of tribal leaders, merchants and members of the two most important minorities, the Circassians and the Christians. In this way appointment to one of the two cabinets came to serve a representative function, bringing the king into touch with various regional and social groups in a manner that might otherwise have been carried out by political parties. It was also a way of organizing and maintaining support. Such is the importance attached to maintaining close relations with the palace that members of this élite were almost always content to be dismissed from office without protest, knowing that if they avoided public display they would be recalled to favour on some future occasion.

Jordanians outside this small élite had little or no opportunity to influence policy at the national level. General elections were only rarely held before 1989, and all political organizations were banned. In these circumstances those wanting to make their opinions known had either to do so by means of personal contact with a member of the élite or to engage in some form of illegal activity. Even so, strikes and demonstrations were very infrequent and the only occasion on which the king had to face anything like a concerted opposition from local Jordanian groups was during the months leading up to the armed confrontation with the Palestinian resistance movement, which began in September 1970.

During the 1970s efforts were made to introduce a system of limited decentralization. Municipal elections were held regularly from 1976, while some power was devolved to local governors, mayors and the heads of village councils. However, as such elections were closely monitored and most of the persons concerned were either civil servants or retired soldiers with close ties to the government, this only opened up a tiny space for a type of competitive politics that could reflect either national or local issues. What it did allow in some municipalities was a challenge to the existing alliance of government officials and local notables, by the election of a few educated technocrats and some men either identified with one of the banned political parties or close to the Muslim Brothers, the one mass organization tolerated by the royal regime. But, once again, they were forced to operate within very strict limits, as can be seen by the strenuous attempts to prevent the re-election of certain members of the Irbid Council alleged to have been involved in the student demonstrations at Yarmuk University in May 1986.

Opposition to the rule of the kings of Morocco was very much more consistent and difficult to contain. Nevertheless, King Muhammad V and his son King Hassan II were able to develop a system of government that enabled them to centralize enormous powers in their own person and to act as arbiter between the country's other political forces. In Zartman's schema the history of this process can be divided into three periods.[20] In the first, from independence in 1956 to 1965, they attempted to create a strongly centralized constitutional monarchy, only for Hassan to abandon the project when he was unable to secure the co-operation of the major parties like the Istiqlal and its more radical offshoot, the Union National des Forces Populaires (UNFP), and was then faced with a major outbreak of popular opposition leading to widespread rioting and demonstrations in Casablanca and elsewhere. Parliament was dissolved and the king ruled through cabinets of technocrats until the attempted military coups of 1971 and 1972 persuaded him of the danger of establishing his rule on too narrow a base of patron-client relations and senior army officers alone. Finally, in the third period, which began effectively in 1974, Hassan II was successful in creating a new system of highly controlled democracy in which a number of parties were persuaded to take part in regular elections and to participate in government on his terms. As it developed, his new formula involved a combination of a number of elements. Loyal politicians were encouraged to form pro-monarchical political groupings like the RNI (National Independents' Rally) and the Constitutionalists' Union (CU). Meanwhile, other parties were allowed to contest the elections in 1977 and in 1984, provided they actively supported his highly nationalistic campaign to incorporate the former Spanish colony of the Western Sahara into Morocco. Finally, the elections themselves were subject to considerable manipulation by the state, including tight control over what could and could not be discussed during the campaign.

Surrounding the king was a small élite of politicians and notables, and the leaders of various labour unions and other economic interest groups who, according to Entelis, numbered no more than a thousand.[21] As in Jordan, Hassan II was personally acquainted with most of them and very much aware of their personal idiosyncracies and rivalries.[22] Like Hussein he was adept at keeping them all in play. It was they who provided his advisers, the executors of his policy and his eyes and ears throughout the rest of Moroccan society. A key part of this system was his ability to grant favoured courtiers and politicians access to the business opportunities that he could offer in his double role of manager of a large public sector and the country's leading private-sector entrepreneur.[23]

Given the presence of such a relatively small élite surrounding the royal court, it has been easy for analysts to limit their study of Moroccan politics to an examination of the leading personalities involved and their varied types of patronage networks. But, as in the case of the single-party authoritarian regimes, this is to ignore the interventions of major institutions like the army, as well as the existence of the mechanisms necessary to solve substantive disputes over major policy issues concerning both domestic and foreign policy. In the Moroccan context it also tends to overlook the role of the parties and trade unions in developing distinctive followings among different sections of Moroccan society which look to them to represent some of their particular interests.[24]

Another shortcoming of the same approach is that it reduces the importance of political activity outside the capital city. But, as

Seddon has suggested in his study of rural politics in Morocco's Eastern Rif, this is to ignore many of the important changes that took place in the countryside after independence, and their impact on the ways in which local people were able to represent and to defend their own interests.[25] Three factors are of major significance in his analysis: the extension of state administrative power into the rural areas; the role of the political parties in providing alternative lines of communication between centre and periphery; and the changing balance of local wealth and power. Of these the first was certainly the most important, and provided the framework in which all political forces had to operate. It also acted to strengthen existing solidarities and to counter or to dampen down efforts to mobilize the rural population behind ideological positions to be found represented at the national level. Constituency boundaries for elections to the newly created communes, beginning in 1960, tended to follow older administrative or tribal boundaries, thus reinforcing pre-existing loyalties. Meanwhile, the communal councils themselves were kept under strong administrative control and specifically forbidden to formulate views of a 'political character or foreign to objects of local interest'.[26] Nevertheless, although most candidates for the local elections felt it safer to stand as independents, some at least were willing to reveal an association with one or other of the national political parties. Meanwhile, different local groups were able to advance their interests by making alliances with the various official agencies of the state present in their town or province, as well as with other networks of power and patronage that led ultimately to the capital and to the palace. As Seddon is at pains to point out, real political issues are present in the countryside; but, because of the system of tight state control, they can only be expressed or represented in a distorted and sometimes highly personalized form.[27]

The practice of family rule: Saudi Arabia and the Gulf states

The practice of family rule that developed in Saudi Arabia had many of the same features as in Jordan and Morocco, with the important proviso that the Saudi royal family was very much larger and thus able to dominate all the senior civil and military posts itself. Otherwise there was a similar division between the cabinet (or in this case the council of ministers) and the royal court, and a similar tendency for the king and his close advisers (the senior princes) to pay special attention to matters of foreign affairs, defence and internal security (as well as the religiously sensitive issues of justice and education), leaving other matters like economic development either to American-educated princes of the third generation or to non-royal technocrats with no power base of their own.

Such a system allowed only a small group of major, political actors – some of the sons of Abd al-Aziz, members of related families like the Jilwis and the al-Shaikhs, and a few tribal leaders and members of the clergy. Membership of this group depended largely on the family of origin, seniority, prestige and an active desire to take part in public life. In addition, the weight attached to such membership could rise or fall according to political necessity, while the importance of tribal leaders suffered a decline over time as their followers settled on the land and became more directly subject to the central administration. However, unlike Jordan and Morocco, the family was large enough to keep members of the new educated élites resolutely out of policymaking, with the exception of certain rare individuals like Zaki Yamani, the minister of oil for most of the 1970s and 1980s. There was also no serious attempt to create representative institutions of any kind, while incorporation as a subsidiary member of the ruling élite was based almost exclusively on loyalty to the family and a shared perception of the values of Saudi culture and pride in its own special achievements.

The development of the main features of monarchical rule can be best understood by a rapid survey of recent Saudi political and administrative history.[28] At the time of the death of Abd al-Aziz ibn Saud in 1953 the country was still ruled much as it had been in the 1930s, with only a minimal bureaucracy of a few hundred officials and advisers, assisted when necessary by the considerable resources of the oil company, ARAMCO, from its enclave in the east. However, before he died, the king made two important preparations for the future. One was his attempt to regulate the succession and to provide leadership for the future by ensuring that his eldest son, Saud, became king but worked in close co-operation with his second son, Faisal, who had important diplomatic and administrative skills that Saud lacked. The second was the creation of a council of ministers to direct the work of the inevitable expansion of the bureaucracy as oil royalties began to mount. Given their different talents, the new king, Saud, worked to consolidate his hold over the royal court while Faisal built up the council as a major institution of state, using it to provide senior princes with administrative experience and to supervise the activities of the various ministries.

Competition between Saud and Faisal came to a head in the period between 1958 and 1964, when Saud's mishandling of a series of diplomatic and financial crises threatened the whole basis of family rule. These included near bankruptcy through the wasteful use of oil revenues, and a failure to find ways to meet the challenge posed by the increasing power of President Nasser of Egypt, made more threatening in 1962 by the dispatch of an Egyptian military force to assist the officers who had overthrown the imam of North Yemen. Nevertheless, in spite of these great dangers, the transfer of power from Saud to Faisal was a lengthy process as it took time for the majority of the senior members of the family to accept the need for taking such a serious step. In all this a key role was played by three princes whom Faisal himself had introduced into the council of ministers: Khalid, who was appointed deputy prime minister in 1962; Fahd, who became minister of education in 1953; and Abdullah, who was made commander of the national guard in 1963. In the process of consolidation that took place after Saud had been deposed and Faisal made king (and prime minister) in 1964, Khalid became crown prince (while continuing as deputy prime minister) with Fahd next in line, a position signalled by his appointment to the newly created post of second deputy prime minister in 1967. All this required complex intra-family negotiations, particularly with respect to Abd al-Aziz's next son, Prince Muhammad, who was older than the other three and who took some time to agree to surrender his right to his full brother Khalid.

Once firmly in power and sure of full family support, Faisal proceeded to provide himself with new instruments of rule, notably the creation of a higher committee of senior princes, which advised him on all major decisions, leaving the council of ministers to deal with more routine matters of administration including the planned development of the economy that began in earnest in the late 1960s. He also took advantage of the death of the grand mufti of Saudi Arabia in 1970 to create a new ministry of justice which brought the important sphere of Islamic jurisprudence within the framework of cabinet control. Finally, he pursued a deliberate policy of introducing western-educated, third generation, princes into government posts, having taken the lead in sending his own son, Saud al-Faisal, to school and then university in the United States in the 1950s. This was important in preventing the family from having to rely too heavily on the advice and skills of Saudi technocrats in the future. But it also had the effect of accelerating a process that Samore has called the development of 'power fiefdoms' among the senior princes, some of whom remained in control of the same ministry, or the same institution, for many years, if not decades.[29] This placed limits on the king's own power, made joint decisions more difficult to reach, and increased the possibility that institutional interests and intra-family rivalries would become dangerously intermixed. A good example of this occurred after the discovery of an ill-planned coup attempt among air-force officers in 1969, when family decision-making processes seemed paralysed for months and the king was subject to fiercely conflicting advice about whether to push forward with more reforms or to permit the religious establishment greater control over morals and values. In the end he decided to do both at once.

Faisal's assassination by one of his nephews in 1975 led to a period of more collective family rule, first under King Khalid (1975–82) and then under King Fahd. Once again this sometimes made consensus difficult, particularly at a time of crisis like the seizure of the Grand Mosque in Mecca in 1979 by a group of Muslim religious extremists who hoped that this would act as a spur to popular revolt against the monarchy. Nevertheless, such was the grip that the family and its allies had established on all the major centres of power, its rule was never seriously threatened, even when it was challenged by the forces of the Islamic revolution in Iran just across the Gulf from its eastern province. As Samore notes, the continuous accumulation of wealth and expansion of the state structure greatly facilitated the resolution of structural tensions within the family, as well as between the family and the rest of Saudi society.[30] Meanwhile, the non-royal Saudis who were required as technical experts could easily be absorbed as individuals into the various family patronage networks without the need to admit them into the inner circles of power or to provide them with the support of even the most rudimentary representative institutions. When it felt threatened, as after the Mosque attack in 1979, the king and the senior princes might attempt to build up popular support for themselves by a promise to explore the possibility of creating a popular consultative council. But it is clear that the majority of family members were against any such arrangement for sharing power and, in the end, the matter was quietly dropped. With all the institutions of government so firmly in the hands of one family, with political parties and trade unions banned, with opposition confined to a few tiny underground groups, the practice of politics at the national level remained an almost exclusively royal monopoly.

Nevertheless, even when so well entrenched at the centre and in the provinces, the Saudi ruling family, like any other, was not able to make policy in a vacuum and was forced to base important parts of its policy on detailed negotiations with powerful interest groups like the religious establishment and the wealthier merchants and businessmen. This could be seen with particular clarity in government efforts to clear up the difficult problems involving bankruptcy and the failure to meet obligations on loans, which came to prominence during the economic contraction that accompanied falling oil prices from 1985 onwards. So complex were the various negotiations regarding such highly contentious issues as the charging of interest that laws and decrees had constantly to be revised in the light of new pressures from the clergy and the business community.

The ruling families in Kuwait, Bahrain, Qatar, Oman and the seven constituent states of the United Arab Emirates (UAE) formed in December 1971 were also able to keep power largely in their own hands during the oil era. This involved a similar process of consolidation and of sorting out problems of succession and of access to high government office. Once this was done it was possible to use family members to dominate the most important posts in the various councils of ministers. In the mid-1980s, the office of prime minister in Kuwait, Bahrain, Qatar and the UAE was held either by the ruler or the crown prince, while the ministries of foreign affairs, the interior and defence (where they existed) were also controlled by senior relatives – the one exception being the ministry of foreign affairs in the UAE, which was in the charge of a commoner. Family dominance was equally apparent in Oman, where there was a somewhat different system of administration.[31]

The families in question were able to achieve this type of dominance as a result of two main factors. One was the protection they enjoyed, first from the British presence in the Gulf before its withdrawal at the end of 1971, then from Saudi Arabia and the United States, as well as the system of mutual support they developed for themselves through the creation of the Gulf Co-operation Council (GCC) in 1981 – until this was breached by the Iraqi invasion of Kuwait. The second was access to profits from oil, which largely freed them from financial dependence on the local population for tax revenues or on the local merchants for loans. The result was the ability to distribute largesse, not only to their own family but also throughout their own small societies. The latter was carried out in various forms: by cash handouts; by the state's purchase of privately owned lands for very high prices; and, in an institutionalized form, by the development of a wide variety of welfare services, from free education and health care to the provision of highly subsidized electricity, water and housing. In addition, the expansion of the bureaucracy and the economy allowed further opportunities for obtaining popular support by providing jobs, loans and the possibility of participating in a whole range of profitable enterprises. A key feature in all this was the creation of particular monopolies that were available only to people defined by the very restrictive nationality laws as local citizens. In most of the Gulf states these monopolies included the right to own property and to open a business. The result was a situation in which a privileged group of local nationals was well placed to take advantage of all the openings for making money that stemmed from oil, as well as from the presence of the many millions of non-nationals drawn to the Gulf in search of work.[32]

Given their large, independent, financial resources and their protection from external attack, the Gulf ruling families were free to establish links with all sections of their own societies – the merchants, the clergy, the Shi'ite minorities, the settled tribal elements – but on their own terms. In some cases, as in Kuwait, this might include a tacit bargain by which, for example, the merchants agreed to keep out of politics while the royal family kept out of business.[33] In others, it needed to be no more than an extension of a particular set of privileges to a particular group, such as the regular employment of tribesmen in the army and the police. As a rule such arrangements worked with relatively little friction. But there were always strains during periods of economic slow-down, when oil royalties declined. At such times the families had to undertake the difficult task of managing not the distribution of money and jobs but of cuts, contractions and relative hardships. This was particularly apparent in Kuwait after the collapse of the unofficial stock-market known as the Suq al-Manakh in 1982, when investors, some of whom included prominent members of the royal family, were faced with huge debts running into many billions of dollars. The government took several years to produce an agreed policy, and even then there were inevitable accusations of favouritism as some individuals and companies received very much more in official compensation than others.

As a rule, relations between Gulf rulers, governments and people were conducted along informal, personal, lines, with only minimal reference to institutions. The only two states to attempt to create formal representative assemblies were Kuwait and Bahrain, just after independence in 1962 and 1973 respectively. But even there parties were banned, the electorates were confined to only a small proportion of the male population with full citizenship, and the elections themselves were usually subject to considerable government interference. In addition, both national assemblies ran into predictable problems stemming from the fact that they contained important members of the ruling family, either *ex officio* as cabinet ministers or as elected representatives. Tensions between the family and the opposition led to the Bahrain assembly being dissolved in 1975 after two short sessions. The one in Kuwait lasted somewhat longer, with periods of co-operation being interspersed with times of great friction between some parliamentarians and a government dominated by members of the ruling house of al-Sabah. It was first dissolved in 1976, then re-opened again in 1981, before its second dissolution in 1986 following the forced resignation of the minister of justice, on the grounds that he had misused his office for personal gain, and fierce criticisms of two other ministers including the half brother of the ruler, the minister for oil.

Libya: from monarchy to a new type of state, the Jamahiriyyah

Libya gained its independence in 1951 as a federal state consisting of the three very different provinces (Tripolitania, Cyrenaica and the Fezzan) and as a constitutional monarchy under King Idris al-Sanusi. In some respects its political history echoed that of Jordan and Morocco, with an early showdown with the main nationalist political party, the Tripolitanian National Congress, in 1952, after which the king took all power into his own hands and ruled through a series of loyal politicians, while keeping parliament firmly under control. There was also a similar system of rule, with a royal cabinet containing a mixture of men from the tribal nobility and from the major families in the towns, and a ministerial cabinet in which the portfolios of finance, defence and the interior were kept firmly under the king's control.[34] Furthermore, the federal system, with its four administrations, provided large numbers of posts for loyal supporters before it was replaced by a centralized system of government in 1963, while the discovery of oil in the late 1950s provided the monarchy with a second source of considerable largesse.

There were obvious differences as well, however, and it may well be that these were enough to account for the overthrow of the monarchy by the military coup of 1969 led by Captain Muammar al-Qadhafi. The first involved the size and cohesion of the ruling family. As a result of a confrontation with dissident relatives in 1954, one of whom had killed his senior adviser, King Idris confined the succession to his brothers and members of his own line, depriving all the remainder of their royal titles and of the right to hold public office. This at once removed a large pool of loyal family talent. To make matters worse, he had no son of his own to succeed him, so that succession had to pass through his brothers to a very lacklustre nephew as crown prince. Second, the king showed none of the energy of a Hussein or a Hassan in constantly reinforcing his legitimacy and in reminding his subjects of his authority by endless public performance, preferring instead to hide himself away in a distant palace and to manipulate the political system from afar. The third difference was the king's failure to maintain personal control over the regular army or to impose an acceptable standard of behaviour on either his close relatives or his main advisers when it came to nepotism and corruption. Finally, King Idris showed little skill in distancing himself from the British and the Americans, both of whom had military bases in the country. Hence by the time he had begun to try to improve his Arab nationalist credentials in the aftermath of the 1967 Middle East war, by his use of oil royalties to support the defeated Egyptians and Jordanians, his support had crumbled away beyond repair. In an important sense he could be said to have de-legitimated both himself and the whole system of monarchical rule, and it was a question of luck as to which of a number of groups of military conspirators would be able to launch their coup first.

The leaders of the Libyan Free Unionist Officers' Movement that came to power in September 1969 promptly constituted themselves as a revolutionary command council under the chairmanship of Qadhafi, who was immediately promoted to colonel and commander-in-chief of the army. For the first four years they attempted to reorganize the government along the lines laid out by Colonel Nasser and his colleagues, centralizing power in their own hands, creating new administrative structures to limit the influence of the country's rural élites and then a mass rally, the Arab Socialist Union, to mobilize popular support. By April 1973, however, they were beginning to look for a new organizational formula, which they discovered in the notion of the people's committees to be elected in all villages, schools, popular organizations and foreign companies. To begin with, these committees were only allowed to play a significant role in local and provincial government, where they assumed some administrative and legislative functions. But in yet another initiative announced in September 1975 their activities found expression at a national level with the creation of a general people's congress, with Qadhafi as its secretary general and representatives from the district people's committees, as well as of the Arab Socialist Union and of the new work-based unions to which all Libyans were now supposed to belong.[35]

It was this system that formed the basis for the final mutation of the Libyan system associated with the publication of the first volume of Qadhafi's Green Book, *The Solution of the Problem of Democracy* (1976), and his March 1977 announcement that henceforward the country was to become a *jamahiriyyah* – a 'state of the masses'. What this actually meant in practice presents considerable problems of analysis. For one thing it was subject to considerable mutation, including the creation of a new set of revolutionary committees in 1979 which were established first in schools and universities, and then in many parts of the bureaucracy, turning many of the ministries into so-called people's bureaux. These existed side by side with the older people's committees, and reported directly to Qadhafi himself, who in 1979 had resigned from his post as secretary general of the general people's congress to assume the new post of 'leader of the revolution'. For another, the late 1970s also saw the start of a concerted attack on economic privilege, leading to the nationalization of large numbers of private firms. But it seems clear that, throughout all these changes, power remained firmly in the hands of Qadhafi and a few close aides who controlled the essential levers of the state.

As a result, by the early 1980s the structure of the Libyan state showed considerable differences from that to be found anywhere else in the Middle East. It is true that it had at its centre a large bureaucratic apparatus backed by an army which had increased to some 55,000–65,000 in 1981 and a sizeable force of policemen, militia and other persons concerned with domestic security.[36] But this organization, although ultimately answerable to Colonel Qadhafi and his colleagues, was supervised in a novel way by a combination of the permanent secretariat of the general people's congress, various revolutionary committees and, in some places, the remains of previous administrative hierarchies to be found in the military and some of the ministries – now re-named people's bureaux. This, in turn, had important consequences for Libyan politics. Whereas all the major Arab regimes had tried to create mechanisms for bringing their populations under their administrative control, not one of them had gone anything like so far as to combine this with the encouragement to popular participation provided by the committees. The result was a multitude of new types of political practice, few of which have been open to inspection by outsiders.[37]

How all this had come about also poses problems in terms of historical explanation. Clearly the presence of large sums of money from oil exports had something to do with it, at least in terms of providing the funds to support such a comprehensive and continuous process of economic, social and administrative engineering. The fact that Libya had only a small population of some two to three millions and had experienced such a short history of centralized bureaucratic structures is also significant. But the personalities and expectations of the small group of middle-ranking army officers who made the coup cannot be ignored. As John Davis, one of the shrewdest observers of the Libyan scene, has noted, *The Green Book* seems to have been written by a man who feels deceived and frustrated by the day-to-day experience of government.[38] Born in a tent pitched in the open desert, and with only minimal contact with any type of bureaucracy before he joined the army in 1964, Colonel Qadhafi shared none of the commitment to regular administrative procedures shown by a Nasser or an Asad. He also lacked their patience and their attention to detail. The result was a freedom – perhaps even a compulsion – to experiment, which remained an essential feature of Libyan political and organizational practice.

Notes

1 Nazih Ayubi, 'Arab bureaucracies: Expanding size, changing roles', in Adeed Dawisha and I. William Zartman (eds), *Beyond Coercion: The Durability of the Arab State* (London: Croom Helm, 1988), p. 17. Ayubi's figures for 1980 probably exclude military and diplomatic personnel, which accounted for another 14,227 in June 1982. The total labour force amounted to 491,641 in 1980, but of this only just over 100,000 were Kuwaiti citizens; State of Kuwait, Ministry of Planning, Central Statistical Office, *Annual Statistical Abstract 1983* (Kuwait: Nov., 1983), pp. 105–6, 132–3.

2 Ibid. p. 17. But note that the Ministry of Planning, using a different definition of employment that includes daily wage workers not classified as 'civil servants', gives a figure of 399,400 in civilian government employment for 1400 AH (1980) or 13.2 per cent of the total labour force; Kingdom of Saudi Arabia, Ministry of Planning, *Fourth Development Plan* (Riyadh, 1405 AH/1985), Table 2–6, p. 32.

3 John A. Shaw and David E. Long, *Saudi Arabian Modernization: The Impact of Change on Stability* (Washington, DC: Praeger, with Center for Strategic and International Studies, Georgetown University, 1982), p. 26.

4 Ayubi, 'Arab bureaucracies', p. 19; Mary C. Wilson, 'Jordan's malaise', *Current History* (Feb., 1987), p. 85.

5 I have excluded the rulers of the tiny statelets in the hinterland of Aden once known as the Aden Protectorate, all of whom were swept away soon after the Liberation Front took power after the British withdrawal in 1967.

6 Samuel P. Huntington, *Political Order in Changing Societies* (New Haven, Conn: Yale University Press, 1968), pp. 171–91.

7 Idem.

8 Quoted in Mordechai Abir, 'The consolidation of the ruling class and new elites in Saudi Arabia', *Middle Eastern Studies*, 23/2 (April, 1987), p. 156.

9 Ibid., p. 157.

10 G. S. Samore, *Royal Family Politics in Saudi Arabia (1953–1982)*, University Microfilms, Harvard University Ph. D. 1984, pp. 308ff.

11 Rosemary Said Zahlan, *The Making of the Modern Gulf States* (London: Unwin Hyman, 1989), pp. 83, 88, 98, etc.

12 For example, Rémy Leveau, 'Aperçu d'évolution du système politique marocain depuis vingt ans', *Maghreb/Machrek*, 106 (Oct./Nov./Dec., 1984), pp. 15–18.

13 Quoted in Samir A. Mutawi, *Jordan in the 1967 War* (Cambridge: Cambridge University Press, 1987), p. 16.

14 John Waterbury, *The Commander of the Faithful: The Moroccan Political Elite: A Study of Segmented Politics* (London: Weidenfeld Nicholson, 1970), p. 162.

15 Walter Bagehot, *The English Constitution* (London: Chapman & Hall, 1867), pp. 63, 70–1.

16 Waterbury, *Commander of the Faithful*, p. 150.

17 The paragraphs on the Jordanian political system draw heavily on Mutawi, *Jordan*, especially Ch. 1, and the slightly longer account to be found in the same author's Ph. D. thesis, also called 'Jordan in the 1967 War', which he presented at Reading University in Sept. 1985. I have also used information from Marius Haas, *Hussein's Konigreich: Jordaniens Stellung im Nach Osten* (Munich: tuduv Buch, 1975).

18 Sune Persson, 'Exile and success: Palestinian exiles in Jordan', Mimeo (Dept. of Political Science, University of Goteborg, Sweden, Oct., 1985), p. 21.

19 Persson, 'Exile and success', p. 22.

20 I. William Zartman, 'Political dynamics in the Maghrib: The cultural dialectic', in Halim Barakat (ed.), *Contemporary North Africa* (Washington, DC: Center for Contemporary Arab Studies, Georgetown University, 1985), pp. 28–9.

21 John P. Entelis, *Comparative Politics of North Africa: Algeria, Morocco and Tunisia* (Syracuse, NY: Syracuse University Press, 1980), p. 65.

22 Leveau, 'Aperçu d'évolution du système politique morocain', pp. 23–6.

23 Ibid., p. 18.

24 David Seddon, *Moroccan Peasants: A Century of Change in the Eastern Rif 1870–1970* (Folkstone: Duckworth, 1981), p. 273.

25 Ibid, Ch. 10. See also J. David Seddon, 'Local politics and state intervention: Northeast Morocco from 1870 to 1970', in Ernest Gellner and Charles Micaud (eds), *Arabs and Berbers: From Tribe to Nation in North Africa* (London: Duckworth, 1973), pp. 109–40.

26 Quote from Article 25 of Constitution of Rural Communes, in ibid., p. 137.

27 See, in particular, *Moroccan Peasants*, pp. 277, 283.

28 In this historical section I draw heavily on Samore, *Royal Family Politics* and Summer Scott Huyette, *Political Adaptation in Sa'udi Arabia: A Study of the Council of Ministers* (Boulder, Colorado, and London: Westview Press, 1985).

29 Samore, *Royal Family Politics*, pp. 235, 286–7.

30 Ibid., p. 490.

31 Zahlan, *The Making of the Modern Gulf States*, Ch. 8 and Appendix.

32 Roger Owen, *Migrant Workers in the Gulf* (The Minority Rights Group, London, Report No. 68, Sept., 1985), and sources cited there.

33 Jill Crystal, *Oil and Politics in the Gulf: Rulers and Merchants in Kuwait and Qatar* (Cambridge: Cambridge University Press, 1989), p. 75.

34 Ruth First, *Libya: The Elusive Revolution* (London, Harmondsworth: Penguin Books, 1974), p. 78.

35 Nathan Alexander, 'Libya: The continuous revolution', *Middle Eastern Studies*, XVII/2 (April, 1981), pp. 212–19.

36 Figures for military from Anderson, *State and Social Transformation*, p. 266.

4 Arab nationalism, Arab unity and the practice of intra-Arab state relations

Introduction

The fact that the vast majority of newly independent states contained largely Arab-speaking populations and that they consciously identified themselves as Arab has played a major role in 20th-century Middle Eastern politics. But attempts to try to define this role and to work out whether the practice of intra-Arab state relations differ markedly from that between other groups of states in, say, Latin America or East Asia, have not proved markedly successful. For one thing, much of the writing on the subject has always been highly political and concerned to make polemical rather than academic points. Perhaps because of this, few writers have taken any great care to distinguish between the various types of Arabism, which have run all the way from a sense of shared history, culture and, sometimes, religion to the creation of parties and movements that have placed Arab nationalism and Arab unity at the centre of their programmes of political action. There has been a similar disinclination to distinguish between the different types of national solidarities to be found among the Arabs; for example, the strong sense of local identification to be found among Egyptians or Moroccans, or the several kinds of Palestinianism that have developed among Palestinians with quite separate experiences of occupation, exile or foreign rule.

On top of this, writers on the Middle East have increasingly been influenced by the lively debate between the exponents of different theories or explanations of nationalism, as well as by the work of those like Sami Zubaida who argue that nationalism itself does not constitute a 'unitary general phenomenon' and therefore that no such theory is possible or appropriate.[1] To speak very generally, the greater part of the writing on Arab nationalism has been by those who see it, first and foremost, as an ideology, a set of ideas to be interpreted and analysed for what they say about the relationship between history, culture, society, politics and the right ordering of a future, united, Arab nation. This is usually done by isolating the work of a number of Arab intellectuals, politicians and polemicists who are somewhat arbitrarily defined as nationalists; although, at its best, it also seeks to locate them within the wider currents of the social and political thinking of their time.[2] However, in recent years there has also been some attention to the development of different types of Arab nationalist political movements and the impact of their activities, not only on the politics of the separate Arab states and of the Palestinians but also on inter-state relations as well.[3] As a rule, those who concentrate their attention on nationalist writings tend to an 'idealist' view of history, in which ideas are the motor force of historical change, while those who are more concerned with nationalism as a political movement tend to a more 'materialist' approach, in which the major influence stems from economic and social developments within each society and in the world at large.[4]

Faced with the large volume of contradictory and often imprecise work on Arab nationalism, I find it useful to start my examination with a look at the notion of Arabism and of the Arab cultural revival at the end of the 19th century, before going on to an analysis of some of its political consequences since the First World War. One of the latter was the development of a powerful nationalist ideology; others ran all the way from the various types of solidarities that began to be expressed in the 1920s and 1930s and various mechanisms for intra-Arab co-operation to the fully fledged schemes for instant unity like those that led to the Egyptian/Syrian union of 1958–61 (the United Arab Republic) and the discussion of an even wider union between Egypt, Syria and Iraq in 1963.[5]

From Arabism to Arab nationalism

At the end of the 19th century large numbers of people living in the Middle East had claims to be called Arabs, for linguistic, cultural and historical reasons. They spoke Arabic and, what was more important, those who could read and write had access to a language that had resisted major dialectization and could be understood from Morocco to the Persian Gulf. They were also heirs to a common culture and a common historical experience based on memories of the Arab and Ottoman Empires. And the vast majority of them who were Muslims possessed not only a common religion but also a set of religious practices, like the pilgrimage, that brought them together at the same revered holy sites.

Nevertheless, Arabness was just one of a number of possible identities at this time, and usually much less important than that of belonging to a particular family or tribe or region or town. And even when the first nationalist writers in the Syrian provinces of the Ottoman Empire began to write in praise of Arabism and to try to get people to think of themselves, first and foremost, as Arabs, they had to compete with a number of other national, religious or regional identities which had already begun to assume political importance. As has often been remarked, it was the Arabs and the Turks, of all the peoples in the empire, who came last to a national movement of their own, many decades after the Greeks and Armenians and others. But like all such late comers, they had immediate access to a well-developed vocabulary based not only on notions of patriotism and national rights but also on associated concepts like citizenship and political representation which could be seen as the properties of people who had managed to establish their own nation state.[6]

Writers like Anderson, Gellner and Nairn have tried to set out some of the specific historical conditions that allow national movements to appear and to gather strength.[7] These include certain processes that tie significant groups of people together into what Anderson calls an 'imagined community', for example, the development of local or regional economies and the spread of printing and newspapers. This in turn promotes the transition from a situation in which people possess a cluster of identities based on religion, or some other primary loyalty, to one based on culture – which may then be conceived of, either partially or wholly, in secular terms. Typically this involves a concern with language, with folklore and with popular history, either real or invented. And it often starts with the works of poets, artists and lexicographers who have a particular interest in stressing cultural homogeneity. From there it can quickly develop into an assertion that the people who are identified as sharing a particular culture should also live together in a particular state on a particular piece of land.

For writers who argue in this way, all nationalisms generate a very similar sort of political theory, using very much the same language. They are concerned with a common problem of national definition: What is the national essence? How was it maintained through history? Where are its boundaries? Their writings are also to be seen much more as a call to action than a coherent, philosophically satisfying, statement. Their purpose is to start a movement, not to fill libraries. If they are to succeed they have to persuade all the people they have defined as being Slav, or Greek, or Arab, or whatever, to act as though that was their primary identity and to place it at the centre of their political lives. This is often best done by a combination of rhetoric and poetry, and by an appeal to a glorious national past and an equally glorious national future.

Just what class or group first takes up the call and tries to mobilize the rest of a national population differs from case to case. Some writers assign this role to the educated élite, others to the middle class. But neither of these groups is usually defined with any precision. There is more general agreement that, in a Third World context, national movements arise most obviously as a result of a desire to throw off imperial control and of a recognition that, in a world of nation states, the only way a people can protect itself is to obtain a state of its own. Whether or not they succeed will then depend not only on their ability to mobilize large sections of this same population and to keep it unified but also on a whole variety of historical, geographical and political accidents such as wars, great power rivalries and the strength of other groups competing for the same territory.

As far as the Arabs at the eastern end of the Mediterranean were concerned, they followed a roughly similar path, from an emphasis on language and culture to the first small, overtly political, groups that appeared just before the First World War, calling for the separation of the Arab provinces from an Ottoman Empire that was seen as being run, increasingly, by Turkish-speaking officials and that seemed to be proving woefully deficient at standing up to both European and Zionist encroachment. Members of some of these same groups, including former Ottoman army officers, took part in the Hashemite-led revolt against the Turks in the First World War and then in the short-lived Arab kingdom established by Faisal in Damascus in 1919/20. After that, however, the movement was forced to come to terms with the fact that not only was the eastern

Arab world split up into separate states by the colonial powers but that these same states rapidly developed their own, local, laws, symbols and practices which provided an alternative focus for Arab loyalties. This can be seen very clearly in Iraq, the first of the eastern Arab states to achieve its official independence in 1932 (and a seat at the League of Nations), where efforts to create a sense of Iraqi patriotism were deliberately introduced by the very same king and set of politicians who were also busy with schemes for wider Arab co-operation and even unity. Examples of the former range all the way from the establishment of a competition among poets and musicians to provide words and music for the first Iraqi national anthem to the arguments in favour of universal military service and the politically orchestrated appeals to Iraqi national feeling designed to put an end to the divisions engendered by the tribal revolts of 1935/6.

Nevertheless, if the colonial period saw the creation of new frontiers dividing the new Arab states from each other, it also saw the development of powerful countervailing tendencies as well. One that followed from the normal processes of economic modernization was the growing importance of newspapers, broadcasting stations, films and foreign travel in reinforcing the sense of an Arabism that transcended the new political boundaries. This was accompanied by the introduction of intra-Arab conferences of various kinds, and by the development of institutions like banks, with branches in a number of separate states. The policy of employing Arabic-speaking teachers, doctors and legal experts in Iraq, Kuwait and Bahrain was part of the same trend. A second countervailing tendency was the assistance given to those fighting against the colonial presence, for example, King Faisal's offer of employment to two Syrian, anti-French, activists who sought refuge in Baghdad in the early 1930s. But certainly the most important factor was the growing Arab support for the Palestinians in their struggle against both the British and the Jewish settlers, culminating in the active involvement of politicians and publicists during the anti-British revolt of 1936–9. As Yehoshua Porath correctly observes, events in Palestine now constituted the 'single most important factor contributing to the growth of pan-Arab ideology'.[8]

In these circumstances it was relatively easy to keep a sense of Arabism alive and to stress the links that united the Arab-speaking peoples on both sides of what could be made to seem like wholly artificial, foreign-imposed, borders. As Bensaid notes of one of the deputies attending the first Syrian constituent assembly in 1928, he felt unable to swear an oath of allegiance to something as vague as the notion of a country ('watan') called Syria.[9] For him, as for many others, the Arabs belonged to a state with much larger and more generous frontiers than the British and the French had allowed.

The new Arab states: between co-operation and competition

The contradictory necessities of state building versus Arabism are reflected in the policies of the various Arab regimes as they gained their independence, first in the east, then in North Africa, then in the Gulf. All were aware of the many cross-border ties that linked them to their neighbours, and sought to profit from them. But all were equally aware of the dangers these same ties imposed and the possibilities they offered for outside interference in their political life. Not only was it virtually impossible to control the free flow of people and ideas but there were also a multitude of tribal and family, of cultural and commercial, connections that linked Arabs on both sides of any border. In these circumstances the new regimes began to use a heightened, political, Arabism to win local support, to enhance their own legitimacy and to protect themselves from attacks by the growing number of groups advocating greater Arab co-operation against the colonial powers or the Jews in Palestine. Meanwhile, for the Hashemite rulers of Iraq and Trans-Jordan in particular, the spread of Arab nationalist sentiments allowed them to dream of expanding their own power to include union with neighbouring states like Syria and Palestine.

A good example of the type of politics this involved took place in Iraq in 1932, when King Faisal tried to get the British to give their approval to his holding an Arab congress in Baghdad, using the argument that Arab support would help to reduce Iraqi weakness and to overcome the dangers threating the integrity of Iraqi society.[10] This in turn was countered by Humphreys, the British high commissioner, who argued that such a move might actually provoke the hostility of its neighbours and encourage the very dangers that the king feared. In his opinion, the best way to serve the Arab cause would be through Iraq's attention to its own economic and cultural progress. More than 50 years after the event it is possible to see the merits of both sets of arguments. A parade of Arabism might have both positive and negative consequences, depending on circumstances. In this particular, Iraqi, case it could have been used to increase support for the regime. It could just as easily have stimulated opposition, either from the local Shi'is, who tended to see Arabism as a way of bolstering Sunni supremacy, or by the leaders of other Arab states like Saudi Arabia who resisted anything they saw as an Iraqi bid for leadership over the rest of the Arab world.

In this situation, the way chosen by most Arab regimes in the 1930s and 1940s was one of encouraging greater co-operation on a state-to-state basis. This can be seen in the treaties of friendship, arbitration and extradition that were signed between them from 1931 onwards. It can also be seen in the creation of what was officially entitled the 'League of Arab States' in 1945, with Syria, Iraq, Saudi Arabia, Egypt and Lebanon as its first members. Although there were quite serious difficulties between the advocates of closer union (notably Egypt) and those who wanted a looser type of arrangement (mainly Lebanon and Saudi Arabia), all agreed that what was needed was a framework permitting greater co-operation between what were, basically, independent sovereign states.[11] Indeed, as Korany points out, the word 'state', in its territorial sense, appears 48 times in the 20 articles of the Arab League charter.[12] The negotiations reflected the different interests of the separate regimes. Egypt, which had been searching for local allies since the Anglo-Egyptian treaty of 1936 had allowed it to pursue an independent foreign policy, supported a closer union on the grounds that its greater power and size would allow it to dominate any such arrangement. By the same token, Saudi Arabia and Lebanon, fearful of domination by their Arab neighbours, felt that they could profit best from an institution based on co-operation rather than enforced unity.

Nevertheless, in spite of such forebodings, there were immediate pressures to move further in the Egyptian direction. The defeat of the Arab armies in Palestine in 1948/9, the struggle against what was left of the British and the French presence and the growing competition between the Americans and the Russians for Middle Eastern influence all seemed to underline the advantages of greater unity. Further emphasis came from President Nasser's assertion of Egyptian independence, leading to his nationalization of the Suez Canal and his triumph over the Anglo-French and

Israeli invasion of October/November 1956, which he immediately set out to exploit as a great 'Arab' victory. In this atmosphere it was easy to mobilize large crowds behind nationalist and anti-colonial slogans throughout most of the Arab world. Popular enthusiasm reached its peak with the formation of the United Arab Republic between Egypt and Syria in 1958, and then again with the unity talks of 1963, during which flags were carried through the streets of Cairo with four stars representing the countries that were supposed to form the new super-state: Egypt, Syria, Iraq and, in some formulations, North Yemen.

The search for greater political unity failed, however, largely as a result of the contradictory interests of its main exponents. One example was the central role played by President Nasser and by Egypt. Given Egyptian economic and military predominance in the Middle East at this time, any scheme for unity was bound to be to its advantage. But this was exactly what worried the other Arab leaders, particularly when the Egyptian regime showed no compunction in appealing to their people over their own heads. 'If as a state Egypt recognizes boundaries in its dealing with governments', wrote a columnist in *Al-Ahram*, the official mouthpiece of the Nasser regime on 29 December 1961, 'Egypt as a revolution should never hesitate or halt before these boundaries but should carry its message beyond its borders to the people in order to initiate its revolutionary message'.[13] Such fears were further intensified by the actual experience of Syrian union with Egypt, which left many important persons, the future President Hafiz al-Asad among them, determined never to place their country in such a subservient position ever again.

The Palestine issue also possessed the same ability both to unite Arabs and to divide them. For the first ten years after the creation of the state of Israel and the expulsion and flight of some 750,000 refugees, the two Arab states most closely involved, Egypt and Jordan, were more preoccupied with trying to stir up the Palestinians against each other than in preparing a plan for joint Arab action against the Israelis.[14] There was also little willingness to encourage the Palestinians themselves to play a role in the future liberation of their land.[15] Things changed in the early 1960s, however, when the idea of creating what was known as a Palestinian 'entity' among refugee Palestinians began to gather support and was finally agreed by the Arab leaders themselves, meeting at the first Arab summit in January 1964. This in turn paved the way for Ahmad al-Shuqairi to establish the Palestine Liberation Organization (PLO) at the initial meeting of the Palestinian national council held in Jerusalem the following May. For most observers, rivalry between Egypt and the new revolutionary regime of Brigadier Qasim in Iraq, 1958–63, had much to do with the decision to allow the creation of a PLO, while others see it also as aimed against Jordan, which was bound to feel threatened by an organization that offered an alternative leadership to the many Palestinians living under its own control. Meanwhile, at this very same time, Yasser Arafat and a few friends were preparing to start guerrilla operations against Israel with their new Fateh organization which they had formed as a deliberate attempt to allow Palestinians to control their own destinies after years of neglect by the Arab states. In the end it was Fateh's greater militancy that not only played a role in precipitating the disastrous confrontation with Israel leading to the 1967 Middle East war but that also allowed it to obtain a major influence in the PLO, leading up to Arafat's election as chairman of its executive committee in February 1969.

Tension between the Palestinians and the Arab states also points to a third contradiction inhibiting the drive for unity – the fact that, by the 1950s, the main exponents of Arab nationalism were the Arab regimes themselves. Not only were they unwilling to consider any of the reductions in their own power and sovereignty that a real union would involve but they were always worried that unbridled support for Arab nationalist goals might involve them in a dangerous war with Israel as well. For both reasons, they were particularly wary of the smaller, pan-Arab, groups like the Movement of Arab Nationalists (MAN) founded in Beirut in the early 1950s, whose demands for union and for immediate confrontation with the Israelis were worryingly insistent. After some initial hesitation, MAN supported President Nasser's drive for Arab leadership until 1965/6, when it too began to adopt a more critical stance and to argue that it was the existing regimes that were the main obstacles to Arab unity and which should either change their ways or be removed by revolution from below.[16]

In the highly charged atmosphere that followed the 1967 war, it was the PLO, the guerrillas and their various Arab radical supporters that seemed, for a moment, to show the Arab world an alternative way forward. But then the existing states began to assert themselves, to strengthen their defences and to regain control. In all this they were greatly assisted by access to the oil wealth that Saudi Arabia, Libya and the Gulf states agreed to distribute at the Khartoum Arab summit in 1967. This was followed by Jordan's successful confrontation with the Palestinian resistance movement in 1970/1 and then by the much better performance of the reorganized Arab armies in the 1973 war against Israel. Thereafter, the drive for union was much diminished and the separate states were left free to develop their own particular identities within the larger Arab environment.

Arabism in the 1970s and 1980s

In a well-known article published in 1979, Fuad Ajami proclaimed the 'end of pan-Arabism'.[17] By this he seems to have meant that the power of the individual states to resist pan-Arab appeals had become much greater and therefore that such appeals were much more difficult to make. This is undoubtedly correct as far as it goes. However, as I have tried to show in the previous section, the drive for unity was always more ambivalent than is usually presented. Just as important, any scheme for greater inter-state co-operation was underpinned by a basic Arabism, a sense of kinship between the Arabic-speaking peoples, which remained a central fact of Middle Eastern life whatever else might be going on. Seen from this perspective, what Ajami is trying to describe is not the end of Arabism itself but an important change in the way it was interpreted and put to political use.

Apart from the immediate fall-out from the 1967 war, the Arab environment changed in a number of important ways during the 1960s and early 1970s. One factor was the decline of Egyptian power and prestige as a result of military defeat, economic exhaustion and the death of President Nasser. A second was the growing financial influence of Saudi Arabia, and a third the new political importance of Syria following the consolidation of President Asad's regime in the early 1970s. If we also add the large increase in the numbers of independent Arab states, we see an Arab world where power was very much more diffused and within which, consequently, it was very much more difficult for one leader, or one regime, to exercise influence or control.

Another important factor accounting for the changed Arab environment was what has been termed the increasing 'durability' of the Arab regimes and the existing Arab states.[18] After the numerous coups of the 1950s and 1960s, no regime or ruling family was overthrown by force in the 1970s and 1980s, with the exception of that of President Numeiri of Sudan, who was ousted as a result of widespread popular (and army) opposition in 1985. Other enforced changes, like President Sadat's assassination in 1981 or President Bourguiba's deposition in 1987, did not lead to any basic change in the way each country was run. As has already been argued, the major reason for this durability lies in the growth of state power. Only Lebanon provides solitary testimony to the inability of a government to contain the conflicting forces at loose on its national terrain; as such, it was also made the victim of intra-Arab and Arab/Israeli rivalries which could be expressed, with less danger to their protagonists, on somebody else's soil.[19]

The new situation permitted regimes to exploit some of the possibilities inherent in Arabism without having to surrender control over policy or, worse still, their own state sovereignty. An obvious strategy was to proclaim a strong attachment to unity while avoiding any scheme that might involve closer political union with another Arab country or actual military confrontation with Israel. Two of the regimes that practised this approach most assiduously were the Ba'thi ones established in Syria in 1966 and Iraq in 1968. Both were helped by the fact that one of the three major principles of Ba'thism, 'unity', implied such a strong commitment to Arabism, almost by definition, that it was unnecessary to demonstrate this commitment by undertaking what might have been harmful actions beyond each state's borders. As an additional precaution, both regimes resorted to periods of ideological overkill in which, at a rhetorical level, they adopted such extreme positions towards support for the Palestinians and opposition to Israel as to make it impossible for any other regime to align itself with them. As a result, it came as something of a surprise when, in the wake of the November 1978 Baghdad Arab summit conference, both Ba'thi regimes agreed to unite. However, as Kienle argues, the decision is best seen not as a sincere attempt at union but as a 'device to enhance their own position', with Iraq seeking to replace Egypt as the leader of the Arab world and the Syrian regime trying to buy time for itself at a time of considerable internal weakness.[20] The two leaders, Hafiz al-Asad and Saddam Hussain, met only three times before the scheme finally collapsed amid mutual allegations of unacceptable interference in each other's affairs in the summer of 1979.

A second change in direction involved each regime placing more and more stress on its own local territorial nationalism. This was relatively easy for the countries of North Africa – Libya apart – where the existence of separate states had never been seen to be in any sort of major conflict with the demands of Arabism or greater Arab co-operation.[21] In the case of Egypt, for example, President Sadat was able to derive advantage from the genuine mood of war weariness that followed the October war with Israel and the feeling that Egypt had spilled more than enough of its blood in the Arab cause. And the decision to use the name Egypt again, rather than the United Arab Republic, aroused little opposition. Matters were somewhat more difficult in the eastern part of the Arab world, where the existing states still seemed more artificial entities and where most of the separate regimes had traditionally relied on political appeals to Arabism to augment their own legitimacy. But in Iraq and Jordan there began a process of subtle linguistic change designed to reinforce the vocabulary of a local territorial nationalism while, elsewhere, it was loyalty to the ruling family that generally stood proxy for a primary attachment to the state within its narrow boundaries.[22] Only in South Yemen, where appeals to either Arabism or Yemeni nationalism were deemed politically and ideologically inappropriate, was a third authority, that of Marxist-Leninism, employed as an alternative focus for popular loyalty until the sudden volte-face at the end of the 1980s.[23]

One index of the shift towards a more localized set of symbols and practices that linked particular Arabs to particular pieces of land was the construction of tombs of unknown soldiers. Another was increased attention to the celebration of specific national days, few of which had any symbolic pan-Arab component.[24] This process was carried furthest in Iraq during the war with Iran in the 1980s, when the country was given a specifically local history and geography calculated to stress its differences with its Arab neighbours. A good example is the frequent pictorial representation of the Iraqi landscape as an oasis of richly watered date palms surrounded by an obviously Arab desert.[25]

Such moves clearly reinforced the existing tendencies towards greater separateness among the Arab peoples that were already expressed in the different passports, the different educational and legal systems, the different rules governing migration and citizenship, and so on. Nevertheless, in spite of the obvious diminution in the calls for unity, Arabism continued to express itself in a variety of ways, for example, by the joint action to expel Egypt from the Arab League after its peace treaty with Israel in 1979, or the support given to Iraq by Egypt and Jordan during its long war with Iran from 1980 to 1988. In each case, the unity of the Arab ranks was broken, the first time by Egypt, the second by Syria, who sided with Iraq's adversary, Iran. But in each case, too, the ties of Arabism were strong enough to encourage a high degree of co-operation between the great majority of the Arab states.

The same tendencies were reinforced in the 1970s by the oil boom, which encouraged a whole new breed of schemes of intra-Arab co-operation based on the planned redistribution of wealth from rich to poor in the interests of the more rapid economic development of the Arab region as a whole. Even more important were the decisions to use oil revenues in support of the so-called 'front line' states in the wars against Israel and to bolster the resolve of those opposed to the Camp David agreement of 1978 and the planned Israeli-Egyptian peace agreement. In this latter case Syria was promised $1.8 billion a year for ten years, Jordan $1.2 billion and the PLO and the Palestinians of the occupied West Bank and Gaza $150 million each.[26] However, as a result of falling oil revenues, the financial demands of the Iraq/Iran war and the changes in political relationships, it is very unlikely that all this money was actually handed over.

The specificities of intra-Arab relations

In international law, as well as in their own perceptions of themselves, the individual Arab states are sovereign entities. This is officially recognized in the title as well as the charter of the League of Arab States. As Article VIII forcefully asserts: 'Each state participant in the League shall respect the existing regime obtaining in the other League states, regarding it as a (fundamental) right of those states, and pledges itself not to undertake any action tending to alter that regime.'[27] However, in terms of actual practice, the League acted as though the Arab states should conduct their relations more in terms of some notion of brotherhood than protocol. This can be seen very easily in the League's lack of any mechanism for settling disputes about interference in each other's internal affairs. The matter first arose on two occasions in 1958. In the first, Lebanon lodged an official protest against propaganda attacks against it by the media of the United Arab Republic (then consisting of Egypt and Syria), and against intervention across its borders by armed bands. Instead of examining the protest in detail and trying to assign blame, the other members passed a resolution which simply called upon both states to end the disturbances between them. As the Sudanese delegate explained, this approach was based not on the notion that the League was a court of justice adjudicating between two parties but on the need to encourage a reconciliation between brothers. A few months later, a Tunisian speech of complaint against Egypt for harbouring a group of political exiles which, it alleged, had plotted against the government was rejected, again without examination, as largely 'offensive' to the League of Arab States and derogatory to one of its members.[28]

The reason for the absence of an official mechanism for settling inter-state disputes stems obviously from the assumption that the Arab states were so similar in kind that such a mechanism was both unnecessary and inappropriate. As leader of the revolution, Qadhafi stated forcefully to President Mubarak in December 1989: 'I am against diplomatic representation (between Egypt and Libya) because the ultimate aim must be a united Arab nation where there is no need for the exchange of such missions.'[29] Occasions of this kind also provide an important clue to the way in which intra-Arab relations were (and are) actually conducted. As a rule, they were attended to, personally, by the president or head of state, often on the telephone to his opposite number or by personal visit, with only minimal reference to his own foreign ministry or his diplomatic representatives in the other capital. Another feature was the important role assigned to senior members of a regime with personal contacts in other Arab states, for example, Anwar Sadat in the Nasser period, who was regarded as having good relations inside most Arab states, or Rifaat al-Asad, the Syrian president's younger brother, who had close ties with Prince Abdullah of Saudi Arabia.

Just as important, there was a general disregard for borders and for national sovereignty when it came to trying to influence an Arab neighbour, to put pressure on it or to try to stop it from pressuring you. Over the years this has taken the form of direct military intervention, assassinations, kidnappings, bombings, sabotage, newspaper and radio campaigns, and support for the political opponents of rival regimes. A few examples of the most flagrant acts of interference, taken more or less at random, would include: King Saud's plot to kill President Nasser in 1958; Egyptian attempts to destabilize King Hussein between 1958 and 1960, including the assassination of his prime minister; the brief Syrian invasion of northern Jordan in 1970; Jordanian and Iraqi support for the Muslim Brothers in their struggle with the Syrian regime from 1979 onwards; Algeria's provision of base facilities for the Polisario Front during its fight against the Moroccan army in the western Sahara; and Libyan encouragement of armed incursion into Tunisia in 1980. As all such activities were organized by senior military officers or members of an intelligence agency, their origins are inevitably shrouded in great secrecy and their exact purpose difficult to discern. Nevertheless, they are certainly testimony to an habitual willingness to act across international borders that seems unparalleled elsewhere in the non-European world.

Attempts to reduce such behaviour to a set of underlying principles or patterns have not proved particularly successful.[30] Nevertheless, it is possible to hazard a few generalizations about the practice of intra-Arab state relations, its aims and its consequences. The first is the general assumption that boundaries are porous and that neighbours will attempt to interfere. This forces regimes to be much warier than they might otherwise be and, often, to try to pre-empt such interference by making a first move themselves. More generally, this assumption has often been accompanied by attempts to weaken a troublesome neighbour as a way of reducing its capacity to intervene itself. Second, it follows that there is also an assumption of potential conflict, without, on many occasions, there being any objective reason for a dispute. Third, the involvement with events and processes on the other side of Arab borders means that there is less of a difference between domestic and foreign policy than in other parts of the world. Regimes habitually attempt to find support, and even legitimacy, across such borders; but they also have to pay close attention to rival attempts to do the same.

Taking the Arab world as a whole, the applicability of these generalizations will obviously vary from country to country and also from time to time. One example of this is the way Egypt's relations with its Arab neighbours became very much less intense after President Nasser died and, again, after its expulsion from the Arab League in 1979. Another is the various phases of Iraqi/Syrian relations since they both came to be ruled by Ba'thi regimes from 1968 onwards. To begin with, as Eberhard Kienle clearly demonstrates, the main dispute between them was about which of the two was to be considered the true or authentic expression of Ba'thism.[31] This was important in at least three ways. First, the use of the authority of the party and of its ideology was central to the political management of each society, as I will try to show in greater detail in Chapter 10. It was also elaborated in such a way that, just as in the case of the dispute between the Soviet and Chinese brands of Marxism in the 1960s, there was room for only one legitimate authority, so that any rival had, automatically, to be labelled as an imposter. Second, to be recognized as the authentic Ba'th party carried with it, for a while at least, the additional cachet of also being regarded as the leading national and progressive force in the Arab world. Third, as Kienle also points out, both regimes were initially very weak and were appealing to a floating constituency of Ba'th party members who had yet to decide which of the two regimes to support.[32] However, as the Syrian regime in particular became more confident and more sure of itself, the ideological confrontation became of less importance and was replaced by more tangible issues such as mutual rivalry for leadership of the Arab world, as well as a long history of often violent disagreement about a host of questions involving policy towards Israel, the Palestinians and the Iranian revolution.

The role of Israel and the Palestinians in intra-Arab relations

Apart from the influence of Arabism on intra-Arab relations, a second specific and unusual influence has been that of the Israeli/Palestinian conflict. As far as Israel is concerned, this stemmed largely from the fact that, for the first 30 years of its existence, its relations with its Arab neighbours were conducted almost exclusively by force and by threat of force, a policy developed by its long-time prime minister, David Ben-Gurion, and the defence establishment in the early 1950s. At different times this was aimed at pre-empting an Arab attack, at preventing Arab support for Palestinian and other guerrillas and at trying to get rid of a hostile Arab leader like President Nasser.[33] Israel's Arab neighbours, for their part, were unwilling either to sign a peace treaty or to normalize relations and were thus left with the choice of either preparing for war or developing some kind of unofficial *modus vivendi*. As a rule, Egypt and Syria took the former path, and Jordan and Lebanon the latter.

This unresolved conflict was largely responsible for a Middle Eastern arms race, a series of wars, and the Israeli occupation of the West Bank, Gaza and Egypt's Sinai peninsula in 1967, as well as numerous lesser clashes. The Palestinian factor added an extra dimension, particularly after the increase in the size and bellicosity of the guerrilla organizations in the late 1960s. The consequence was to bring Lebanon and Jordan more directly into the conflict as a result of Israeli raids against the bases established on their territory. But Israel's policy towards the two states soon diverged. No sooner had King Hussein decided to expel the guerrillas from Jordan than Israel reverted to its traditional policy of support for the Hashemite monarchy as a conservative force on its eastern flank. At the same time, intervention against the Palestinians in Lebanon became ever more intense, leading up to the Israeli invasion of the country in 1982, the defeat of the Palestinians and the brief attempt to engineer the establishment of a friendly regime dominated by the Lebanese forces controlled by Bashir Gemayel. Even though politically unsuccessful, Israel's invasion triggered off a series of changes in the internal balance of power between Christian, Shi'i and Druze militias that were to make their own major contribution to the further disintegration of Lebanon's fragile system.

One reason why the Israelis were able to exercise their power in Lebanon was the fact that the Egyptians had already signed a peace treaty with them in 1979. From President Sadat's point of view this meant a considered decision to normalize relations with his powerful neighbour. It also involved the implicit de-coupling of the political equation that implied that support for the Palestinians and hostility to Israel were two sides of the same coin. For most of the other Arab regimes this was seen as a gross betrayal of the Arab cause, even if the majority of them soon began to follow the Egyptians along the same path. The alternative strategy employed by Syria was to build up its military capacity so as to be able to confront Israel, while, at the same time, seeking to control the Palestinian resistance movement in such a way that its policies became subservient to the requirements of Syrian security. This too aroused considerable Arab hostility, particularly when it involved Syria's military confrontation with the PLO's forces in Lebanon in 1976 and then its attempt to divide the Palestinians and to promote an alternative leadership to Yasser Arafat from 1983 onwards.

Analysis of the influence of the Palestinians on Arab politics and inter-state relations is even more complex than that of Israel. For most of the first two decades after 1948 they were without a state of their own, and largely under the control of a variety of different regimes. But after they began to assert their own independence of action in the late 1960s they inevitably posed major problems for those Arab states they asked for support. One, of course, was the danger of inviting a harsh Israeli response. Another was the twin appeal that the Palestinian leadership was willing and able to make, both to the regimes and to their people. Although one of the main principles of Fateh's political creed was to maintain the movement's freedom of action by avoiding interference in the internal affairs of Arab states, this was often ignored in practice. In some cases, as in Jordan in 1970 and in Lebanon a few years later, this meant direct attempts to destabilize the regime in association with opposition forces; in others, there was pressure to follow a revolutionary logic that placed Arab unity and the necessity of constant confrontation with Israel above everything else. As a result, the leaders of most Middle Eastern regimes could have been forgiven for supposing that, while Palestinians saw their own nationalism as perfectly compatible with a wider Arabism, they were quite ready to ride roughshod over Jordanian or Egyptian or Lebanese national self-interest if this seemed to stand in the way of their own objectives.

In addition to their own nationalism, the Palestinians also developed an evolving strategy for achieving their political aims. This began with great stress on the primacy of armed struggle. But, as in the case of most movements of national liberation, it turned progressively towards an emphasis on diplomacy and a negotiated settlement. The first major stage in this transformation was completed in 1974 when the 12th Palestinian national congress agreed on what was called an 'interim' or 'phased' programme by which it was decided that an 'independent national authority' was to be established over any part of Palestinian national territory that could be liberated from Israeli control – generally understood to refer to the West Bank and Gaza. Twelve years later it reached its culmination with the political statement issued by the 19th national council held in Algiers in November 1988 that affirmed the determination of the PLO to arrive at a 'political settlement' of the Arab–Israeli conflict by means of an international peace conference at which all parties would be represented on an equal basis.[34]

This progression owed much more to developments within the various Palestinian communities inside and outside the West Bank and Gaza than it did either to Arab diplomatic activity or to obvious Arab self-interest. Indeed, a number of Arab regimes did their very best to split the movement, to marginalize its leadership or to make their own political arrangements with the Israelis without reference to the PLO. This was true of the Syrians, who tried to develop an alternative leadership to Yasser Arafat after the PLO's removal from Beirut following the Israeli invasion of Lebanon in the summer of 1982. It was also true of the Egyptians, whose separate peace with Israel in 1979 lacked any sure guarantee that Palestinian rights would be respected. Nevertheless, the leadership of the PLO managed to overcome these threats in a number of ways. It was able to rebuild the unity of the movement, whenever this was required, to launch a new political initiative. It also made skilful use of the disagreements between the various Arab states to find new allies for itself and to avoid falling under the influence of any one hostile regime. By so doing it was in a position to take maximum advantage of the revolt against Israeli rule on the West Bank and Gaza – the Intifada – when it broke out in December 1987 and to use this as a launching pad for its drive towards an independent Palestinian state which it began at the 19th national congress in Algiers.

The politics of Arab economic integration

During the early independence period it was a natural assumption that the drive towards greater political co-operation among the Arab states should be accompanied by one towards greater economic integration as well. Such feelings were influenced by developments during the Second World War, when a large part of the region had been run as a single unit by the Anglo-American Middle East Supply Centre based in Cairo, and then by the early signs of progress towards the establishment of a European Common Market. Supporters of the move also saw it as a way of promoting intra-Arab economic exchange, which had been greatly diminished as a result of the creation of the separate national economies by the colonial powers.

There were, however, significant difficulties. Opportunities for increasing trade were greatly limited by the fact that most of the newly independent Arab states produced roughly the same range of agricultural and industrial products, the only major exception being oil, which already contributed the overwhelming proportion of existing intra-Arab exchange. In addition, most of the Arab regimes were unwilling to lower tariffs, being heavily reliant on them to protect their own infant industries, to raise revenue, or both. There were important political difficulties as well, notably the fear that the economically weaker states felt towards integration with the strong, and the very considerable problems involved in setting up an Arab international secretariat to monitor and to manage any new arrangement.

Efforts to promote Arab economic integration took four main forms.[35] The first of these, which was attempted in the early 1950s, can best be characterized as the free trade phase, when an initiative was taken to use the Arab League and some of its associated institutions to reduce barriers to the exchange of goods, services, capital and labour. Its main achievement was the Convention for Facilitating Trade and Regulating Transit between the states of the Arab League, which was agreed at the first conference of Arab economic ministers in 1953. One of its strongest exponents was Lebanon, which had a special interest in securing access to Arab markets as a way of reducing its dependence on Syria following the break-up of the customs union between the two countries in 1950. The convention led to some progress in the mutual abolition of tariffs on agricultural goods and oil but little on the industrial goods that almost all the signatories were concerned to protect.

This phase was followed in 1957 by a sustained attempt to create an Arab common market with a single external tariff. Leadership came from Egypt, anxious to build on the momentum created by the defeat of the Anglo-French invasion of Egypt, which, thanks to Saudi financial assistance, it was able to present as an economic as well as political victory for Arab solidarity. Agreement in principle to establish such a market was reached at the Arab League's economic council in January 1958. But it was not until August 1964 that Egypt, Iraq, Jordan, Kuwait and Syria signed a treaty binding them to establish the Arab common market on 1 January 1965 and to work towards the progressive abolition of all duties

and quantitive restrictions on trade between them by January
1974. In the event, the treaty was only ratified by four of the
states concerned – not Kuwait – and it proved extremely difficult
to reach agreement on the goods on which tariffs and quotas were
to be reduced. Each of the partners presented long lists of, mainly
manufactured, products which it wanted to see given exemption and,
after the first four rounds of reductions had been completed in
January 1968, little seems to have been achieved and the whole
initiative simply faded away. There was a similar lack of progress
towards the establishment of a common external tariff. Arguing
with the benefit of hindsight, it would seem that the various states
concerned agreed to enter the union for largely political reasons
and that, far from promising them tangible economic benefits,
it was soon seen as a threat to their existing programmes of
industrialization based on protecting their own national markets.
However, in mitigation it should also be noted that many other
non-European regional groupings ran into exactly the same kind of
problems, for example, the Latin American Free Trade Association
started in 1960.[36]

The third move towards greater economic integration began
during the oil boom of the early 1970s and involved the creation
of a multiplicity of funds and banks to invest some of the new
wealth in the oil-poor Arab states. Here at last was a significant
complementarity to exploit, with the oil-rich states in need of
labour and expertize to create modern institutions for themselves,
and the remainder desperately anxious for the capital necessary
to develop their economies. It also opened up the prospect of
combining Arab resources in a whole host of joint ventures, from
banks to shipping agencies, from metallurgical plant to huge
schemes designed to improve the agricultural output of Sudan.
The basic institutional model was provided by the Kuwaitis,
whose Kuwait Fund for Arab Economic Development had been
established at the time of independence from Britain in 1961. Its
aim was as much political as economic: a desire to underpin the
city state's rather fragile legitimacy by showing that it was prepared
to share its wealth in co-operative ventures with its poorer Arab
neighbours. This pattern has been followed, since 1970, by the
creation of nearly 200 other Arab enterprises, staffed by a growing
group of officials who owe their allegiance to Arab as much as to
local state interests.

The fourth and final form of Arab economic integration is

the various sub-regional groupings, of which the Gulf Co-operation Council (GCC) was certainly the most successful. The idea was first introduced in the form of the abortive North African (Maghrebi) union, established with a consultative council at Tunis in 1966. But, as with the Arab common market, efforts to remove barriers to local trade were thwarted by the existence of the separate national plans and national planning agencies, as well as by the pull of the European Economic Community with which individual trade agreements seemed preferable. The GCC, established in 1981, offered quite a different model, with many more obvious advantages. This was a union between economically underdeveloped states, all of which had ambitious plans to build a variety of modern industries based on the existence of cheap energy, a programme that was much more likely to succeed if the states could manage to agree on how to share their growing local market between them.[37] Later, in 1989, the creation of two more sub-regional groupings was announced: the Arab Maghreb Union, embracing Algeria, Libya, Mauritania, Morocco and Tunisia; and the Arab Co-operation Council (ACC), consisting of Egypt, Iraq, Jordan and North Yemen. But in each case the political reasons for their establishment were very much more obvious than the economic. In the case of the ACC, it collapsed as a result of the tensions produced by the Iraqi occupation of Kuwait. The Maghreb Union had more of a future, however, due to the fact that the North African states shared a mutual interest in joint co-operation with the European Community, as well as with the new Mediterranean grouping that was launched in Rome in October 1990.

Is there an Arab 'order'?

Enough has probably been said to sustain the argument that the Arab states interact in a way that is unusual, to say the least, in the modern world, on account of their close ties of language, region and culture. A last question to ask, therefore, is whether their pattern of interaction is sufficiently regular, predictable and mutually well understood to constitute something that it would be useful to call an 'order'.[38] Here the terminology itself is less important than the discovery of structures that are important enough to inform the thinking of all the major actors and to influence their policies and the way they practise day-to-day inter-state, and inter-regime, relations.

To answer this question it is necessary to consider several important features of the Middle East's regional context. The first is the growth in the number and variety of independent Arab states, from the five that signed the original Arab League charter to the present-day 21. This at once suggests that strategies designed to exercise leadership and influence have had to become very much more complex. There has also been the obvious tendency towards the development of sub-regional groupings in both North Africa and the Gulf, leaving a much more fluid situation in the old heartlands of Arabism at the eastern end of the Mediterranean.

The second feature is the growing importance of relations with local non-Arab states, beginning with Israel and then extending to Iran, Ethiopia and the more peripheral North African states like Chad. In all cases such states have passed from being simply enemies, or, at the least, difficult and unruly neighbours, to allies of one or more of the Arab regimes in their disputes with other local Arab rivals. At one stage, in the 1950s, President Nasser was able to marginalize a state like Iraq, which had entered the Baghdad Pact of 1955 with non-Arab allies. But this pattern was certainly broken in the late 1970s and early 1980s by the peace agreement between Egypt and Israel and then by the strategic alliance between Syria and revolutionary Iran. Meanwhile, the Libyans and the Sudanese became involved in a variety of temporary arrangements with the contending factions inside both Ethiopia and Chad.

The third and fourth features involve the role played in the region by the superpowers, on the one hand, and the European Community, on the other. As far as the superpowers were concerned, a key moment was the American decision taken in the mid-1950s to abandon its brief search for alliances with secular nationalist Arab leaders like President Nasser and to base its Middle Eastern position on its support of conservative, or 'moderate', monarchical regimes like the Saudis, Jordanians and Moroccans, none of which posed any threat to its other ally, Israel. This at once gave the Soviet Union an opportunity to gain major influence by offering military and financial aid to the more radical regimes like the Egyptians, the Syrians and the Iraqis. But once the latter had been so comprehensively defeated by the Israelis in 1967, this left the field clear for the United States to exercise an almost unrivalled hegemony for two decades, before the USSR began to make a small comeback in the early Gorbachev era. European political influence was very much less important but it did play an important role in the economic field by forcing an increasing number of Arab states to band together in order to improve the terms on which they might hope to obtain access to the Common Market.

Looked at in these terms it would seem that if there was an Arab order it must certainly have been an evolving one that was strongly influenced by the changing balance of Middle Eastern, as well as international, power. Three phases suggest themselves. The first is obviously marked by the growing power of Nasser's Egypt, which, although often challenged, was strongly enough based to allow it to dictate the terms on which major Arab policy decisions were to be made. This was as easily effected through the Egyptian control over the Arab League in the 1950s as it was by President Nasser's domination of the Arab summits of the early 1960s.

The second phase, ushered in with such dramatic intensity by the Israeli victory in 1967, was one of Israel's military hegemony, bolstered in the early 1970s by its strategic alliance with the United States. This was used constantly to keep the individual Arab states off balance. The third, and final, phase began in the mid-1980s with the increasingly successful attempts to unite the Arabs, first in support of Iraq in the Gulf War, then behind the Palestinian Intifada. One sign of this was the Amman summit of November 1987, the first to be held since 1982. Another was the restoration of diplomatic relations between Egypt and most of the Arab states which had been severed in 1979. This phase came to an abrupt halt with the Iraqi occupation of Kuwait.

Notes

1 Sami Zubaida, 'Theories of nationalism', in G. Littlejohn, B. Smart, J. Wakeford and N. Yuval-Davis (eds), *Power and the State* (London: Croom Helm, 1978).
2 For example, Sylvia G. Haim (ed.), *Arab Nationalism: An Anthology* (Los Angeles, California: University of California Press, 1962), Introduction; Albert Hourani, *Arabic Thought in the Liberal Age 1798–1939* (Oxford: Oxford University Press, 1962), Ch. 11.
3 For example, C. Ernest Dawn, 'The formation of a Pan-Arab ideology in the inter-war years', *International Journal of Middle Eastern*

Studies, 20/1 (Feb., 1988); Glenn Bowman, '"Tales of a lost land": Palestinian identity and the formation of national consciousness', *New Formations*, 4 (Spring, 1988).

4 An excellent example of the difference between an idealist and a materialist approach was provided by Professor Ernest Gellner at a seminar on 'Nationalism' in St Antony's College, Oxford, 18 Oct. 1980, when he observed that 'just as Marx had turned Hegel's methodology on its head', he proposed to do the same with Professor Elie Kedourie's assertion that it is ideas of nationalism that create cultural homogeneity, by arguing that, on the contrary, it is the latter that has to come first and is a necessary precursor of the former. This idea is repeated in Gellner's *Nations and Nationalism* (Oxford: Basil Blackwell, 1983), pp. 35–8.

5 I have also made this point in my 'Arab nationalism, Arab unity and Arab solidarity' in Talal Asad and Roger Owen (eds), *Sociology of 'Developing Societies': The Middle East* (London: Macmillan, 1983).

6 Said Bensaid, 'Al-Watan and Al-Umma in contemporary Arab use', in Ghassan Salamé (ed.), *The Foundations of the Arab State* (London: Croom Helm, 1987), pp. 152–9.

7 Benedict Anderson, *Imagined Communities: Reflections on the Origins and Spread of Nationalism* (London: Verso, 1983); Tom Nairn, 'Marxism and the modern Janus', *New Left Review*, 94 (Nov./Dec., 1975).

8 *In Search of Arab Unity, 1930–1945* (London: Frank Cass, 1986), p. 162.

9 Bensaid, 'Al-Watan and Al-Umma', p. 152.

10 Khaldun S. Husri, 'King Faysal 1 and Arab unity 1930–33', *Journal of Contemporary History*, 10/2 (April, 1975), pp. 324–5.

11 Ahmed Gomaa, *The Foundation of the League of Arab States: Wartime Diplomacy and Inter-Arab Politics* (London and New York: Longman, 1977), pp. 247–8.

12 Bahgat Korany, 'Regional system in transition: The Camp David order and the Arab World 1978–1990', in Barbara Allen Roberson (ed.), *Middle East Regional Order* (London and Basingstoke: Macmillan, 1992).

13 Quoted in Adeed Dawisha, *The Arab Radicals* (New York: Council for Foreign Relations, 1986), p. 24.

14 Moshe Shemesh, *The Palestinian Entity 1959–1974: Arab Politics and the PLO* (London: Frank Cass, 1988), pp. 11, 19, 21.

15 For example, Helena Cobban, *The Palestine Liberation Organisation: People, Power and Politics* (Cambridge: Cambridge University Press, 1984), p. 23; Andrew Gowers and Tony Walker, *The Man Behind the Myth: Yasser Arafat and the Palestinian Revolution* (London: W. H. Allen, 1990), p. 25.

16 Walid Kazziha, *Revolutionary Transformation in the Arab World: Habash and his Comrades from Nationalism to Marxism* (London: Charles Knight, 1975), Ch. 4; Fred Halliday, *Arabia Without Sultans* (London, Harmondsworth: Penguin, 1975), pp. 21–5.

17 'The end of Pan-Arabism', *Foreign Affairs*, 57/2 (Winter, 1978/9).

18 This is part of the sub-title of Dawisha and Zartman's *Beyond Coercion*.

19 Georges Corm, *Fragmentation of the Middle East: The Last Thirty Years* (London: Hutchinson Education, 1988), Ch. 6.

20 Eberhard Kienle, *Ba'th v Ba'th: The Conflict Between Syria and Iraq 1968–1989* (London and New York: I. B. Tauris, 1990), Ch. 4.

21 Elbaki Hermassi, 'State-building and regime performance in the Greater Maghreb', in Salamé (ed.), *Foundations of the Arab state*, pp. 76–7.

22 For example, Amatzia Baram, 'Qawmiyya and Wataniyya in Ba'thi Iraq: The search for a new balance', *Middle Eastern Studies*, 19/2 (April, 1983).

23 I owe this idea to Professor Michael Cook.

24 Emmanual Sivan, 'The Arab nation-state: In search of a usable past', *Middle East Review* (Spring, 1987), pp. 25–8.

25 Amatzia Baram, 'Mesopotamian identity in Ba'thi Iraq', *Middle Eastern Studies*, 19/4 (Oct., 1983). See also his *Culture, History and Ideology in the Formation of Ba'thist Iraq, 1968–89* (London and Basingstoke: Macmillan/St Antony's, 1991), especially Chs 6 and 7.

26 Patrick Seale, *Asad: The Struggle for the Middle East* (London: I. B. Tauris, 1988), p. 313.

27 Muhammad Khalil, *The Arab States and the Arab League: A Documentary Record*, II, *International Affairs* (Beirut: Khayats, 1962), p. 59.

28 Ibid., p. 203.

29 Quoted by Middle East News Agency, 12 Dec. 1989.

30 Still one of the best examples is Patrick Seale, *The Struggle for Syria: A Study of Post-War Arab Politics 1948–1958* (Oxford: Oxford University Press, 1965), pp. 1–4. For another view, Bahgat Korany and Ali E. Hilal Dessouki (eds), *The Foreign Policies of the Arab States* (Boulder, Colorado, and London: Westview Press, and Cairo: The American University of Cairo Press, 1984).

31 Kienle, *Ba'th v Ba'th*, Ch. 1.

32 Ibid., pp. 31–2.

33 Dan Horowitz, 'The Israeli concept of national security and prospects for peace in the Middle East', in Gabriel Sheffer (ed.), *Dynamics of a Conflict: A Re-examination of the Arab–Israeli Conflict* (Atlantic Highlands, NJ: Humanities Press, 1975).

34 Extracts from the English translation of the text can be found in *Middle East International*, 339 (2 Dec. 1988), pp. 22–3.

35 For sources and an expanded version of the same arguments, see my 'Arab integration in historical perspective: Are there any lessons?', *Arab Affairs*, 1/6 (April, 1988).

36 For example, M. J. H. Finch, 'The Latin American Free Trade Association', in Ali M. El-Agraa (ed.), *International Economic Integration* (London and Basingstoke: Macmillan, 1982).

37 Abdullah Ibrahim El-Kuwaiz, 'Economic integration of the Cooperation Council of the Arab States of the Gulf: Challenges, achievement

and future outlook', in John A. Sandwick (ed.), *Gulf Coopera-
tion Council: Moderation and Stability in an Interdependent World*
(Boulder, Colorado: Westview Press, 1988); Michael Cain and Kais
Al-Badri, 'An assessment of the trade and restructuring effects of
the Gulf Co-operation Council', *International Journal of Middle East
Studies*, 21/1 (Feb., 1989).

38 Patrick Seale, 'Regional order: the implications for Syria', in Roberson
(ed.), *Middle East Regional Order*.

5 State and politics in Israel, Iran and Turkey from the Second World War

Introduction

This chapter examines the political process after 1945 in the three major non-Arab Middle Eastern states – Israel, Iran and Turkey. The history of these countries has little in common except in the most general terms, for example, the central importance of the American alliance and American aid (except to Iran after 1979) and, in the Israeli and Turkish cases, the problems of sustaining a multi-party democracy. Beyond this, there is little value in a search for similarities, and I will simply provide a brief account of what I take to be the salient features of each system in terms of state construction and the distribution of power. I will also place considerable emphasis on the point that, in each country, this process was a fluid one and continually contested.

As with the previous analysis of the political systems in the Arab world, I will return to some of the main issues in Part II, where it will be possible to deal with them in a more systematic fashion. These will include the role of the military, the political influence of religion and the enforced restructuring of the economies as a result of both domestic pressure and changes in the world economic order.

Israel

The state of Israel officially came into existence in May 1948, towards the end of a bitter civil war between the Arab and Jewish populations of Mandatory Palestine, which in turn was triggered off by the precipitate British military withdrawal. By this time the Jews were in control of most of the areas allocated to them under the

United Nations partition agreement of November 1947, with the exception of the Negev Desert in the south. But they still had to face invasions by small Arab armies, as well as a complex struggle with the Hashemite Kingdom of Jordan, a struggle that eventually was to leave what was later to be called the West Bank in Jordanian hands and a divided Jerusalem. By the time the fighting came to an end with the armistice agreements of 1949, the new state of Israel had been purged of all but 160,000 of its original Palestinian population of some 850,000.[1]

According to the declaration of independence issued by its provisional council, Israel was stated to be a 'Jewish state established by and for the Jewish people'. As Yuval-Davis notes, while this declaration had no legal authority, it was of great symbolic value as it represented the widest possible consensus among the different trends and groups within the Zionist movement that had worked to establish just such an entity.[2] However, the differences between these same groups were too great to allow the drafting of a permanent constitution. What happened instead was the creation of a set of institutions, laws and practices, some of them based on the Jewish organizations established in Mandatory Palestine, others owing more to the political exigencies of the first few months of independence and the fact that politics continued to be dominated by the Mapai party under its powerful leader – and Israel's first prime minister – David Ben-Gurion. The political history of this period provides a fascinating, if complex, insight into the way in which a modern state comes to be constructed, something that Mitchell has aptly described as involving a process of 'co-ordination and renaming'.[3]

An essential feature of the process was the degree of choice that came to be exercised by the leading politicians over what was, and what was not, officially defined as being part of the central state apparatus. In some cases the decision was more or less straightforward, as when they simply took over much of the administrative apparatus of the colonial state, together with those of its laws that did not conflict with central Zionist goals; striking out, for example, the mandatory government's regulations limiting Jewish immigration and Jewish land purchase. Much the same applies to specifying those major offices and institutions named in the transitional law of February 1949 that established the presidency, the cabinet, the Knesset (or parliament), and so on. In other cases, however, certain important organizations were either left as non-state entities or brought under the state umbrella while remaining subject as much to party as to central bureaucratic control. As everywhere, the reasons why such and such a choice was made depended on the struggle between different political interests as well as on certain Zionist imperatives such as the desire to attract more Jewish immigrants, relations with world Jewry and an increasingly hostile attitude to Israel's remaining non-Jewish inhabitants. We should also note that, although some of this process was carried out in terms of Ben-Gurion's newly coined concept of 'mamlachtuit' (the need to subordinate pre-state organizations and party-based institutions to control by a Jewish state which he regarded as the highest expression of Zionism), this should also be interpreted as being aimed at improving his own position and that of his party as well. As Peri notes, the Mapai leadership gained great advantage in its competition for public support from being able to speak in the name, not only of itself, but also of the government, the state and the nation.[4]

Moving now to specifics, it will only be possible to give a few of the more important examples of this process. I will choose those that relate most directly to the central questions of citizenship, stateness and the creation of new sets of practices that allowed the exercise of a high degree of control by Israel's major political groups.

For most political historians, the creation of a new Israeli army represents the clearest example of Ben-Gurion's drive to establish statist, or national, institutions divorced from their previous particularist, party, affiliations. Hence, out of the pre-state Haganah, the Palmach and the smaller militias like the Irgun came the IDF (the Israeli Defence Force), a single, unitary, military organization whose members were supposed to possess no social or political allegiance except to the government through the minister of defence.[5] The significant features of this process were further emphasized by such notions as professionalization and depoliticization, which, in turn, were taken up by the military itself as part of its own organizational image.[6] But, as Peri demonstrates, Ben-Gurion was also able to use this process as a cover to continue his own control of the military as prime minister and minister of defence, promoting officers loyal to himself and to his party, weeding out others associated with his political rivals, and preventing effective supervision by the Knesset and the cabinet in the name of the higher necessity of national security.[7]

The new status of another major pre-state institution, the Histadrut (or General Organization of Jewish Workers in Palestine, founded in 1920) was subject to a more openly political logic. In this case it was decided that it should remain outside the official apparatus of the state but only after surrendering some of its functions, for example, control over its schools, to new ministries like the ministry of education. Here the rationale is said to have involved the transfer of those services that had previously served as a base for Mapai's major political rival, Mapam, while leaving it with other functions that either assisted Mapai to steer the economy or to reach out to large sections of the population – including new migrants – through its provision of social welfare arrangements like its funds for sickness and pensions.[8] Given the fact that the Histadrut not only represented workers' interests but was also a major employer and the owner of important enterprises like the construction company, Sol Boneh, the manufacturing company, Koor, and Israel's second largest bank, its usefulness to a government trying to manage a poor economy ran parallel with its role in recruiting labour voters from among the new entrants to the labour market it employed or the new immigrants it supported. As Shalev notes, one more asset was provided by its ability to divide and control the Arab workers once they were forced to seek jobs in the Israeli economy in the 1950s.[9]

A third type of formula was applied to the two other major pre-state Zionist organizations, the Jewish Agency (responsible for relations with world Jewry) and its land purchase arm, the Jewish National Fund. In this case it was decided that their role in promoting further migration and settlement should be exercised in the name of the whole Jewish people rather than the Israeli state. One reason was that it allowed the agency to receive funds from the United States which could only benefit from tax exempt status under American law if they were channelled for use by a philanthropic organization and not by a foreign state.[10] Even more important, it permitted the adoption of certain exclusionary practices towards the Arab population – for example, land owned by the fund could not be sold or rented to non-Jews – which, as Shalev notes, made it possible to discriminate in favour of the Jewish population without having to call attention to that discrimination by incorporating it into the public laws of the state.[11] Having said all this, however, the agency and the fund remained firmly under the control of the major Israeli political parties that were represented on their management in proportion to the votes they had received in the 1946 elections to the pre-state national assembly – a practice known in Israeli parlance as the 'key'. The notion of the key also played an important role as a guide to the distribution of the funds received from overseas, which were divided among the parties in the same proportion.[12] Seen from this perspective, the fact that both the Agency and the Fund are often referred to by Israeli political scientists as 'quasi-state' enterprises captures some of the reality of their position, without suggesting the further point that, in any country, the boundary between what is, and is not, defined as belonging to the state is both fluid and subject to political manipulation.

The system constructed in the first few years after 1948 possessed a number of important features which remained central to the practice of Israeli politics at least until the 1967 Middle East war. First, power continued to reside with the leaders of Mapai (later the Labour Alignment), which, although never able to obtain a clear Knesset majority in elections held under the system of proportional representation inherited from the pre-state period, consistently obtained twice as many seats as its nearest rivals.[13] It also benefited from its pivotal position in the left/right spectrum, which meant that it was impossible to consider forming a coalition without it. In these circumstances Mapai was always able to provide the prime minister as well as the foreign minister and the ministers of the treasury and (for all but a few months) of defence. In addition, its capacity to govern was enhanced by its control over such important organizations as the military and the bureaucracy as well as over the Histadrut and the Jewish Agency, both of which gave it access to a huge variety of extra resources ranging from the former's newspaper, publishing house and bank to the latter's funds raised in North America and elsewhere.[14] Lastly, as Shalev notes, Mapai was able to play a hegemomic role in one other important sense, in that the party's interpretation of Israel's national mission, of its military strategy and of its principal economic objectives was soon accepted by the vast majority of the country's Jewish citizens.[15]

Second, Mapai was willing to share office and to distribute resources through the construction of coalitions which were wider than those that would have been strictly necessary to ensure a Knesset majority. One way of decribing this process is to use Galnoor's phrase 'the politics of accommodation'.[16] But in reality it was much more than this. For one thing, it encouraged the other parties to continue to try to form themselves in Labour's image, seeking access to resources from government as well as from their own banks and credit institutions, their own economic and social organizations and their own links with Jewish communities overseas.[17] For another, the parties became essential links between the various official and quasi-official bodies that made up the Israeli state.

A third feature of Israel's first two decades was the existence of a strong executive controlled by a party that provided most of the senior members of the cabinet, including a strong prime minister with wide, and purposefully ill-defined, powers. It was the party and the cabinet that initiated most of the new legislation, with only rare challenges either from the Knesset or from the judiciary. Borrowing from British precedent, the former was provided with formidable sovereign powers, at least on paper. Hence, according to the Knesset basic law of 1958 (introduced as a substitute for part of a permanent constitution) no other body can veto Knesset laws, while only the Knesset can dissolve itself. But, as in the British case as well, strong party control over the members of parliament was easily able to render these privileges virtually meaningless.

Fourth, the government, and the institutions it controlled, pursued highly interventionist economic policies. In part these were necessary to build up the defence establishment and to cope with the mass immigration of the first four years after independence, when the Jewish population nearly doubled. But such policies were also encouraged by the lack of private investment in the Israeli economy at this period and by the government's access to large funds from outside. According to figures quoted by Beinin, Israel received over $6 billion in capital imports between 1948 and 1965, two-thirds of which consisted of unilateral transfers from world Jewry, from the United States and from the post-war reparations paid by the West Germans.[18] As a result, the government was able to contribute two-thirds of all capital invested in Israel in the 1950s and two-fifths in the 1960s. This, in turn, gave it extra control over a public sector that, together with the Histadrut, employed some 40 per cent of the labour force, as well as over the private sector, through its ability to award loans, concessions and contracts.[19] More power came from Mapai's ability to use the Histadrut to control relations between workers and employers. In these circumstances, as Shalev notes, the party was well placed not only to steer the economy but also to reap the many political rewards that went with it.[20]

A last feature of Israel's early political life was that it took place within the context of an aggressive security policy towards Israel's Arab neighbours. This in turn was used to justify the treatment of the country's own Arabs as what Cohen has called 'members of a vanquished enemy population'.[21] They were placed under martial law until 1965, they lost much of their remaining land and, although they were given the vote, they were not allowed to form their own political parties. Hence, while they were formally members of the Israeli democracy, they were in actual fact subject to a wide range of controls which rendered them subordinate to the will of Jewish politicians and bureaucrats.[22] The resulting contradiction between the notion of a state with equality for all and the practice of denying equality to some remained largely hidden until 1967, when the Arabs still formed less than 10 per cent of the total population. But it was to assume greater salience once Israel obtained control over the much larger numbers of Palestinian Arabs in the West Bank and Gaza during the 1967 war.

For many Israeli analysts, their army's unexpected, and over-whelming, victory in 1967, and its rapid conquest of places steeped in ancient Jewish history, like East Jerusalem and the West Bank, marks a watershed in their country's politics. There is certainly some truth in this; as Galnoor notes, it led to an immediate revival of the highly charged debate, about Zionist objectives concerning boundaries and the treatment of the large non-Jewish population, they now controlled, that paralysed the Labour Party, devalued Labour Zionism and gave an immediate advantage to those religious nationalists who seemed to be able to provide clearer ideological answers to current problems.[23] Nevertheless, as he also notes, the war itself is better seen as a 'catalyst' for trends that had already begun to manifest themselves before 1967.[24] Three of these are of particular importance.

The first trend involved the influence on politics of certain processes of economic and social change which had begun to gather momentum in the early 1960s. One concerned the fact that a substantial portion of Mapai's historic base of support – the Ashkenazi working class (of European origins) – was promoted into managerial or clerical roles after 1948 and their place taken by oriental Jews from Asia and North Africa, and later by Palestinian Arabs. This and other factors then encouraged the growing political involvement of these same orientals, whose share in the total population rose from a third in 1951 to over half by the 1970s. As their numbers increased, and as the second generation immigrants began to feel less dependent on Mapai and the Histadrut for jobs, houses and social security, they also began to become more resentful of the wide educational and cultural gap that separated them from the Jews of European origin. To take only one example, only three cabinet ministers of oriental origin were appointed between 1948 and 1973.[25] An oriental drift away from Labour is visible before 1967, even if it did not begin to become a flood until Menachim Begin's Likud bloc began to look like a viable alternative in the 1970s. Arabs, too, started to use the power that they obtained from their entry into the Israeli labour market, and could no longer be relied upon to vote for Mapai in the way they once had.

A second trend already apparent before 1967 was the growing disenchantment of some of the younger members of the National Religious Party with their inability to exercise more than a marginal influence over Israeli life while serving as one of Mapai's regular coalition partners. This was to have important effects after the war as they forced their party to interest itself in broader national questions – for example, the need for Jewish settlements on the West Bank – while abandoning its earlier role as mediator between the government and the majority of the observant community.[26]

Third, Mapai, like any party that had been in power for so long, was beginning to show signs of stress and strain, manifest most obviously in intra-party splits, over-centralization and a general loss of enthusiasm and intellectual vigour. To make matters worse, it also experienced growing difficulty in managing its various constituencies and in finding them the necessary resources. Symptoms of this malaise can be seen in the resignation of its long-time leader, Ben-Gurion, in 1963 and his founding of a rival party, Rafi, as well as in the large number of anti-government strikes during the 1966/7 recession. All this was made much more difficult after 1967 when there was a huge surge in private capital investment from outside, expanding sectors of the economy like the growing military-industrial complex over which the party was able to exercise much less control.[27]

Nevertheless, as far as major shifts in voting patterns were concerned, these only began to reveal themselves in the general elections held after 1967.[28] In 1969 the Labour-Mapam alignment (Ma'arach, in Hebrew) was still able to obtain 46.22 per cent of the vote (and 56 seats out of 120). By 1973 this had been reduced to 39.7 per cent (and 51) seats. And there are some who argued that it would have been even less if the election had been held not in the immediate aftermath of the 1973 October Middle East war but a few months later when evidence of the government's unpreparedness for the Egyptian and Syrian attack was more widely known. There then followed the appearance of a new challenge to the alignment in the shape of the creation of the Democratic Movement for Change (DMC), which took 11.6 per cent of the vote in the 1977 election, enough to reduce the Ma'arrach to 26 per cent and to let in the Likud (33.4 per cent) in coalition with the National Religious Party and the DMC.

Coming as it did after so many decades of Labour dominance, both in the state and the pre-state period, the shock produced by the Likud victory of 1977 was aptly described by Horowitz as more than just a 'change of government'.[29] But while it is easy to see that the stable voting patterns of the old era had come to an end, it has proved much more difficult to work out just what replaced them. Looking at the electoral statistics alone it would seem that what emerged is best described as a 'two-coalition' system, with the regular increase in the Likud vote being halted in 1984, to be replaced by something like a stalemate, with the Likud and Labour obtaining 41 and 44 seats respectively in that year's general election and 40 and 39 in 1988. Given the fact that this gave neither group a clear majority to govern at what was widely perceived to be a time of great national crisis, and that the increasingly strident demands of the smaller parties made the traditional practice of coalition building very difficult, both of the larger groups resorted to the new formula of cabinets of 'national unity' in which the major offices were shared between them according to predetermined rules. This led to many of the practices associated with the formation of coalitions in two-party systems elsewhere in the world: difficulty in formulating clear policies; mutual suspicion; and the sense that at least one of the partners was always looking for the right occasion to bring down the government and to fight another general election on terms favourable to itself. In the Israeli case, however, what kept the cabinet of national unity together until the spring of 1990 was: its popularity, at least in its first two years; the succession of economic, religious and political crises ending with the Palestinian

Arab rebellion known as the Intifada; and, at least as far as the party leaders are concerned, their perception that they were better off inside the government, with access to posts and resources, than outside.

Meanwhile, the coherence once associated with the exercise of state power in the period of Labour hegemony was very much reduced. This can be seen by an examination of any number of new factors.[30] One is the diminished authority of the parties themselves, whose role in representing a wide range of political interests has been increasingly challenged by powerful new organizations, as well as by pressure groups like Gush Emunim, which acts as a champion of the Jewish settlers on the West Bank. This has been accompanied by a similar reduction in the power of quasi-state institutions like the Histadrut, many of whose business enterprises began to experience severe difficulties during the long period of economic stagnation during the late 1970s and the 1980s. Another series of changes has affected the power of the executive, which has been increasingly challenged both by the judiciary and by groups like the religious underground that began to assert itself on the West Bank by killing and terrorizing Arabs opposed to Israeli rule. The result has been a process of fragmentation which has reduced the power of any one group to steer Israeli policy. This is obviously a very different situation from the one that existed in the immediate post-independence period, and may be lamented by some. Nevertheless, it can be argued that the present system is much closer to the norm in some parts of Europe and the Americas than the one it replaced.

Iran

Iran was occupied by British, American and Soviet forces during the Second World War, who deposed Reza Shah in 1941 and replaced him with his son, Muhammad Reza. In these circumstances the throne lost much of its power and authority, and was exposed to considerable pressure from political groups within the Majles anxious to curtail its powers still further and to turn it into something of a constitutional monarchy. The struggle was at its most intense over control of what were seen as the two essential props of the regime, the army and the ministry of the interior, the latter being responsible both for the police and for the appointment of provincial governors-general and the local councils that supervised elections. Beyond this, power in the countryside was shared with the large landowners and tribal chiefs, only some of whom were loyal to the shah. Meanwhile, in the towns, the weakening of monarchical authority, combined with the growth of economic and social tensions produced by the war, permitted radical organizations like the Marxist Tudeh party (established in 1941) a space within which to recruit, to publicize their policies and, in the case of the Tudeh itself, to create a nationwide party with strong links with the trade unions and an increasing capacity to mobilize large numbers of people for demonstrations in the major cities.[31]

Once the war was over, however, and foreign troops withdrawn, the shah was able to move quite rapidly to re-establish monarchical control. He increased the size of the army, repressed the Tudeh, built up support from the members of landowning families in the Majles and then, in 1949, took advantage of an attempt on his life to proclaim martial law and to convene a tame constituent assembly which voted at once to increase his powers. This success was then interrupted by three years of prolonged crisis, 1950–3, triggered off by popular opposition to the proposals put forward for the renewal of the 1933 agreement with the Anglo-Iranian Oil Company. In these circumstances the shah had little option but to appoint a government led by an old opponent of the monarchy, Dr Muhammad Mossadeq, who not only nationalized the oil industry but also went on to use his coalition of anti-monarchical forces, the National Front, to strip the ruler of most of the powers he had been able to win back since 1941. But then Mossadeq's own support began to wane, making it easier for him to be overthrown in a coup organized by Iranian army officers with assistance from the American CIA.

With power back in his own hands, Muhammad Reza Shah moved quickly to crush all centres of opposition and then to establish a strongly centralized military dictatorship. Its base lay in the further expansion of the bureaucracy and the army, together with a more efficient security apparatus based on the intelligence-gathering and supervisory agency, SAVAK (National Information and Security Organization), set up in 1957. In all this he obtained great advantage from a high level of American aid as well as from increasing money from oil sales, which grew from 11 to 41 per cent of total government revenues between 1948 and

1960.[32] However, if, as exponents of the notion of Iran as a *rentier* state assert, such large amounts of income from outside allowed the shah to expand his bureaucracy, to spend money on public works and to lessen his dependence on key social groups like the large landowners, it also produced negative consequences such as inflation and a tendency for the economy to make sudden lurches from periods of boom to ones of deep depression.[33]

A good example of the disadvantages of dependence on external income can be found in the period of political instability that took place between 1960 and 1963. A combination of falling revenue, widespread shortages and inflation in the late 1950s led, first, to an outbreak of strikes and other symptoms of popular discontent, then to a period of enforced austerity when much-needed loans from the United States and the International Monetary Fund could only be obtained in exchange for the promise of a programme of extensive economic retrenchment. Pressure from Washington for more comprehensive reform followed as President John Kennedy's new administration sought to persuade many of America's authoritarian allies to pre-empt popular opposition by social reform. The shah's response was to proclaim what he called a 'White Revolution' in 1962, the most important feature of which was an extensive programme of land redistribution. This in turn encouraged an increasingly vocal opposition from a wide range of urban groups united by their dislike of American interference and the shah's dictatorial ways. They included a revived Tudeh Party and National Front, as well as a group of radical clergy led by the Ayatullah Khomeini. The movement culminated in three days of huge popular demonstrations in Teheran and other major cities in June 1963, which were dispersed by the army with considerable loss of life. Once again the shah moved quickly to crush the rest of the opposition, while Khomeini himself was deported to Turkey, from where he moved on to a more permanent refuge in the city of Najaf in Iraq.

Renewed American support, ever-increasing oil revenues and the programme of land reform that destroyed the power of the rural magnates provided the basis for a further attempt to consolidate the shah's regime. This was based, as before, on a continuous expansion of the army, the bureaucracy and the security services, with the number of civil servants doubling between 1963 and 1977.[34] As a result the regime was able to maintain its tight grip on all possible sources of opposition, as well as to extend its control over new areas of society in both town and country. One instance of this is the role played by SAVAK in setting up, and then supervising, government-sponsored trade unions; another is the incorporation of a wide range of village headmen and others into a system of rural control. Meanwhile, the central position occupied by the state in the management of the economy allowed the regime enormous scope in supervising and controlling private-sector entrepreneurs by means of subsidies, credits and access to government contracts.

Nevertheless, given the emphasis on manipulation and control exercised without any form of political participation, the shah's programmes failed to create the type of support that similar initiatives had produced elsewhere. A obvious example of this is the programme of land reform, which, although distributing small plots to two million peasants, negated much of its positive effect by trying to force many of them to surrender these same plots in order to allow the creation of large and, it was thought, more efficient co-operative farms. As Moghadam observes, while few such farms were actually created, the legacy of bitterness that the whole episode left behind meant that the regime lost all possibility of obtaining political support from the direct beneficiaries.[35]

The shah's system of government also remained highly sensitive to external shocks. This was amply demonstrated in 1975/6, when the economic boom promoted by the quadrupling of oil prices in the early 1970s began to peter out amid evidence of widespread corruption and the misuse of resources. The Shah's response to this, as Halliday notes, was the creation of a new instrument of control, the Rastakhiz (Resurgence) Party, a mass organization to which all of Iran's bureaucrats and persons of influence and importance were encouraged, and then forced, to belong.[36] Whatever the real aim of this initiative in terms of bridging the gap between the shah's regime and the wider society, the most significant effect of the use of the party as an agent of supervision and mobilization was to intensify fear and resentment within a wide range of groups, some of which had remained more or less untouched by government regimentation until this time. These included the clergy, whose control over their own religious endowments and system of education now came under attack, and the merchants of the bazaar, who found themselves subject to fines and arrest as part of the government's anti-inflation campaign aimed against excessive price rises and profiteering. It was just at this time that the shah himself began to come under great pressure from the new American administration of President Jimmy Carter, aimed at stamping out some of the worst excesses of SAVAK and the other security services in the name of improved human rights.

Most writers date the beginning of the last great wave of opposition to the shah to 1977, when signs of economic discontent started to appear in tandem with a growing willingness to criticize a regime that was perceived to be losing American support.[37] They are also agreed that the massive popular protests represented the start of a revolutionary process that not only sapped the foundations of the shah's regime but also went on to express itself in a sustained experiment aimed at creating a new political order. As for the importance of the roles played by the different components of the anti-shah coalition, here there is more disagreement. Some stress the importance of the near general strike that paralysed the oil industry, the banks and government offices in 1978.[38] For others, it was a mainly religious phenomenon, with everything from day-to-day tactics to overall leadership and ideology provided by the clergy.[39]

The reality was not so simple. For one thing, the process of undermining the shah's government was the work of a variety of social forces with quite different interests. For another, the clergy itself was by no means united. A third important point concerns the role of Khomeini himself. Although his leadership of the anti-shah movement was vital throughout 1978, its impact was of much more than purely religious significance. It was his single-minded insistence that there could be no negotiations with the shah before he left the throne that prevented any of the other leaders of the opposition from breaking ranks and trying to make a deal with the regime. He was also a master of a type of populist rhetoric, with its emphasis on such central themes as anti-imperialism, democracy and social justice, that seemed to provide a consensus around which all opponents of the shah could come together. As Zubaida notes, a central feature of his thinking involved a call to the 'people' (certainly not a traditional Islamic concept) to rise up against an unjust and Godless tyranny. And he goes on to make the essential point that this same appeal constituted the core of a species of popular nationalism that saw Islam 'as the identifying emblem of the common people against the "alien" (and pro-western) social spheres in their own country which had excluded and subordinated them'.[40]

A final aspect of Khomeini's leadership was that it was aimed at seizing, and then utilizing, the institutions of the Iranian state as they existed in the 1970s and not in trying to return Iran to the type of political order that had existed in 7th-century Medina under the leadership of the Prophet Muhammad. This can be clearly seen in the speed at which he and his allies took over the army, the broadcasting service and the government ministries, purging officers and officials whose support for the revolution was deemed to be unsound. Khomeini's next task was to stabilize the new situation as quickly as possible by introducing a constitution which established the main agencies of the new Islamic government and its senior personnel. If all had gone according to plan, the constitution in question would have been an amalgam of the 1906 Iranian one and that of France under the Fifth Republic. And it was only when this first draft was challenged by some of the few liberals in the assembly of experts (which was acting as a constituent assembly) that it was revised in such a way as to include a very much greater degree of direct clerical supervision as well as specific reference to the key notion justifying religious involvement in politics – Khomeini's doctrine of the *velayat-e faqih* (the rule of the just jurist).[41]

It is the way in which the constitution of the Islamic republic was conceived and drafted that explains much of its ambiguity. At one level it contained features typical of a 19th-century European liberal constitution, with its emphasis on the separation of powers between the executive, the judiciary and the Majles, or legislature. As political leaders like Ali Khamenei, the second president of the republic, were later to explain, they were convinced at the time of the need for a system of checks and balances in order to avoid any more dictatorships like that of the shah.[42] However, at another level, the constitution contained references to religious institutions and personnel, and ideas that set limits on those of a more secular or universal nature. An example of this can be found in Principle 26, which asserts that 'the formation of parties, groups and political and professional associations . . . is free, provided they do not harm the principles of freedom, sovereignty, national unity, Islamic standards and the foundation of the Islamic republic'. Just as important, the constitution created new supervisory bodies, like the 12-man Council of Guardians that was charged with ensuring that all legislation was in conformity with 'Islamic decrees' (Principle 96).

The constitutional document was also imprecise about the status of a number of institutions and organizations such as the revolutionary guards and the revolutionary courts that had sprung up in the period of dual power in 1979 when the religious groups had been forced to share government with a cabinet composed largely of liberals and technocrats.[43] In the case of the former, for instance, it was laid down in Principle 150 that the limits of its duty and the scope of its authority in relation to that of other armed forces would be 'determined' by law. In fact this was never done and it took a period of many years, and the creation of a separate ministry to supervise the guards, before this organization could be said to have been successfully integrated into the official state structure.

Given the separation of powers and the existence of so many parallel institutions like the revolutionary courts, cohesion was only possible at the top as a result of Khomeini himself, whose role was institutionalized in the constitution as the *Faqih* and leader of the revolution (Principles 107–10). However, in practice, the ayatullah was slow to come down on one side or another in the various factional disputes that ensued, and he tended to be used as a decision maker of last resort who might, in certain circumstances, be persuaded to come up with an unambiguous judgement when prompted. For the rest, the only other instrument of governmental cohesion was the IRP (the Islamic Republic Party), which was established in 1979 in time to win a majority of seats in the 1980 Majles election. Once it had grown strong enough, so that its members occupied the presidency (after President Bani-Sadr's ouster in 1981) and most of the cabinet ministries, as well as being powerfully represented in the parliament, its leaders were in a position to make policy provided they could obtain a consensus among the politically active clerics. But this was not always easy. There were immediate divisions over the question of relations with foreign powers and over the extent to which private property could be sacrificed to the needs of the community or of social justice. Such was the strength of feeling that a bill proposing only a moderate act of rural redistribution involving uncultivated land was held up as un-Islamic by the Council of Guardians from 1980 onwards.[44]

The war with Iraq encouraged sufficient unity to allow the machinery of government to operate with some cohesion until the middle of the 1980s. But once oil revenues began to fall dramatically in 1986, followed by a number of serious military reversals, major divisions among the leadership began to emerge. These intensified after the decision to agree to a ceasefire in the summer of 1988 and tended to focus, in the first instance, on what became known as the question of leadership. As debated in the years just before the Ayatullah Khomeini's death in 1989, this problem had two parts. One was the role of the *Faqih* after Khomeini's expected demise. This subject became even more complex after Khomeini's own attempt to redefine, and also to expand, the powers of the *Faqih* in January 1988 as a way, it would seem, of freeing himself from the religious authority of the senior theologians on the Council of Guardians, which was being used to justify vetoes over legislation of which he himself approved (see Chapter 7). The other was the problem posed for policymakers by the constitutional separation of powers between executive, Majles and judiciary. According to President Ali Khamanei, in a sermon preached in April 1988, this might have been justified at the beginning of the Islamic revolution but it had gone on to produce a harmful 'dispersion and diffusion' of control that now had to be addressed.[45]

In the event, Khomeini's own death, and the fact that he was succeeded as *Faqih* by a relatively junior theologian with little religious authority – the same Ali Khamanei – meant that the ayatullah's attempted redefinition was made redundant. But the question of the separation of powers was tackled directly in the constitutional referendum that was held at the same time as the presidential elections in August 1988. This permitted the new president, Ali Hashemi Rafsanjani, to combine the posts of prime minister and president in one, a measure that greatly facilitated his efforts to build up a single, centralized source of authority and policymaking. Some problems still remained, however. President Rafsanjani was repeatedly defeated in his efforts to amalgamate the revolutionary guards into the regular army. And the fact that Iran remained a theocracy, governed and administered by mullahs, meant that criticisms of his policies by political rivals could still be couched in terms of a symbolic and religious rhetoric that many continued to find persuasive.

Turkey

As in any country, the transition from single-party rule to the practice of multi-party competition was not an easy one in Turkey. In spite of their overwhelming victory in the 1950 general election, the leaders of the new Democrat Party retained a justified suspicion that many of the senior bureaucrats and army officers would retain their historic loyalty to the RPP in opposition. This does much to explain the increasingly strong measures that they took to try to curb their rival's power and influence, most notably their proposal to establish a committee to investigate allegations that the RPP was engaging in subversive activities, a plan that was one of the major causes behind the anti-Democrat military coup of 1960.[46]

A second type of difficult transition concerned the impact of multi-party competition on the relations between the parties, the central administration and interests to be found in the wider society. As Keyder points out, politics before 1950 were the preserve of a small élite within the bureaucracy and an even smaller number of entrepreneurs and businessmen, almost all known to one another.[47] Now, after the first open elections, Turkey's politicians were forced to respond to a large national constituency and to find ways of maximizing the distribution of resources and the rewards of office on a much wider scale. Attempts to analyse this phenomenon frequently attach an exaggerated importance to the Democrats' often rhetorical support for the notion of free enterprise. But in fact the period in which they attempted to pursue liberal economic policies was relatively short and, as early as 1954, they were already returning to more openly statist measures involving a reinforcement of bureaucractic control over a significant proportion of economic activity. In addition, the Democrats exploited two new avenues of patronage to their supporters and potential clients. One was a system of protective tariffs and quotas which could be used, selectively, to favour particular interests or individuals. The other was their successful programme of opening up Turkey's rural areas by means of roads, electricity and new forms of transport.

The officers' coup of 1960 was clearly aimed at ousting an increasingly authoritarian Democrat Party from power. But, beyond that, there was little coherent purpose among the military plotters, while influential groups of intellectuals and officials took advantage of the situation to introduce programmes of reform of their own. One was the replacement of the 1923 constitution by a new one more in keeping with current democratic practice, as well as the introduction of new laws permitting the formation of labour unions and the institution of collective bargaining between employers and workers. Another was the effort to centralize previously haphazard economic interventions within a new state planning organization with power to allocate cheap government credit and scarce foreign exchange. Such measures resulted both in a growth in administrative power and in the multiplication of interest groups with more pressing demands. They also helped to intensify a process of rapid economic and social change marked by an increase in industrialization, urbanization and labour migration abroad. The result was the creation of new classes (including an increasingly militant working class), new relationships between interest groups and government and, at a national level, a new political and electoral geography.

The immediate beneficiary of these processes was the Justice Party, a successor to the dissolved Democrat Party, which, in spite of military efforts to hold it back, won more votes than its RPP rival in every general election between 1961 and 1971. Initially it was forced to join a series of short-lived coalitions with the RPP. But after its convincing victory in the 1965 election it was able to form a government of its own under its new leader, Suleyman Demirel. Demirel it was who consolidated the party's organizational strength by using his control over what remained essentially a highly politicized programme of planned economic development.[48] But it was also Demirel who saw this same strength weaken as elements on the right defected from his leadership to form new organizations like the National Action Party and the Islamicist National Order Party (see Chapter 9). One reason generally put forward to explain this phenomenon was the further multiplication of often contradictory economic interests that could no longer be contained within a single organization, for example, the growing opposition between the representatives of the larger enterprises that benefited from rapid industrialization and those of the small artisans and craftsmen who did not.[49] Another was the growing militancy of a number of workers' and leftist student organizations, which aroused the justified apprehension of their opponents on the right.[50]

It is clear that many army officers shared this apprehension, and were only too ready to launch a second intervention in 1971 to put an end to a situation of growing administrative chaos and political violence. However, once again, the senior generals who took charge of events had no agreed programme of reforms, and contented themselves with minor constitutional amendments aimed at curbing some of the freedoms granted in 1961. Of more significance for the future was the split within the RPP over its leader's support for the military coup, and its takeover by Bulent Ecevit, who immediately used his powers to push it in a more leftward direction as it sought new constituencies for itself among working class and minority groups. This in turn paved the way for a much greater polarization of Turkish politics once parliamentary life was again restored in 1973. With the Justice Party vying with the National Action Party (NAP) and the National Salvation Party (NSP, the successor to the Islamic National Order Party), for support on the Turkish right, and the RPP trying to pick up votes among radical groups on the left, the stage was set for an increasingly heated ideological confrontation which soon spilled over into the streets of towns throughout Turkey. To make matters worse, neither the RPP nor the Justice Party was able to obtain a clear majority in any of the elections held from 1973 onwards, giving them the choice between forming minority governments or having to patch together a coalition with one or more of the smaller parties.

Given the highly politicized atmosphere in Turkey in the 1970s, and the fact that it resulted in yet another military intervention in 1980, it is probably inevitable that analysts tend to highlight quite different explanations for the lack of firm government, the politicization of most parts of the state administration and the growing violence. For some the chief blame attaches to the squabbling of the politicians, made worse by the defects in the Turkish party system and the country's constitutional structure. Others concentrate more on the underlying stresses and strains posed first by a period of rapid social transformation and then by a long period of economic crisis from 1973 onwards, when high oil prices combined with a loss of American aid after the invasion of northern Cyprus and a decline in the remittances sent back by Turkish workers in Europe to produce a crippling shortage of foreign exchange. Others again point to the existence of various groups on both the right and the left that seemed determined to seize power by violent extra-parliamentary means.

In the event, of course, all these factors played their part. Nevertheless, it should also be noted that by 1980, the year of the third military intervention, the economic situation had much improved as a result of the introduction of the economic stabilization plan agreed with the IMF in January 1980 and the revival of United States military aid once the American administration had decided that it needed a strong Turkey as an ally against the forces unleashed by the Iranian revolution.[51] In addition, as Ahmad notes, the martial law declared in 13 provinces in December 1978 should have done much more to reduce political violence than it actually did.[52] Why this is so remains a puzzle, the more so as the military was able to bring the situation under control so quickly after it took power in September 1980. This may have had something to do with the fact that the generals were not unhappy to allow matters to deteriorate so as to provide a better justification for their own coup, as Ahmad suggests.[53] But it may also be that the police force had become so highly politicized and so heavily infiltrated by NAP supporters that it was no longer capable of effective action. The same could also have been true of those municipalities and other local administrations that had passed into the control of the NAP or some other extremist group.

There is no doubt that, when it came, the army's intervention in 1980 had widespread popular support. But this does not mean that the majority of the Turkish people were prepared to see a long period of military rule. Indeed, it is reasonable to suggest, as Ahmad does, that one of the main explanations for the unexpected success of Turgut Ozal's new Motherland Party (ANAP) in the 1983 elections was that it was viewed by many as the organization least closely attached to the generals and most likely to engineer a return to full civilian rule.[54] The fact that ANAP was able to dominate Turkish politics for the rest of the 1980s can be ascribed to three particular sets of reasons. The first was the partial success of its domestic policies aimed at transforming Turkey from a protected, inward-looking economy to one based on the export of manufactured goods in the highly competitive world markets. Fortunately for the Ozal government, the policy of export promotion was launched just at a time when the Iran/Iraq war was producing a surge in demand for Turkish goods. But that Turkey was also able to make substantial inroads into the West European market was due in large measure to the fact that the previous military government had destroyed all the institutions protecting workers' interests and so allowed manufacturers to keep wages low. Just why the great militancy shown by the unions in the

1970s collapsed as quickly as it did is unclear but it may be that it had something to do with the fact that the Turkish industrial working class was of a relatively recent formation and had only a short tradition of political activism.[55]

The second reason for ANAP's success was Ozal's ability to disengage himself, his party and then the whole political system from military tutelage (see also Chapter 8). This was a gradual process which involved the re-establishment of successor parties to the old ones dissolved by the generals, and the return of almost all the old politicians after the 1987 referendum that put an end to the 10-year banishment that had been imposed on them under the 1982 constitution. It also involved the establishment of a *de facto* division of responsibilities between the Ozal government and the army, by which the former was allowed to manage the economy while the latter retained most of its control over domestic security. The result was a situation in which the checks on Turgut Ozal's freedom of action were gradually removed until he was in a position to use an ANAP parliamentary majority to have himself elected as president in 1989. This in turn gave him sufficient authority to continue to dominate his party and parliament, as well as to seize the opportunity offered by the Gulf crisis that opened the next summer to increase his powers still further.

The third and last reason was the weakness and division of the opposition. As happened in many other countries, the party that was best positioned to offer solutions to the economic crisis of the 1970s was able to set the political agenda and to manoeuvre its opponents into a situation in which all they had to offer was a pale imitation of its own policies. In addition, the coalition of politicians that had come together to form ANAP in the first place brought with it constituencies among a variety of religious, nationalist and regional groups which gave it a wider appeal than its competitors. Finally, the old politicians who re-started their old parties in a new guise seem to have incurred much of the blame for the violence of the 1970s and the military intervention that followed.

All this was enough to ensure ANAP's victory in the 1987 election, albeit with a greatly reduced popular majority. However, due to the vagaries of the 1983 electoral law and some clever amendments to it just before the election itself, the party's third of the vote translated into two-thirds of the seats in the grand national assembly. This, in turn, was enough to permit Ozal's election as president, as well as to withstand pressure from the opposition to dissolve the assembly after ANAP's share of the vote in the 1989 municipal elections had fallen to only 21.7 per cent, significantly less than that of its two major rivals.

ANAP's domination of the political process during the 1980s also led to a profound change in the role and character of the Turkish bureaucracy. In spite of attempts by the major parties to politicize it during the previous decade, for example, by bringing in their partisans to top posts in the ministries of finance and trade, senior civil servants had managed to preserve the autonomy of a number of key state agencies.[56] In the case of the Motherland Party, however, economic decisions with important ramifications for particular business enterprises, such as the provision of export subsidies or subsidized credit, began to be made much more by the ministers themselves (and often the prime minister) than as a result of normal bureaucratic processes. Although this was generally justified by the need to cut red tape and to speed up official procedures in a time of economic liberalization, there is no doubt that it was used to favour party supporters while punishing those who had voted for its rivals. The same trend can also be observed in the award of central government resources to municipalities and other organs of local government, which varied according to the political coloration of the institution concerned.

Notes

1 For a detailed account of the fighting that took place in 1948/9, see Benny Morris, *The Birth of the Palestine Refugee Problem: 1947–1949* (Cambridge: Cambridge University Press, 1987); and Avi Shlaim, *Collusion Across the Jordan: King Abdullah, the Zionist Movement and the Partition of Palestine* (Oxford: Clarendon Press, 1988), Chs 7–12.
2 Nira Yuval-Davis, 'The Jewish collectivity', Khamsin 13, *Women in the Middle East* (London: Zed Books, 1987), pp. 62–3.
3 E. Roger Owen, 'State and society in the Middle East', *Items* (Social Science Research Council, New York), 44/1 (March, 1990), pp. 10–14.
4 Yoram Peri, *Between Battles and Ballots: Israeli Military in Politics* (Cambridge: Cambridge University Press, 1983), pp. 45–6.
5 For example, Dan Horowitz and Moshe Lissak, *Origins of the Israeli Polity: Palestine Under the Mandate* (Chicago and London: Chicago University Press, 1978), pp. 190–1; and Don Peretz, *The Government and Politics of Israel*, 2nd edn (Boulder, Colorado: Westview, 1983), p. 144.

6 Peri, *Between Battles and Ballots*, pp. 39–40.
7 Ibid., p. 48.
8 Horowitz and Lissak, *Origins*, pp. 193–4.
9 Michael Shalev, 'Jewish organized labor and the Palestinians: A study in state/society relations in Israel', in Baruch Kimmerling (ed.), *The Israeli State and Society: Boundaries and Frontiers* (Albany, NY: State University of New York Press, 1989), pp. 103–13.
10 Horowitz and Lissak, *Origins*, pp. 194–5.
11 Shalev, 'Jewish organized labor', p. 93; Uri Davis and Walter Lehn, 'And the Fund still lives', *Journal of Palestine Studies*, VII/4 (Summer, 1978), pp. 4–16.
12 Dan Horowitz and Moshe Lissak, *Trouble in Utopia: The Overburdened Polity in Israel* (Albany, NY: State University of New York Press, 1989), p. 35.
13 For a history of the Israeli electoral system and the difficulties in changing it, see Misha Louvish, 'The making of electoral reform', *The Jerusalem Post* (13 April 1977).
14 Dan Horowitz, 'More than a change of government', *Jerusalem Quarterly*, V (Fall, 1977), pp. 14–15; Michael Shalev, 'The political economy of Labor Party dominance', in T. J. Pempel (ed.), *Uncommon Democracies: the One Party Dominant Regimes* (Ithaca and London: Cornell University Press, 1990), pp. 104–7.
15 Shalev, 'Political economy', pp. 85, 118.
16 Itzhak Galnoor, 'Israeli democracy in transition', *Mimeo* (1987), pp. 28–35.
17 Horowitz and Lissak, *Origins*, pp. 206–10.
18 Joel Beinin, 'Israel at forty: the political economy/political culture of constant conflict', *Arab Studies Quarterly*, 10/4 (Fall, 1988), pp. 437–8 and Table 1.
19 Ibid., pp. 440–1.
20 Shalev, 'Political economy', pp. 122–5.
21 Erik Cohen, 'Citizenship, nationality and religion in Israel and Thailand', in Kimmerling (ed.), *Israeli State and Society*, p. 72.
22 Shalev, 'Jewish organized labor', pp. 110–15.
23 Itzhak Galnoor, 'Transformations in the Israeli political system since the Yom Kippur War', in A. Arian (ed.), *The Elections in Israel – 1977* (Jerusalem: Jerusalem Academic Press, 1980), p. 123.
24 Ibid., pp. 123–4.
25 Peretz, *Government and Politics*, p. 62.
26 Galnoor, 'Israeli democracy in transition', pp. 12–13.
27 For example, Michael Shalev, 'Israel's domestic policy regime: Zionism, dualism and the rise of capital', in Frances G. Castles (ed.), *The Comparative History of Public Policy* (Cambridge, Mass.: Polity, 1989), pp. 131–2.
28 For the figures, see Peretz, *Government and Politics*, pp. 80–1.
29 This is the title of Horowitz's article in the *Jerusalem Quarterly* (Fall, 1977).
30 Here I follow the argument of Galnoor in 'Israeli democracy in transition', pp. 35–43.

31 Ervand Abrahamian, *Iran Between Two Revolutions* (Princeton, NJ: Princeton University Press, 1982), pp. 281–305.
32 Hossein Mahdavy, 'Patterns and problems of economic development in rentier states: The case of Iran', in M. A. Cook (ed.), *Studies in the Economic History of the Middle East* (Oxford: Oxford University Press, 1970), Table 2, p. 430.
33 For Mahdavy's over-optimistic evaluation of the economic advantages of *rentier*ism, see ibid., p. 432.
34 Abrahamian, *Iran Between Two Revolutions*, p. 438.
35 Fatemeh E. Moghadam, 'An historical interpretation of the Iranian Revolution', *Cambridge Journal of Economics*, 12 (1988), p. 413.
36 Fred Halliday, *Iran: Dictatorship and Development* (London, Harmondsworth: Penguin Books, 1979), p. 47.
37 For example, Henry Munson Jr, 'Conclusion: Why only in Iran?', in Munson, *Islam and Revolution in the Middle East* (New Haven and London: Yale University Press, 1988), pp. 126–7.
38 Halliday draws attention to the 'modernity' of the Iranian revolution as compared to the Russian and the French, citing the use of the political strike as one example of this. See Fred Halliday, 'The Iranian Revolution', *Political Studies*, XXX/3 (Sept., 1982), p. 438.
39 For example, Hamid Algar, *The Roots of the Islamic Revolution* (London: The Open Press, 1983), pp. 123–4.
40 Zubaida, *Islam, The People and the State*, pp. 18–20, 33.
41 A more detailed analysis of Khomeini's political thought can be found in Chapter 7. The translation of the word *faqih* as 'just jurist' can be found in 'The Constitution of the Islamic Republic of Iran', *Middle East Journal*, 34/2 (Spring, 1980), pp. 181–204.
42 See Ali Khamanei's Friday prayers sermon of 28 April 1989 in BBC, SWB, ME/0447 A/1 (1 May 1989).
43 'The Constitution of the Islamic Republic of Iran', pp. 202–4.
44 Asghar Schirazi, *The Problems of the Land Reform in the Islamic Republic of Iran: Complications and Consequences of an Islamic Reform Policy*, Freie Universität Berlin, Forschungsgebietsschwerpunkt, Occasional Papers, 10 (Berlin: Das Arabische Buch, 1987), pp. 13–22.
45 Ali Khamanei's Friday prayers sermon of 28 April 1989.
46 Feroz Ahmad, *The Making of Modern Turkey* (London: Routledge, 1993).
47 Caglar Keyder, *State and Class in Turkey: A Study of Capitalist Development* (London and New York: Verso, 1987), p. 117.
48 Ahmad, *The Making of Modern Turkey* (London: Routledge, 1993).
49 Ibid.
50 Ahmet Samim, 'The tragedy of the Turkish Left', *New Left Review*, 126 (March/April, 1981), pp. 72–6.
51 Tosun Aricanli, 'The political economy of Turkey's external debt: The bearing of exogenous factors', in Tosun Aricanli and Dani Rodrick (eds), *The Political Economy of Turkey: Adjustment and Sustainability* (London: Macmillan, 1990), pp. 230–49.
52 Ahmad, *The Making of Modern Turkey* (London: Routledge, 1993).

53 Ibid.
54 Ibid.
55 This is the argument used by Ayse Oncu, 'Street politics: Comparative perspectives on working class activism in Egypt and Turkey', mimeo, paper prepared for workshop on 'Socio-Economic Transformation, State and Political Regimes in Turkey and Egypt', Istanbul, July 1990.
56 Here I follow the argument of Korkut Boratav, 'Contradictions of "structural adjustment": Capital and the state in post-1980 Turkey', mimeo, paper prepared for workshop on 'Socio-Economic Transformation, State and Political Regimes in Turkey and Egypt', Istanbul, July 1990.

Part II

Themes in contemporary Middle Eastern politics

Introduction

In part II, I examine some of the themes mentioned in Part I in greater detail. These are the politics of economic development and restructuring; the impact of the contemporary religious revival (Christian and Jewish as well as Muslim); the changing role of the military; the practice of multi-party democracy and the evolution of the single-party regimes. To do this I draw examples, where appropriate, from most of the Arab states as well as Israel, Iran and Turkey.

As far as the time period is concerned, the main focus is on the post-Second World War decades, with particular emphasis on the statist projects undertaken by the newly independent regimes and the challenges posed to them in the 1970s. In almost all the countries of the Middle East, a period of enthusiasm for centralization and planning was followed by a process of enforced readjustment, in which changes in the international economic climate, shortages of resources and social pressures from below all played an important role. In some cases this pressured local leaderships to introduce new economic and political strategies, for example, Egypt's *infitah* or the Algerian version of the Soviet perestroika; in others, it led to revolutions or military coups, as in Iran and Turkey.

A notable feature of many of the official policies of readjustment was their justification in language that was heavily influenced by the various types of anti-statist ideologies to be found in the international arena, whether the western emphasis on liberalization and privatization or the eastern one of economic and political perestroika, glasnost and the end of single-party monopoly. In most cases, however, this was simply the prelude to a process of reorganization and re-definition of the state structures that left the administration as large and nearly as pervasive as before. This was accompanied by the beginnings of a process in which the totalizing, nationalist, ideologies of the statist period (for example, those associated with Ataturk, Nasser or the Ba'th) were challenged by a much more varied form of political discourse which provided openings for a wide variety of religious and regional groupings to lay the basis for particularist claims which would not have been considered before.

probably the most influential have been those that draw their inspiration from the work of G. O'Donnell and focus on such notions as the crises that inevitably face countries that base their development strategy on import substituting industrialization and that lead, first, to greater state intervention and then, when this fails, to new, IMF-inspired, policies of reduced budgets, increased exports and greater encouragement to the private sector.[1] In a Middle Eastern context, two important works that draw heavily on both types of explanation are Caglar Keyder's *State and Class in Turkey* and John Waterbury's *The Egypt of Nasser and Sadat*.

Nevertheless, approaches of this type are not without their problems. To begin with, there are usually quite considerable difficulties concerning chronology and the possibilities of detailing the exact linkage between the world recession and its supposed impact on a particular economy. As far as the Middle East is concerned, the first significant reversal of the process of state-led development came in Tunisia in 1969 at a time when the international economy was still in a phase of rapid expansion. Later, the fact that so many of the Arab states continued to benefit from the high price of oil throughout the 1970s and early 1980s meant that the constraints of indebtedness could be postponed for much longer than was the rule in Africa or Latin America. This is not to deny the existence of international links; they are a vital presence, not only in terms of real pressures and influences but also in the minds of all those policymakers and polemicists whose borrowings from the practices and even the vocabularies of other states are all part of a considerable international demonstration effect that helps to spread powerful ideas like privatization or deregulation still further. However, it is obviously one thing to observe an Algerian minister quoting Deng Xiaoping's well-known defence of a revived private sector in China along the lines of 'it doesn't matter what colour the cat is so long as it catches the mice', and quite another to demonstrate in detail how external factors have affected the day-to-day politics of the long process of Algerian economic reform.[2]

A second set of problems concerns the whole notion of 'crisis' and of the relationship between its economic and political components. For the most part, what are usually referred to as crises are not simple economic events, with obvious cause and effect, but highly managed political affairs, to be controlled and manipulated in ways that owe more to the balance of forces within the country than to the prescriptions of any textbook. Looked at from this perspective, some events later described as crises, for example, the inability of the Egyptians to produce a second five-year plan in 1964/5, were not presented as such at the time, while it has always been open to any national leader to describe his country's chronic economic difficulties as critical whenever he felt that there was some short-term political advantage to be gained.

A third, and last, problem with the internationalist approach, at least as it is usually presented, is that it tends to concentrate mainly on the blockages facing industry – viewed as the major determinant of income and employment – and to ignore the fact that the agricultural sector too has been a battleground for exponents of the public and the private at both the national and the international level.

Turning back to the Middle East itself, what must strike any observer who knows something of processes right across the region is just how varied have been the attempts to alter statist systems of economic management and, just as important, how long they have been going on. In an attempt to simplify matters I will examine only those instances where regimes have attempted adjustments on the supply side. Unlike those, short-term, stabilization programmes that have focused on the demand side and involved measures that are relatively simple to introduce, such as changes in the exchange rate or the reduction of budget deficits, supply-side adjustments in the interest of increasing output and, especially, exports, run up against a web of vested interests which require complex political management. In what follows I will try to do justice to this picture of great historical and structural diversity. But I will also try to bring it under some kind of control by looking at it under three heads.

The first will describe the politics of economic restructuring to be found in a number of the Arab countries of North Africa – notably Egypt, Tunisia and Algeria – where single-party directed, state-dominated, development strategies came under increasing criticism as a result both of their own incoherences and inefficiencies and of their association with a growing international indebtedness which access to oil wealth could only partially contain. Here the politics were played out not only at the international level – through lengthy transactions with foreign creditors – but also in arenas that united the national and the international, for example, the ministries of agriculture, where exponents of state control were forced to defend their position against local landowning interests supported from the outside by USAID and various other agencies. Some of what is said here will also apply to Morocco, which introduced a major programme of structural adjustment in the late 1980s. The second section will deal with Syria and Iraq, two countries where access to large sums of money from oil allowed them to pursue development strategies that were not obviously constrained by the need to borrow in the international market. Nevertheless, both Ba'thi regimes encouraged the expansion of a private sector for their own political and economic ends. Finally, I will make a few general comments about the changes in the relationship between the public and the private sectors in Turkey, Iran and Israel, three countries that had either completed, or almost completed, their import substituting industrialization phase by the end of the 1970s and which were ready (or, in the case of Iran, would have been ready if the shah's regime had survived) for supply-side adjustment programmes aimed at dismantling controls and increasing exports.

Economic reform under conditions of increasing international indebtedness in North Africa: the cases of Egypt, Tunisia and Algeria

The phase of state-led economic planning based on rapid industrialization, tight control over foreign capital and widespread public ownership lasted about ten years in Egypt and Tunisia (roughly the decade of the 1960s) and the same amount of time in Algeria (roughly the decade of the 1970s). In each case the incoherence and often sheer confusion that marked its first years were largely hidden at the time by the huge emphasis on the plan as an instrument of scientific resource management. But even then it was clear to a few that there had been no particular rationale behind the decision to take what was essentially a rag-bag of, mainly foreign-owned, firms into public ownership, nor behind the list of new industrial enterprises that it was proposed to establish.[3] Control was exercised through a variety of administrative mechanisms and, to a lesser extent, by the single government parties (the Arab Socialist Union, the Neo-Destour, the FLN) that were used to marshall support from a number of different social groups, notably the workers organized in unions. Finally, given the primary role assigned to industry, agriculture was largely excluded from the planning process but subjected to a considerable degree of supervision through co-operatives of peasant farmers working either their own land or estates which had been taken into state ownership.

The first regime to seek to reverse this process was the Tunisian, beginning in 1969, when the minister responsible for establishing an integrated system of 'socialist' economic management, Ahmed Ben Saleh, was abruptly sacked and a new strategy of decentralization introduced. This was followed in 1971 by the first tentative steps towards *infitah* in Egypt, a process that began to be better defined in President Sadat's 'October' working paper of April 1974 with its call to free the public sector and its admission that the private sector had an important role in development. The reasons behind these changes of policy seem to have been very different. Whereas Ben Saleh's dismissal is probably best seen as President Bourguiba's response to the threat posed to his own power by the activities of an ambitious and capable subordinate, liberalization in Egypt was the culmination of a lengthy process initiated by President Nasser himself in which defeat in the 1967 war, economic stagnation and then the need to find significant new resources for industrial development all played an important role.[4] Another important difference was that, while Bourguiba was anxious to protect the central role of the Neo-Destour, Sadat's new economic policy was intimately connected with his parallel attempt to limit, and then to destroy, the organization of the Arab Socialist Union, which he identified, correctly, as forming part of the power base of his Nasserite rivals.

Algeria's turn to new economic policies did not take place until the end of 1978/9. That it was so long delayed can be attributed partly to the fact that its period of 'socialist' planning began much later than in Egypt and Tunisia, and partly because it was sheltered from many of the economic problems of the 1970s by its own considerable oil wealth. Nevertheless, it is clear that forces for change were building up some time before the sudden death of President Boumedienne in early 1978, and that even during his last illness the most powerful of his potential successors were agreed that his policies must be reversed.[5] The new policies were immediately unveiled in the discussions leading up to the publication of the next five-year plan, 1980–4, which contained strong criticism of the previous emphasis on heavy industry run by large, inefficient, public-sector organizations, and called for administrative decentralization, attention to light industry and special encouragement to the private sector.

In spite of their dramatic start, the policies of liberalization developed quite slowly in North Africa, subject to general economic conditions, struggles within the political leadership and, increasingly, to the pressures of growing foreign indebtedness, attempts to limit public spending and the serious outbreaks of popular violence that this entailed. As elsewhere in the world, economic liberalization led to greater inequalities of income, increasing unemployment and more obvious corruption, while cuts in subsidies and in imports were a stimulus to inflation, currency depreciation and the growth of a black market. As elsewhere, too, the consequent popular discontent, while posing a major challenge to the regimes, also presented all kinds of opportunities to the different factions within them, being subject to rival interpretations and providing both reformers and anti-reformers with political capital to be used as the situation allowed.

The country where restructuring proceeded fastest was Egypt, where entrenched support for the leading role of the public sector and for a state-managed market was most easily contained. In addition, President Sadat's re-modelled political system provided a number of spaces in which private-sector interests could use their influence to affect major policy decisions, notably through the specialized committees of the People's Assembly and the public role assigned to major business groups like the important Egyptian Businessmen's Association with its three representatives on the board of the national investment authority. Further support came from the increased role of the courts, which had been partially freed by President Sadat to give a clear signal that the regime was concerned with the defence of private property and the security of both domestic and foreign investment. In these circumstances, the balance between public and private seems to have been determined as much by the relative strengths of the two sectors as by the political need to maintain regime control. This is an important point, and would suggest that the limits to private-sector growth were set largely by its own intrinsic weaknesses, given its dependence on the government for support, on the public sector for cheap inputs and on foreign businesses for capital and technological know-how.

Meanwhile, there were equally powerful constraints on either making the public sector more efficient or selling parts of it off. Only some of its enterprises were efficient enough in international terms to attract foreign partners for possible joint ventures, while the rest contributed a much-needed addition to Egypt's over-stretched system of public welfare by providing safe jobs and cheap, subsidized, goods. If this argument is correct, the occasional calls to privatize parts of the public sector must be seen as largely rhetorical exercises, and interesting only when they forced the regime to set out the rationale for its policies in a more than usually explicit form. Such was the case in Egypt in 1987 when President Mubarak, stung by his minister of tourism's suggestion that the public sector should be privatized, countered with the assertion that it was not for sale given that its major *raison d'être* was to provide popular necessities at a low price.[6] Only in 1991, in an effort to take advantage of its role in the Gulf War against Iraq to obtain substantial debt forgiveness from its international creditors, did Egypt agree to a plan that combined substantial reform of the public sector with promises to sell shares in a large number of publicly owned organizations. This formed part of yet another letter of intent signed with the IMF, after three years of negotiations, setting out policies designed to reduce public expenditure as a way of limiting the budget deficit that had again risen to an unacceptably high level.

The balance between the public and private sectors shifted less fast in Tunisia. There the new policies introduced after the dismissal of Ben Saleh proved reasonably successful in terms of economic growth for most of the 1970s, and only received their first serious jolt with the general strike of January 1978 and the subsequent split between the regime and the single trade union organization, the UGTT, that had been the major partner of the Neo-Destour since independence. Growing economic difficulties produced further popular militancy, leading to the widespread 'bread' riots of January 1984 which President Bourguiba used not only to buy time for himself from Tunisia's international creditors but also to reintegrate a UGTT purged of its main leader within the regime once again. And it was only with the rapid deterioration of the balance of payments in 1986 that a major new attempt was made to restructure the system of economic management with a return to export promotion, the encouragement of small and medium enterprises and, for the first time, the attempt to disengage the state from the day-to-day management of the Tunisian public sector. Only this was sufficient to obtain the renewed support from western bankers that the regime so desperately required.[7]

The process of economic restructuring also proceeded slowly in

Algeria, where opposition to reform inside the regime and within the single party was, if anything, even more firmly entrenched than in Tunisia. Here, too, periods of reformist activity came in short bursts, prodded on by each new balance of payments crisis and each new outburst of popular unrest. The early 1980s consisted of one such period, with its major acts of decentralization and deregulation as well as the break-up of the large state farms; while the next had to wait for the large drop in the international price of oil in 1986 that led not only to severe cuts in imports (and the subsequent riots in Constantine and Setif) but also new efforts to stimulate public-sector efficiency by such measures as abolishing the ministry of planning, giving greater freedom to the managers of public enterprises and encouraging more competition among the state-owned banks. A third stage was triggered off by the widespread riots of October 1988, themselves a response to two years of increasing austerity and falling living standards. But, on this occasion, further economic reform was accompanied by a major restructuring of the political system, including the reduction in the power of the FLN (see Chapter 10).

Looking at North Africa as a whole, it would seem that the processes that I have just been trying to describe have four main features. First, there is a degree of homogeneity about the explicit aims of the reforms, which are, very generally, to stimulate an inefficient public sector and to encourage the private sector to take more of a role in employment creation, export promotion and new investment. However, the mechanisms by which this has been attempted have not worked particularly well, most notably the tentative moves towards decentralization and deregulation that did not act to set entrepreneurs and managers free as they were supposed to. The reasons for this are relatively unexplored but have as much to do with the structures of economic control as they have to do with the abilities of those opposed to the reforms to resist. Even where the larger public organizations were quickly dismantled, as in Egypt in the mid-1970s and Algeria in the 1980s, public-sector managers could only make the profits they were asked to do by staying within the system and submitting to the dictates of powerful economic ministers.

Meanwhile, the fact that so many public-sector concerns continued to operate at a loss made privatization difficult, and the only country where even small progress was made was Tunisia, where some banks and textile firms were able to be sold off. As for de-regulation, the abolition of some layers of red tape simply meant that, instead of having to seek the permission of 30 or 40 bureaucrats before obtaining an import licence or a contract, they now had to obtain it from two or three, whose power (and sometimes whose price) was correspondingly increased. Given these types of blockage, the regimes in Egypt, Tunisia and Algeria have then been encouraged to press on with a second wave of reforms involving, among other things, the use of an increasingly de-regulated and competitive banking system to stimulate economic enterprise for them.[8] By and large, attempts to improve agricultural output by allowing peasants greater freedom to grow what they like, and to receive near world-market prices for it, have usually been more successful.

The second general feature was that the men identified most closely with the process of economic reform have always come to be aware that they require a companion piece of political reform as well. These can be seen clearly in Egypt, where President Sadat's 'October' working paper of April 1974 called for some form of political liberalization as well. In this case, the president's primary aim was to be able to re-shape the single party in such a way as to neutralize the remaining Nasserites and to bring them more firmly under his control. Elsewhere, in Tunisia and Algeria, the first period of reforms was accompanied by efforts to reorganize and to re-invigorate the single party, and it was only later, when the party itself came to be seen as a highly conservative force, that efforts were made to reduce its powers over government and the economy. Meanwhile, both the Egyptian and Tunisian regimes made half-hearted attempts to channel political opposition into groupings that were allowed to challenge the dominant party at elections, although in both cases they took good care to ensure that they had little hope of achieving a popular majority.

The third feature is that economic restructuring was attempted against a background of increasing short-term economic problems, notably the sharp fall in the price of oil and growing foreign indebtedness. Measures to deal with these crises have produced their own type of politics, with regimes occupied in an almost non-stop process of bargaining with their foreign creditors in an attempt to keep outside pressure to an acceptable minimum. This may involve exaggerating the dangers of doing anything that might trigger off 'bread' riots, choosing one set of international banks or consortium of creditors rather than another, or getting by with promises of financial or exchange-rate reform. Such politics interact with the politics of economic reform, at some times making the task of the reformers more difficult, at others easing their way forward by allowing them to persuade their opponents in the government and the party that the crisis is so great that further changes are imperative.

The politics of structural reform and international indebtedness also came together in terms of regime strategies for containing working class opposition. On the one hand, most workers remained effectively disenfranchised by official barriers to the creation of any genuinely proletarian party. On the other, the union movement was used to bind its mass membership as closely as possible to the regime, whether through granting a privileged position to the Tunisian UGGT or by President Sadat's strategy of ensuring that the president of the Egyptian Confederation of Labour was always assured a cabinet seat – usually as the minister responsible for labour affairs.[9] Further encouragement was provided by subsidizing the cost of certain basic necessities, a measure that began to take up more and more of each country's budget and that proved extremely difficult to curtail in spite of strenuous prompting from the IMF and the World Bank. Meanwhile, workers' groups were able to make use of their links with the government party to defend their position within the public sector, fighting a fierce rearguard action against efforts to reduce their job security or to open up the sector to joint ventures free from the official regulations regarding wages and unemployment.

Before leaving this subject, one important caveat is required. So far my analysis of the politics of reform among the Arab states of North Africa has relied heavily on the notion of an economy divided into a 'public' and a 'private' sector. While this is a necessary starting point, and follows the terminology used by the regimes themselves, such a division has a strong ideological component as well as suggesting a more simple boundary than is, in fact, the case. As is well known, the concepts of the public and the private were first developed in modern Europe in the course of a long struggle between various interests to define the scope and the powers of the state. And it followed that the dominance of any one such definition was inevitably supported by a host of laws and administrative rulings aimed at giving it power and permanence. As always, the subsequent transfer of some of these concepts, and their associated organizational practices, to the Middle East raises difficult problems at many levels of analysis. It also has had significant political consequences.

Perhaps the first point to make is that, although there is a general correlation between the political left, the working class and defence of the public sector in North Africa, the ideological position of the wealthy members of the private sector is very much more blurred. This has much to do with the powerful role of the state as well as with the fact that private sector interests are still so weak. To speak very generally, North African regimes have done their best to prevent the emergence of a coherent liberal ideology which might, in other circumstances, serve as a rallying cry for influential sections of the bourgeoisie. This can be seen very clearly in Egypt, where President Sadat acted very quickly to silence journalists like Ali and Mustafa Amin, briefly the editors of *Al-Ahram* and *Al-Akhbar* in the 1970s, whose writings could be read as suggesting the need for the marriage of the two powerful notions of economic and political freedom. Later attempts by new groupings like the Wafd to present themselves as standard-bearers of liberalism were also quite easily contained, partly because they were generally perceived as coming from elements that wanted to put the clock back to before the revolution of 1952, partly because the regime had no difficulty in enmeshing the Wafdist leadership in its own political activities, thus denting its claim to stand for liberty and freedom.

Private-sector weakness is just the reverse side of the same coin. Highly dependent on bureaucratic protection and fragmented into a small number of oligopalistic, market-controlling groups, its members were unlikely to develop either the unity or the self-confidence to produce an ideological challenge to the state. Attempts to create an Islamic section of the economy by the Muslim Brothers and others may have made such a project even more difficult still for, although just as anxious to defend themselves from too much state regulation, they were inhibited from developing an ideological position that would allow them to present themselves as apostles of freedom in straightforward liberal terms.

In these circumstances organized efforts to push the boundaries between the public and the private in one direction or another have been somewhat limited affairs. And where they have succeeded, they are as likely to be the result of some temporary political alliance as of the pressure of powerful interest groups. This seems somewhat paradoxical at first sight, given what appears to be the intensity of the debate between the supporters of the public and the private sectors. However, a closer examination of the language involved reveals that argument is usually conducted at a very general level, in which, for example, attacks on the inefficiencies of state industry are met with counter charges against the corruption and inequalities associated with unbridled private accumulation.[10]

The limits of oil wealth: encouraging private profit in Syria and Iraq

In Syria it was the 1960s that saw the major acts of nationalization and the establishment of state control over much of the economy. This trend was then arrested shortly after Hafiz al-Asad's seizure of sole power in 1970, when the new ruler attempted to consolidate his position by loosening import restrictions, permitting freer trade and encouraging rich Syrians who had fled the country to return to invest their money at home.[11] The major political gain from this early version of *infitah* was the way in which it was then used to forge an important alliance between the Alawi-dominated regime and the influential Sunni merchants of Damascus, cemented during the economic boom that followed the 1973 Middle East war, when Syria opened up to both western and Arab capital. This, in turn, provided the basis for ten years of quite rapid economic growth sustained into the early 1980s by Syria's own oil production and the large sums of money that President Asad was able to obtain from Saudi Arabia, Libya and Kuwait.

Hinnebusch suggests that had it not been for the increase in authoritarian control needed to contain the Muslim Brother challenge of the late 1970s and early 1980s, the trend towards economic liberalization might have been allowed to intensify.[12] More generally, he argues for the existence of an alliance between public-sector managers, trade unionists, Ba'th party officials and others which was active both in maintaining a statist approach to economic direction and in preventing any effort to encourage the further development of private-sector interests. Moreover, he sees this alliance at work in both the industrial sector and in the countryside, where pressures to permit the creation of larger and more efficient private units have always been blocked by defenders of the rural co-operatives and other reforms.

One result of such policies was that they permitted the development of a system of officially tolerated corruption in which cliques
of public-sector managers and private entrepreneurs with close
links with the regime were able to come together to manipulate
the economy for their own profit. But while this gave President
Asad the great political advantage of being able to act as a mediator
between the competing cliques, it also led to widespread allegations
of financial wrong doing and, even more seriously, to a failure
to produce a coherent industrial strategy which could only be
masked as long as oil revenues accrued to the state from domestic
and external sources. Heavy spending on defence, and the fact
that Syrian agriculture, although progressing more rapidly than
in most other Arab countries, could only produce a smaller and
smaller proportion of the country's growing needs, simply made
matters worse.

Efforts to revive the productive sectors of the economy have
always been constrained by the need to maintain political control.
On the one hand, new measures introduced in 1985 were aimed
at encouraging private-sector investment by making it easier for
it to import freely and to establish joint ventures with foreign
multinationals. On the other, the regime began to concern itself
with what it called 'good management' in the public sector in an
effort to tackle the problems of inefficiency, low productivity and
a significant under-utilization of capital. However, on closer inspection, the latter initiative looks as though it has been deliberately
managed in such a way as to prevent awkward questions about the
links between poor performance and the whole system of regime
control. This at least is the conclusion to be drawn from Elizabeth
Longuenesse's analysis of the way the matter was treated at the
8th national congress of the Ba'th party in 1985 in which neither
President Asad's calls for 'responsibility' and the 'punishment of
faults' nor the serious criticisms levelled by the workers' representatives against managers who ignored central directives were pushed
far enough to touch on the more basic problems involved.[13] Such
problems have much to do with the role played by the members
of the single party, as in Algeria, and are sustained by a system
of political control in which the regime allows its clients to ignore
the barriers between the public and the private spheres in order
to make profits at the state's expense. One good example of this
that emerged at the 8th congress was the practice of public-sector
managers falsely claiming that other public-sector goods were not

of a high enough quality and so obtaining permission to import very much costlier goods from abroad – no doubt through the agency of private-sector associates.[14]

The emergence of a private sector in Iraq followed a different course. What little private capital that existed was largely obliterated by the nationalizations of the 1960s, so that the new ventures that were allowed to establish themselves in the 1970s were largely the creation of the regime itself, anxious to prevent much of the oil wealth passing into the hands of foreign companies. The main beneficiary of this policy was the construction sector, where the hand of the government can be seen in the fact that many of the new firms were actually lent money to start up their businesses. Regime favouritism can also be seen in the way in which, according to 'Isam al-Khafagi, at least half the large firms that dominated the sector were controlled by families from Takrit and al-Anbar, the original home of many of the regime's leading supporters.[15]

A second period of encouraging private capital followed in the 1980s, largely stimulated by the problems associated with running a war economy in the long struggle with Iran. This began in the agricultural sector, where a law of 1983 allowed individuals and groups to rent state land, a practice that had in fact been tolerated for some years.[16] It then extended to other sectors, with a particular boost in 1987 with the introduction of a liberalization programme involving the privatization of certain state-owned industries and efforts to give more autonomy to public enterprises in the interests of greater output and a reduction of the losses needed to be carried on the central budget. This was followed in 1988 by the privatization of various state factories and the tourist industry, and the creation of a new bank, the Rashid, to provide competition for the Rafidain Bank which had previously exercised a complete monopoly.

Given the paucity of information about Iraq, it is impossible to say whether private-sector initiative had anything to do with these developments but it would seem unlikely. What is more certain is that the reforms met opposition from within the Ba'th Party itself. This was signalled by the regime's abolition of the Higher Council of Agriculture on which the party's regional command had three members and, later, by a number of speeches by President Hussain in which he called for a reduction of party control over the government and the economy in terms that seem to have been deliberately reminiscent of those employed by supporters of

President Gorbachev in the Soviet Union. But perhaps his most obvious tilt at party orthodoxy came in early 1987 with his ringing assertions that 'if there had been no private sector in Iraq it would have been the duty of the leadership to create it' and that 'our brand of socialism cannot live without the private sector, whether now or after the war'.[17]

Nevertheless, for all the energy that the president seemed to put into the change of policy, it is unlikely that it proceeded very far.[18] In Iraq, as elsewhere, there are obvious limits to the growth of a private sector, particularly one that contains a number of large and medium-size firms heavily dependent on the state for contracts and protection. It is also the state that has the power to decide what new industries can be invested in by private and mixed-sector companies, and under what conditions. For example, a January 1988 resolution of the revolutionary command council not only listed the types of enterprises for producing car parts that were to be allowed but also set out the privileges that they were to be allowed, including loans from the Industrial Bank of not less than 50 per cent of the value of their 'machines, equipment, imported raw materials and technical aids and consultancies'.[19] Even more important, the move to encourage the private sector was carried out with only a minimal relaxation of political control. Clearly the structure of power precluded any serious move in the direction of greater freedom.

Turkey, Iran and Israel

Turkey is often presented as one of the most successful examples of a country that experienced a severe balance of payments crisis in the late 1970s and that then, under pressure from the IMF, launched a sweeping process of structural adjustment and economic liberalization. Major emphasis was placed on the encouragement of exports, which increased three times in value between 1980 and 1987, producing a continuous surplus in the balance of trade. This was accompanied by efforts to stimulate private foreign investment and the removal of government control over most agricultural prices. Other initiatives proved less successful. The majority of the state economic enterprises continued to make heavy losses, in spite of being given greater freedom to manage their own business affairs, while only a very few of them proved to be possible candidates for privatization – and then only after a long period of preparation.

The political context in which all this took place embraced three quite distinct periods, from the stalemate between the parties in the late 1970s to the military intervention of 1980 and then the return to a controlled democracy after 1983. A central figure in all three periods was Turgut Ozal who, as president of the State Planning Commission (and a former member of the staff of the World Bank), was largely responsible for the introduction of the programme of economic stabilization and restructuring in 1979, a programme he continued to manage, first as deputy prime minister under the military government, then as prime minister from 1983 onwards. Specific international factors were also important, notably the renewed support of the United States, which again saw Turkey as a valuable strategic asset at a time when it was reassessing its military options in the Middle East at the beginning of the Iranian revolution.

An essential feature of the initial IBRD-inspired package was a return to credit worthiness by means of control over inflation and government expenditure, and a new emphasis on exports to be encouraged by deregulation, trade liberalization and other measures to force Turkish industry to meet the challenge of international competition. How this programme would have fared without the military intervention it is impossible to say. But given a government that was determined, for its own political reasons, to destroy the power of the unions, Turkey's modern industrial sector was well placed to take advantage of the huge increase in the Middle Eastern market produced by the second oil boom and by the outbreak of the Iran/Iraq war. This advantage continued well into the 1980s, supported after 1983 by the tight constraints imposed on working class activism in the 1982 constitution and a government led by Mr Ozal which was willing to provide exporters with a high level of loans and guarantees.

The introduction of the programme of restructuring, followed so closely by the military intervention, also had important consequences for balance between the various economic interests in Turkey.[20] Prior to 1979 the modern sector of the Turkish economy was dominated by a group of state enterprises and large private companies operating in a highly protected, highly regulated, domestic market. This provided a context for the competing political parties to use their access to different parts of the state sector to reward their followers and to build up clienteles by giving them jobs or by encouraging private entrepreneurs to invest in selected industries by means of licences and subsidies. Parties in government found the money for such an expensive exercise either from foreign aid or, when this came to an end in the mid-1970s, from deficit financing.

Another feature of the economy in the 1970s was the fragmentation of both the employers and the workers into different, and often competing, interest groups. In the case of the former, the major division was between the small number of modern, largely Istanbul-based, firms organized in the Turkish Industrialists' and Businessmen's Association (TUSIAD) and many of the smaller, often Anatolian-based, enterprises that felt threatened by policies that might subject them to greater competition. Meanwhile, the workers were divided into four confederations of unions; the largest was Turk-Is, started by the government in 1952 to represent the employees of state enterprises, while the second largest was the Confederation of Revolutionary Workers' Unions (DISK), with a much more militant leadership. It was these divisions, in part, that stalled a brief attempt by TUSIAD to develop an alliance with Turk-Is in the mid-1970s on the basis of their mutual interest in social democracy and a high-wage, high-efficiency economy, a strategy bitterly opposed by most of the other groups of workers and employers.

The military intervention changed this pattern of political interests in two important ways. First, all collective bargaining activity was suspended and three of the four trade union confederations closed down. DISK, with its 400,000 members and its history of labour activism, was dealt with particularly harshly and most of its leaders were put on trial for conspiring to establish a Communist regime. Unionism was dealt a further blow in the military's trade unions and collective agreements law, with its introduction of a cumbersome process of collective bargaining and its many restrictions on the right to strike. It is true that workers' organizations were granted *ex officio* membership on the boards of various state agencies but this still kept them far away from the major centres of policy and decision making. Second, the military's efforts to transform the political system involved a conscious – although only briefly successful – attempt to break the link between the new parties and any of the interest groups to be found in the wider society.

The new pattern of interest representation that emerged after

1983 has been analysed by Ilkay Sunar in terms of the renewed fragmentation of employers' groups and the continued weakness of the highly regulated unions.[21] As he sees it, the former were briefly united in their liking for the military's repression of working-class activism before dividing again along familiar lines, with those in the modern sector benefiting from the Ozal government's policy of export promotion, and the small and medium-size manufacturers upset by this appearance of favouritism and worried about their ability to maintain their place in the local market. Sunar also describes the prime minister's efforts to maintain his links with both groups, notably his establishment of a Union of Chambers of Commerce and Industry whose leadership he allowed to fall into the hands of the representatives of small business, in the hope that this could be incorporated as the basis for a conservative-Islamic flank for his own Motherland Party. But in Sunar's argument, the contradictions between the interests of the two groups were too great to be so easily reconciled. This provided an obvious opportunity for the other right-wing party, the True Path, to gather in some of the disaffected members of both groups.

Sunar also draws one important general conclusion from his analysis. Given its power and influence, TUSIAD and those it represents had an obvious interest in trying to exercise their hegemony over the entire Turkish business community in terms of a liberal project centred on making the country's economy efficient enough to enter the European Community. But this path was blocked by the fact that it could only be at the expense of the less efficient producers who constituted an electoral asset too important for the party politicians to ignore.[22] It could also be pointed out that many of the government's measures aimed at de-regulation can equally well be viewed as simply a reorganization of state economic management in the interests of the large, export-oriented, firms.

As for organized labour, this was dominated by Turk-Is, which, according to Sunar, had come to represent more than 85 per cent of unionized workers by 1987. Nevertheless, in spite of the fact that its members faced a situation of rising unemployment and falling real wages after 1983, its leadership was slow to respond to calls for greater militancy. This was the result not only of legal barriers but also the fact that it contained such a large number of public-sector workers who relied on the government for jobs and patronage. In these circumstances, labour opposition to the consequences of restructuring remained largely ineffectual.[23]

Looked at in its international context, Turkey's economic performance during the 1980s is usually regarded as a conspicuous success. But on closer inspection it seems to have been as much the result of certain important factors that occurred in conjunction as of an exercise in conventional wisdom. For one thing, the economy had more or less completed its important substitution phase and was ready for a switch to export promotion. Just as important, no sooner had the new policy been implemented than important markets for Turkish goods opened up in the Middle East as a result of the oil boom and the outbreak of the Iran/Iraq war. On top of this, and in terms of the analysis put forward above, it is unlikely that Turkish goods would have been anything like as competitive if it had not been for the military intervention and its assault on trade union power. In Turkey's case, at least, an essential ingredient of the World Bank's 'coalition', necessary to make a success of the new policies, was the army.

The Iranian economy underwent a very different type of restructuring as a result of the revolutionary processes beginning in 1979. Prior to this, the shah's regime, for all its ideological commitment to free enterprise, had used its increasing oil wealth to support a growing public sector. From the 1960s the state had begun to invest heavily in manufacturing projects which were too large for private business groups. It also created public monopolies in certain parts of the finance, transport and utilities sectors. This was far more important than the few half-hearted attempts at the privatization of state enterprises initiated as a result of the 'White Revolution' in 1963 and then again in the mid-1970s. Nevertheless, the private sector also expanded rapidly, although drawn along by oil-related expenditure and very dependent on the state for licences, subsidies and protection.

A major change in this pattern took place in the first year of the Islamic revolution, with the widespread nationalization of most of the large private factories as well as the banks and many other types of business enterprise. The reasons for this were various, and included the expropriation of most of the old industrial and financial class, the seizure of property by managers and workers, the flight of foreign technicians and the threat of economic collapse. As Bakhash relates, those in control of the Revolutionary Council stepped in to fill this vacuum in the summer of 1979 with a series of laws such as the one nationalizing the banking system and the law for the protection and expansion of Iranian industry which resulted in the public ownership of most of the larger private industrial enterprises.[24] Justification was provided by the revolutionary demand for the promotion of economic and social justice. An important echo of this can be found in Principle 44 of the 1979 constitution with its reference to a private sector that should 'supplement' the activities of the government and co-operative sectors, and Principle 47 which states that private property is to be 'honoured' but only if obtained by 'legitimate means'.[25]

Acts of nationalization continued in more sporadic fashion until 1982 and then stopped. The reasons for this would seem to be twofold. First, with the country now at war, a number of senior government officials had come to realize that the state itself was going to have considerable difficulty managing its huge collection of assorted enterprises with any degree of efficiency. As elsewhere in the Middle East, the list of firms to be taken into public ownership was drawn up in a somewhat haphazard fashion and did not provide any very obvious rationale on which to build a well-run state sector. This trend culminated in the Ayatullah Khomeini's eight-point decree of December 1982, with its emphasis on the need to respect individual rights and property. From 1983 onwards, a few of the nationalized industries began to be returned to their former owners, although this process was often held in check by the countervailing need to provide some of the vast numbers of persons mobilized by the revolution with permanent jobs. In 1986 over 90 per cent of those working in large factories were still employed in enterprises either controlled directly by the government or by official organizations like the Foundation of the Deprived.[26]

The second reason for the halt to nationalizations was the emergence of the Council of Guardians as a major defender of private property rights and of the freedom to engage in private economic activity. This was a development of great significance as it put paid to almost all of the schemes for the further redistribution of wealth presented in the Majles and elsewhere. Nevertheless, it is also important to note that the political and ideological struggle that this engendered did not affect the nationalizations that had already taken place, and referred almost exclusively to the two much more theologically sensitive questions of the right of private ownership of urban and agricultural property and of the freedom to trade. It was here, over principles where the primary rulings to be found in the *Sharia* were most clearly stated, that the conservative forces represented by the Council of Guardians could most easily make their stand. Meanwhile, the strength of their position was clearly indicated by the fact that, for all the efforts of Islamic politicians like Ali-Akbar Rafsanjani, it took five years to persuade the Ayatullah Khomeini to intervene decisively in the matter. And this in spite of the fact that the country was at war, that popular discontent was known to be rising and that the ayatullah himself was believed personally to favour policies of promoting greater economic and social justice such as the schemes for land reform regularly vetoed by the Council of Guardians.[27] Even then the Ayatullah Khomeini's reinterpretation of the powers of the *Faqih* in January 1988 and his institution of a committee to try to reconcile the views of the Majles and the Guardians (see Chapter 7) made little practical difference. Although forcing the latter to give way over a few minor matters, it did not lead on to the immediate passage of any of the measures that they had vetoed for so long. This stalemate also had an important impact in the rural areas, where unresolved disputes over ownership affected some of the country's most productive agricultural land.

Speaking in 1984, Ali-Akbar Rafsanjani identified two basic factions within the Iranian revolutionary regime as far as the economy was concerned: one that supported 'the nationalization of most industries'; and the other that supported the 'private sector'.[28] Once they had stabilized their positions after 1982, both these factions registered considerable victories but neither was able to obtain the upper hand. If the conservatives could not reverse most of the early nationalizations nor prevent the state from exercising a powerful influence over the economy by means of price and credit controls, and its central role over imports, the radicals were prevented from producing a five-year plan which would have required foreign loans, nor were they able to use their narrow majority in the Majles to press on with further measures aimed at a major redistribution of income. Meanwhile, the middle ground between the two factions was occupied by a variety of interest groups, like the Teheran Society of the Bazaars and Guilds or the Chamber of Commerce, Industry and Mines, the most important private-sector interest group, all trying to obtain the ayatullah's ear and to provide their own definition of the still fluid boundary between the public and the private.

It took the end of the war with Iraq and the election of President Rafsanjani in 1989 to allow the creation of a consensus that urgent steps should be taken to arrest the continued deterioration of the economy and the huge fall in real incomes over the previous ten years. These were to include a significant shift back towards the encouragement of private enterprise by means of the sale of all non-strategic manufacturing, service and commercial enterprises owned by the state, as well as significant private-sector participation in the five-year plan for post-war reconstruction announced in March 1990. Two stumbling blocks still remained. One was access to foreign capital. Even though the Majles agreed that the plan required $27 billion in overseas credit, many senior politicians remained adamant about the dangers of borrowing from abroad, while foreign investors continued to be extremely cautious about any project that was not able to pay its way by producing goods for immediate export. Second, the Teheran stock exchange remained much too small in scope to be able to play the major role assigned to it in the sale of government assets.[29] In these circumstances an easier way ahead seemed to be to try to sell up to 49 per cent of the shares in public industries like those belonging to the National Iranian Industries Organization.

The Israeli pattern of economic restructuring in the 1970s and 1980s was very different again, and needs to be looked at under two heads: the first is the political response to the long period of economic slowdown from 1973 to 1984; and the second is the change in the relationship between the public and the private sectors that began to be engineered during the recession of 1965/6. I will treat these in turn.

The year 1973 marked the end of a long period of rapid economic growth that had begun in the mid-1950s.[30] From then until the emergency economic stabilization plan of July 1985 the economy grew at only 1 per cent a year. This was accompanied by rapidly worsening inflation, increasing balance of payments problems and, in spite of near full employment, a growth in the number of strikes and a widening of the gap between rich and poor. The reasons for this poor performance were various but had much to do with the rise in the price of imported oil, the stagnation in world trade and the big increase in defence spending following the 1973 war.

It is difficult to estimate the impact of the economic slowdown on the Labour Alignment's defeat in the 1977 election. Certainly the most important factor was the desertion of many of its traditional supporters among the oriental Jews and the Palestinian Arabs, the culmination of a process that had been going on for many years. Nevertheless, the Likud bloc did present policies that seemed to address themselves to some of the underlying economic problems, notably liberalization and deregulation.[31] However, although some of these initiatives were implemented by the two Likud governments that held power between 1977 and 1984, they had little economic impact, while their effect was soon swamped by other programmes such as the guaranteed minimum wage, large expenditures on urban renewal, a new foreign currency regime that produced a huge increase in the money supply and a deliberately engineered consumer boom before the 1981 and 1984 elections, designed simply to increase the bloc's popular support.[32] The result was runaway inflation which may have reached some 450 per cent a year at its peak, and which was only brought under control by a drastic deflation engineered by the cabinet of national unity in 1985. The economic stabilization plan then introduced was very similar to ones adopted in the Argentine, Bolivia and Brazil, and involved a wage and price freeze, a devaluation and a huge cut in government expenditure. But, unlike Latin America, where such plans achieved only a temporary and partial success, rises in prices were rapidly reduced to a more bearable 20 per cent, there was little increase in unemployment and even a limited resumption of growth. In the opinion of the economist who was governor of the Bank of Israel at the time, Michael Bruno, this was due partly to the care with which the plan was presented to both employers and organized labour, and partly due to the greater degree of social solidarity to be found in a small country like Israel, where price controls could be more easily enforced and where there was a sense that the temporary decline in incomes was being equally shared by all.[33]

However, the stabilization programme was not accompanied by any sustained effort to alter the basic structure of the economy and, in the course of the next few years, wage rates and unemployment began to rise again, while the government continued to provide credit to unprofitable firms.[34] The result was a second stabilization programme in 1989, engineered by Shimon Peres, the minister of finance and leader of the Labour Alignment, which combined another devaluation – aimed at encouraging exports – with an enforced reduction in real wages. That the Histadrut agreed to such a course of action on behalf of its union members was the price it paid for further government support for many of its ailing financial and economic institutions such as Koor and Sol Boneh as well as Kupat Hapolim, its health insurance fund which looked after some 40 per cent of the population, and many of its associated agricultural *kibbutzim* and *moshavim*.[35]

There are many reasons to explain Israel's low rate of economic growth in the 1970s and 1980s, including the high cost of defence expenditure and of settling the West Bank. Another reason that is particularly relevant to the arguments put forward in this chapter involves the attempt to alter the balance between public and private industrial enterprise that began with the recession of 1966/7 when the Labour government then in power was faced with a serious shortfall in outside financial support following the last of the German reparations payments in 1965. Its response was to try to use the economic downturn to wean Israeli industry from its previous dependence on government subsidies and to force it to be more competitive and better able to earn foreign currency from increased exports. This policy was pursued even more vigorously in the new economic climate following the 1967 war, characterized by increased American aid, increased defence spending and many new opportunities for general business expansion. Various state-owned companies were sold off to private individuals, a more aggressive, profit-seeking, management was installed to run the Histadrut's industrial wing, while Israeli firms were encouraged to bid for contracts in the rapidly expanding defence sector.

The result, in Michael Shalev's argument, was a private industrial sector dominated by a few large firms and increasingly militant in its approach to government for support.[36] It was also one that, in spite of capital investment in new processes and a successful turn towards foreign export markets, grew slowly after 1973 and provided only a small increase in employment. The reason for this, according to Shalev, was the association of the larger firms with Israel's expanding defence production, in which huge profits could be made as a result of government contracts, government financial support and government assistance in obtaining orders from abroad.[37] However, this type of industrial structure was also highly vulnerable to shifts in military expenditure, and began to experience increasing difficulty in the mid-1980s as a result of the decline in government contracts after the Israeli withdrawal from Lebanon and the glut on the international arms market. This then set the stage for the government of national unity to try to regain some of the state's lost autonomy by cutting subsidies to industry, refusing to bail out failing companies and, most spectacular of all, finally summoning the courage to win the showdown with the country's largest defence contractor over its decision not to go ahead with the enormously expensive Lavi fighter. The privatization of state-owned industry still proved difficult, however, partly because of the large sums of money involved, partly because of resistance to allowing strategic manufacturing facilities like Israeli Chemicals to fall into foreign hands. By the end of 1990 only a few successful sales had been accomplished, for example, of shares in Bezek, the state-owned telecommunications monopoly. More progress was made in restructuring the debt of Koor, the country's largest industrial group with large debts to Israeli and foreign banks and investors. This was completed in March 1991.[38]

Notes

1 Guillermo A. O'Donnell, 'Reflections on the pattern of change in the Bureaucratic Authoritarian state', *Latin American Research Review*, 13 (1973), pp. 3–37; and 'Tensions in the bureaucratic authoritarian state and the question of democracy', in David Collier (ed.), *The New Authoritarianism in Latin America* (Princeton, NJ: Princeton University Press, 1979).
2 The minister's statement is quoted in Yves Gazzo, 'Les économies arabes face à la crise: les solutions libérales et ses limites', *Maghreb/Machrek*, 120 (April/May/June, 1988), pp. 110–11.
3 The two best accounts of this period are by economists who were in Egypt during the early 1960s and who knew most of the planners personally: P. K. O'Brien, *The Revolution in Egypt's Economic System: From Private Enterprise to Socialism* (Oxford: Oxford University Press, 1966), Ch. 5; and Bent Hansen (with Girgis Mazouk), *Development and Economic Policy in the UAR (Egypt)* (Amsterdam: North-Holland Publishing Company, 1965), Ch. 11.
4 L.B. Ware, 'The role of the Tunisian military in the Post-Bourguiba society', *Middle East Journal*, 39/1 (Winter, 1985); John Waterbury, *The Egypt of Nasser and Sadat: The Political Economy of Two Regimes* (Princeton, NJ: Princeton University Press, 1983), Chs 6 and 15; and Mark H. Cooper, *The Transformation of Egypt* (London: Croom Helm, 1982), Ch. 4.
5 Mahfoud Bennoune, *The Making of Contemporary Algeria, 1830–1987* (Cambridge: Cambridge University Press, 1988), especially pp. 262–3.
6 Quoted in Monte Palmer, Ali Lila and E Sayed Yassin, *The Egyptian Bureaucracy* (Syracuse, NY: Syracuse University Press, 1984), pp. 17–18.
7 Clement Henry Moore, 'La Tunisie aprés vingt ans de crise de succession', *Maghreb/Machrek*, 120 (April/May/June, 1988), pp. 8–9.

8 Ibid., pp. 9–10. See also Clement Henry Moore's 'Money and power: The dilemma of the Egyptian *infitah*', *Middle East Journal*, 40/4 (Fall, 1984).

9 Robert Bianchi, 'The corporatization of the Egyptian labor movement', *Middle East Journal*, 40/3 (Summer, 1986), pp. 438–41.

10 Compare, for example, the language of Egypt's October working paper (extracts of which can be found in Cooper, *The Transformation of Egypt*, Ch. 7) and the Algerian National Charter of 1976 in John Nellis, *The Algerian National Charter of 1976: Content, Public Reaction, and Significance* (Washington, DC: Center for Contemporary Arab Studies, Georgetown University, June 1980), pp. 7–18.

11 Malcolm H. Kerr, 'Hafiz Asad and the changing pattern of Syrian politics', *International Journal*, XXVIII, 4 (Autumn, 1973).

12 Raymond A. Hinnebusch, *Authoritarian Power and State Formation in Ba'thist Syria: Army, Party and Peasant* (Boulder, Colorado: Westview Press, 1990); see also Fred H. Lawson, 'Libéralisation économique en Syrie et en Iraq', *Maghreb/Machrek*, 128 (April/May/June, 1990), pp. 35–6.

13 Elizabeth Longueness, 'Secteur public industriel: les enjeux d'une crise', *Maghreb/Machrek*, 109, p. 6.

14 Ibid., pp. 16–20.

15 'Isam al-Khafagi, 'The parasitic basis of the Ba'thist regime', in CARDRI – Committee Against Repression and for Democratic Rights in Iraq, *Saddam's Iraq: Revolution or Reaction* (London: Zed Press, 1986), pp. 73–88.

16 Robert Springborg, 'Iraqi *infitah*: agrarian transformation and growth of the private sector', *Middle East Journal*, 40/1 (Winter, 1986), p. 37.

17 Speech quoted in *Middle East Economic Digest*, 31/13 (28 March 1987), p. 18.

18 Marion Farouk-Sluglett, 'Iraq after the war (2) – the role of the private sector', *Middle East International*, 17 March 1989, pp. 17–18.

19 *Alwaqai Aliraqiya* (The official gazette of the Republic of Iraq), XXXI/14 (6 April 1988), pp. 4–5.

20 The analysis draws heavily on Caglar Keyder, *State and Class in Turkey: A Study of Capitalist Development* (London and New York: Verso, 1987), Ch. IX; and Ilkay Sunar, 'Redemocratization and organized interests in Turkey', mimeo (paper presented to the annual conference of the British Society for Middle Eastern Studies, Exeter, 12–15 July 1987).

21 Sunar, 'Redemocratization in Turkey'.

22 Idem.

23 Idem.

24 Shaul Bakhash, *The Reign of the Ayatollahs* (London: I. B. Tauris, 1985), pp. 178–85.

25 'Constitution of the Islamic Republic of Iran', *Middle East Journal*, 34/2 (Spring, 1980), p. 193.

26 Patrick Clawson, 'Islamic Iran's economic policies and prospects', *Middle East Journal*, 42/3 (Summer, 1988), p. 381.

27 Bakhash, *The Reign of the Ayatollahs*, Ch. 8; and Asghar Schirazi, *The Problems of the Land Reform in the Islamic Republic of Iran: Complications and Consequences of an Islamic Reform Policy*, Freie Universitat Berlin, Forschungsgebietsschwerpunkt, Occasional Papers, 10 (Berlin: Das Arabische Buch, 1987), pp. 16–23.
28 Quoted in Shahrough Akhavi, 'Elite factionalism in the Islamic Republic of Iran', *Middle East Journal*, 41/2 (Spring, 1987), p. 184.
29 Vahid Nowshirvani, 'Problems and prospects of privatisation', *mimeo* (paper presented to conference on 'Iran's Economy: Perspectives and Prospects', Geneva, Switzerland, Nov. 1990, pp. 10–11).
30 This section relies heavily on Michael Shalev, 'Israel's domestic policy regime: Zionism, dualism and the rise of capital', in Frances G. Castles (ed.), *The Comparative History of Public Policy* (Cambridge, Mass. : Policy, 1989), pp. 100–40.
31 Ira Sharansky and Alex Radian, 'The Likud government and domestic policy change', *Jerusalem Quarterly*, 18 (Winter, 1981), pp. 91–5.
32 Uriel Ben-Hanan and Benny Temkin, 'The overloaded juggler: The changing character of the electoral-economic cycle in Israel 1951–1984', in Asher Arian and Michal Shamir (eds), *The Elections in Israel – 1984* (New Brunswick, NJ: Transaction Books, 1986).
33 Dr Michael Bruno, Hicks Lecture, Oxford, 3 May 1988.
34 Gideon Eshrat, 'Interview', *Middle East Report* (March/April, 1989), pp. 23–5.
35 Peretz Kidron, 'The pay off', *Middle East International*, 17 Feb. 1989, pp. 10–11.
36 Shalev, 'Israel's domestic policy regime', pp. 131–8.
37 Idem.
38 *Financial Times*, 5 March 1991.

7   The politics of religion

Introduction

The subject of religion and politics is a complex and difficult one, both in its general, and its specifically Middle Eastern, context. This makes it all the more important to define the subject as precisely as possible before proceeding with further analysis. To begin with, it is not the study of religion per se but of its influence on the policies and the distribution of power within a modern state. It follows that an examination of particular theologies or systems of religious law is only important to the extent that these provide motives and programmes for political action.

A second set of negative definitions concerns the scope of such an inquiry. In my opinion it should extend to an examination of the political influence of all three of the major Middle Eastern religions – that is, Christianity and Judaism as well as Islam. The reasons for this are twofold. Studies of politico-religious activity that confine themselves exclusively to Muslims tend to exaggerate the specificity of Islamically inspired political practice, and so imply that it is more unusual – and often more violent and obscurantist – than it really is. In addition, given the widespread use of religion as an ethnic or political marker, there are many areas of politics that can only be understood in terms of a contestation between peoples with different religious identities as, for example, in Lebanon, Egypt and Sudan (Muslims and Christians), or Israel and the West Bank (Muslims, Christians and Jews).

The next question to ask is: What, if anything, do the modern politico-religious movements and practices in the Middle East have in common? Here I would like to follow Zubaida's argument to the effect that, although there are very many different types of religiously inspired political activity, with many different forms of organization and kinds of leadership, they share certain common elements that derive from the common historical context in which they find themselves.[1] The first, as Zubaida notes, is that they are contestants for power within specific local political arenas defined by particular state borders.[2] This is not to deny that a number of the movements concerned have important cross-border or international linkages, nor that some of them have attacked the legitimacy of the modern state on theologicial grounds. But it does mean that the vast majority of politico-religious actors behave as though their primary aim was to influence policies and events within a given system.

Three other implications follow. First, in their concern to obtain power and influence, these same actors share much of the vocabulary and many of the same practices as the other politicians within the same arena. They speak of democracy, of civil rights, of constitutionalism. Above all, they seem to share a general concern with nationalism and the future of each national project, even when, like the founder of Egypt's Muslim Brothers, they took pains to underline the distance between their type of patriotism and love of country and that of their secular adversaries.[3] Second, their presence in the political arena involves them in struggles with other political groups which will try to blunt, to misinterpret or to re-define their message. Egypt provides yet another good example in the way in which the regime mounted an intense campaign to convince the public that the young men of Islamic Jihad – the group on trial for assassinating Sadat – had misunderstood the basic message of Islam by concentrating over-much on just a few of its major principles to the neglect of the rest. Third, given the need to respond to given political circumstances, all religious groups are forced to change their strategies and tactics over time. This can be seen just as much in the case of the response of Israel's religious politicians, first to the creation of the state in 1948, then to the military victory of 1967, as it can in the decline in direct assaults on Arab regimes and the practice of more accommodationist policies by most Islamic groups after the early 1980s.

The historical context has also been important in another sense in that it has provided a stimulus, if not to greater religiosity in the Middle East, at least to a greater intensification of politico-religious activity among certain groups. While there can be no single explanation for this, it would seem to have had something to do with the apparent failure of secular, developmentalist ideologies, something to do with the traumatic influence of the 1967 Middle East war on Jews, Christians and Muslims alike, and something to do with the world economic crisis of the 1970s and the impetus this gave to the creation of self-help, communally based, local groups to provide comfort and protection for the poor and the unemployed. Meanwhile, one other feature is surely significant. This is what V.S. Naipaul has called 'the awakening' to historical self-consciousness of all kinds of groups and communities who were encouraged to see themselves as others saw them – often as backward, marginal, obscurantist – and who responded to this with the development of movements of spirited self-assertion.[4] It is this feature, as much as anything else, that encouraged the sense of being under threat, and so the mood of urgency and impatience that was the hallmark of much of their politics.

The most vocal, the most militant and, as it happens, the smallest (numerically) of the Middle Eastern religious groups have often been described as fundamentalist. But this is a very unsatisfactory term in a number of ways. The concept itself was originally designed to describe the doctrines of certain Prostestant groups in the United States just after the First World War that, it implied, were based on a belief in the absolute truth of the holy scriptures combined with a rejection of much of the modern world.[5] But as has often been pointed out the vast majority of Muslims are – and have always been – scripturalists, in that their faith is based on a belief in the literal inerrancy of the Quran.[6] Just as important, Islam, like the other major religions, is a lived tradition, in which people are surrounded by institutions and agencies (mosques and schools and teachers) for reminding them of its history and reinforcing certain types of correct religious practice.[7] But none of these institutions can stand still, and all take part in a constant process of reinterpretation of beliefs and practices in the light of contemporary conditions – some of which will yield political programmes and perspectives for those who want to use them. In the case of Islam, at least, a better word to describe the religious politics of the 1970s and 1980s is the one used by its practitioners themselves – *tajdid* or 'renewal'.[8]

A more valuable concept for understanding the contemporary practice of religious politics is that of communalism. This, as already noted above, stems from the use of religion as an ethnic marker defining the boundary of one community as against another also

identified in religious terms.[9] As Zubaida points out of the
Islamic context, communal ideas do not necessarily entail any
specific political ideas other than the separation and inferiority
of other religions.[10] Nor, except in very rare circumstances, do
they embrace all those identified as belonging to a particular
community. But they can be used very effectively to mobilize large
numbers of people in favour of movements calling for particular
forms of religiously based self-assertion or self-protection, often
under some form of clerical leadership, for example, the Amal
and Tawhid organizations in Lebanon or the heightened form of
political self-awareness to be found among many Egyptian Copts
in the 1970s and 1980s.

For the rest, it is better to go on to illustrate some of the
great variety of different organizations, programmes and practices
involved in the play of religious politics before attempting to draw
any more general conclusions. I will begin with an examination of
the Islamic context because it was here, during the last decades of
the Ottoman Empire, that the modern division between church
and state, religion and politics, was first asserted and practised and
where communal politics first became institutionalized in a number
of influential ways. I will then move on to a discussion of the
Iranian revolution, the one example of a largely religiously inspired
movement aimed at creating a specifically Islamic state. As such,
it immediately became an important laboratory for many types
of religio-political practices as well as an example to many Arab
Muslim organizations which were inspired by its success. The Arab
Islamic context will be examined in the third section, followed
by the Christian in the next section and the Jewish in the last
section.

The Islamic context: introduction

The beginning of the modern world as far as the practice of Islamic
politics was concerned was the introduction of western commercial
and penal codes into the Ottoman Empire in the mid-19th century.
Prior to this moment, although there were two recognizable types
of law, the religious (*Sharia*) and the Sultan's (*Qanun*), both
had been administered by the same personnel and to all intents
and purposes constituted a single, mutually reinforcing, system.

However, with the spread of the new *nizamiye* (westernized) courts administered by the ministry of justice, not only was this uniformity broken but it began to be possible to make the modern distinction between religion and the state, something that was neither thinkable nor sustainable before.[11] And this, in turn, became the basis for a new type of politics during the reign of Abdul-Hamid II (1876–1909), in which he and his advisers sought to instrumentalize Islam as a means to integrate the Muslim peoples of the empire and to legitimize sultanic rule. Later, with the creation of the Turkish republic in 1923, the same distinction was employed as a basis for a policy of secularization aimed at reducing the power of religion to influence state policy, through a direct attack on the religious establishment itself.

A second 19th-century innovation with important consequences for the future of religious politics was the Ottoman response to European pressure to grant legal equality to their Christian and Jewish subjects. This took the form of combining general declarations of universalism with the creation of communal frameworks for peoples of different sects and religions in which they were allowed – even encouraged – to maintain their ethnic identity and language. Many of the same divisions were carried over into the colonial period but with the further distinction that they now represented 'minorities' that required special protection from the Muslim 'majority' – yet another powerful modern notion.

The response of some Middle Eastern Muslims to these developments took two particular forms, both based on the new notion of religion as being something distinct from politics and the state. One was the attempt begun in Egypt and the Ottoman Empire to seek to legitimize Islam in a modern context by finding counterparts in Islamic political theory to such powerful western concepts as 'democracy', 'constitutionalism' and the 'sovereignty of the people'. The other was to oppose the threat posed by secularism either by creating a protective umbrella of institutions within which a good Muslim could continue to practise his religion without interference or by trying to put pressure on the state to reverse its progress by reinstituting the *Sharia* as the basis for the entire legal system. Undoubtedly the most powerful and influential organization involved in the second type of politics was the Society of Muslim Brothers founded in Egypt in 1928. I will discuss its role further later in this chapter.

Which was the first Middle Eastern movement to call explicitly for the creation of an Islamic state remains something of a moot point. Some would argue that it was the Muslim Brothers in the 1930s, others that this development had to wait until well after the Second World War.[12] There is more of a consensus about what the key components were thought to be. Thinking on the subject tended to concentrate on two major points, almost to the exclusion of all else. One was the question of leadership and of specifying who had the necessary qualifications to govern such a state. The second was the belief that such a state had to be ruled by Islamic law. Discussion of just how the *Sharia* was to be implemented in its entirety, or how it could be made the basis for a modern legal system, took up much less time. It is, after all, just as much of a set of religious and social commandments as it is a code of law.[13] We can also be reasonably sure that, as Asad asserts, there has never been a Muslim society in which the *Sharia* has 'governed more than a fragment of social life'.[14] Nevertheless, for the vast majority of Muslim political activists, anxious about the way in which their religion seemed to have been driven from the public sphere, its application, either directly or as the basis for the whole legal system, became their major rallying cry and the touchstone of whether a state was to be considered Islamic or not. For them, the gap between religion and politics, religion and the state, impiously opened up by western interference, had at all costs to be closed.

Religion and politics in the Islamic republic of Iran

Shortly before the overthrow of the shah's regime in January 1979 the leadership of the revolutionary coalition adopted the slogan 'Independence, Freedom, Islamic Republic'.[15] This was a clear indication of the growing importance of the role of the Ayatullah Khomeini and his clerical allies. But it is also important to note that they were still only part of a large coalition of anti-shah forces containing groups with a wide variety of ideological positions, and that it was some years before the role of religion in the new power structure came to be clearly defined, and then only after a period of intense political and cultural struggle. As I have given an account of the main outlines of the Iranian revolution in Chapter 5, I will now concentrate simply on those issues that are central to an understanding of the role of religious politics within it.

No sooner had the revolutionary leader assembled in Teheran after the flight of the shah than it established a revolutionary council and a provisional government with responsibility for drawing up a new constitution and then organizing elections to fill the major offices of state. This was followed in March 1979 by the holding of a referendum with a single question: Do you agree with the replacement of the monarchy by an Islamic republic? The result was an overwhelming majority for the 'yes' vote. Although there is evidence of considerable pressure to toe the official line, Bakhash is surely correct to argue that the result represented the wishes of a considerable majority of the people.[16]

There was similar agreement that the institutional structure of such a republic should be defined in a new constitutional document. The first draft was drawn up by members of the provisional government and relied heavily on ideas to be found in both the 1906 Iranian constitution and that of the Fifth French Republic. Rather surprisingly this was readily agreed to by the ayatullah and his closest colleagues, with only minimal amendment, even though it created no privileged position for the clergy and gave its Council of Guardians only a limited veto power over legislation deemed to be un-Islamic.[17] Just why this was so remains unclear. But it may well have had something to do with Khomeini's desire to set up the new government as quickly as possible in case he died before it could be completed.[18] In addition, at this stage he also seems to have been distrustful of the clergy's ability to rule on its own and so wanted to allow a more even balance between clerical and lay elements.

Later, however, when the first draft was submitted to discussion by an elected assembly of experts with a large clerical majority it was subject to significant revision. First and foremost, the concept of rule by a just and wise expert in religious law – *wilayat-e faqih* – was made the centrepiece of government, although only after a long debate that revealed considerable misgivings on the part of some mullahs about the dangers of too close a clerical involvement in politics. Apart from doubts about the definition of the *Faqih* on theological grounds, it was also seen by some as involving the religious establishment too closely in day-to-day politics and thus likely to suffer from a popular backlash if things went wrong. But in the end, as Bakhash notes, it was the argument that the role of the *Faqih* was essential to the realization of an Islamic state that won the day.[19] A second vital amendment was to provide the Council of

Guardians with a power of automatic scrutiny over parliamentary legislation far in excess of that, say, of the highest court in France, something that was to have major political consequences in the future.[20]

The promulgation of the new constitution paved the way not only for the election of a president and Majles but also for a fierce struggle for power which pitted the newly formed Islamic Republican Party (IRP) against an array of religious and secular forces which opposed what they soon identified as an attempt to monopolize power. To begin with the leaders of the party were very much on the defensive and unable to rely on the sustained support of Khomeini himself. But as time went on they began to obtain enough influence in the new revolutionary organizations such as the revolutionary courts and revolutionary guards, as well as over important networks of provincial clergy, to support their sustained drive towards what was soon to become a virtual theocracy, with mullahs in control of almost every aspect of government. Hence, although the IRP's candidate received only a small proportion of the votes in the presidential elections in January 1980, its success in the parliamentary elections in March gave it a platform from which to obtain most of the important posts in the cabinet, in spite of fierce resistance by the man who was to emerge as its most formidable opponent, President Bani-Sadr. The IRP's drive for power was further assisted by the launch, first of a so-called 'cultural' revolution designed to impose its brand of Islamic orthodoxy on the universities, and then an administrative revolution which used the creation of committees in every government department and office to purge opponents and to place its own supporters throughout the bureaucracy. The only institution that was able to resist its onslaught was the army, whose role in the defence of the country against the Iraqi invasion in September 1980 was too important to be deliberately undermined. But even here, the IRP made considerable inroads by using the revolutionary guards as a parallel military arm and then by appointing mullahs to regular units themselves.

The role of the Ayatullah Khomeini in this process was not at all clear cut. In Bakhash's account of the struggle between President Bani-Sadr and the IRP, although his basic sympathies were with the latter, he often sided with the former, at least in the initial stages.[21] Over time, however, his reservations about the role of the mullahs in government seem to have greatly diminished, while Bani-Sadr's own somewhat erratic performance did nothing to sustain his confidence in either the skill or the reliability of non-clerical experts. Meanwhile, he was inevitably influenced by the sustained momentum of the IRP drive for power and its success in subduing a fragmented and increasingly desperate opposition. As a result, when the Majles began impeachment proceedings against Bani-Sadr in June 1981, Khomeini had little option but to go along with the decision and then to agree to the appointment of the IRP's candidate, Mohammad-Ali Raja'i, as his successor. Two months later, Raja'i himself was killed in the second of the huge explosions directed against the IRP leadership by the coalition of radical Islamic and leftist groups led by the People's Mojahedin. He was succeeded by Ali Khamanei who was elected president in October 1981.

During the next two years the mullahs, associated with the IRP, crushed all opposition and established a type of theocratic government and politics which was to last until the Ayatullah Khomeini's death in 1989. It is interesting to ask what role religion played in its institutional structures and practices, the more so as clerically dominated regimes have been so rare in modern world history.

The question can be approached from two angles. The first is to look at what Khomeini and the leading mullah politicians themselves said about the Islamic nature of their own government. To judge from their own statements, they were quite clear that the existence of an Islamic constitution together with the implementation of the notion of *wilayat-e faqih* meant that, almost by definition, Iran was an Islamic state. This can be seen, for example, in President Ali Khamanei's speech on the eighth anniversary of the revolution in February 1987, in which he pointed out the sweeping changes that it had brought about: 'The environment is now an Islamic environment, not the environment of western culture. It is a healthy environment. Parents are no longer worried about the morals of their children.' [22]

If further proof were needed, the mullahs would almost certainly have pointed to the Islamization of the legal system, something to which Khomeini himself attached particular importance.[23] This involved the progressive elimination of all non-clerical judges as well as the rewriting of many of the laws to ensure that they conformed to Islamic precepts. Just where this left actual practice is unclear. Many writers assert that, for all the efforts of the Islamic jurists, the system contained a hodge-podge of different types of courts and laws.[24] There must also be others who would argue from an Islamic legal perspective that any attempt to codify the *Sharia* or to interfere with the absolute right of judges to decide a case on its own merits must inevitably raise serious doubts about its fundamentally religious character.[25] The same could be said for the bill passed by the Majles in December 1990 allowing defendants the right to legal representation in court – something directly contrary to previous *Sharia* practice.[26] Nevertheless, for the great majority of Iranian Muslims, the existence of an Islamicized legal system could still be taken as proof of the existence of an Islamic state.

Two final arguments for the Islamic character of the post-revolutionary regime might well be adduced by its supporters. One is the attention paid to orthodoxy in morals. As in many other religiously inspired movements, there was a conspicuous concern with religious instruction and with combating what were thought of as harmful influences through correct education and a focus on the family as a source of moral instruction. As elsewhere, this involved efforts to ensure that women behaved as proper role models and that those who were mothers remained at home to look after their children – even though there was later some significant backtracking in such areas as abortion and birth control. A second indicator was a concern with ideological rectitude which led to the proliferation of committees of Islamic guidance throughout the bureaucracy, with particular emphasis on those given the task of supervising the media and publishing as well as the conduct of personnel in key institutions like the army.

Looked at from the outside, and with a greater emphasis on political practice, the picture seems somewhat different and the tension between Islamic and modern features much more apparent. From this point of view, two features of the structure of government stand out. The first is the power given to its most obviously religiously sanctioned components: the post of *Faqih* and the Council of Guardians. In Bakhash's phrase, the Ayatullah Khomeini enjoyed a 'towering presence' in the new order, based on his personal charisma, his role as the architect of the revolution and his domination over important clerical networks – all supported by his sweeping constitutional powers.[27] As such, he remained the final arbiter on all critical questions of policy and the focus of most significant political argument. Nevertheless, he often met his match in the senior clerics on the Council of Guardians, whose interpretations of what was and what was not properly Islamic allowed them to block some of the most important laws passed by the Majles, many of which the *Faqih* himself personally approved. Just why this should have been so is unclear. But given the fact that Khomeini's regular response to a veto was to try to persuade parliament to re-draft its bills in such a way as to obtain the guardians' consent, it would seem likely that he felt unwilling to launch a direct challenge to a body so closely associated with the Islamic character of the state.

The second, and complementary, feature of the Islamic republic was its pluralism. This derived not only from the constitutional division of powers between executive, legislature and judiciary but also from the special character of the pre-revolutionary Iranian religious establishment as well as the creation of a multiplicity of mullah-dominated organizations during the revolutionary turmoil of 1979 and after. Historically, control over Islamic education and its associated pious foundations was exercised by a small group of grand ayatullahs who were also regarded as more or less equal in prestige and legal expertise.[28] Given the subsequent role of religious leadership in the revolution, it was probably inevitable that institutionalized competition between them should be carried over into the politics of the Islamic republic. Mullahs were also the beneficiaries of the period of 'dual power' during the first phase of the revolutionary government, when they created and controlled a whole host of parallel institutions such as the courts and guards, which in turn gave them access to huge new opportunities of power and patronage. A final feature of this structure of what might be called 'mullah pluralism' was the government's use of mosques for a variety of important tasks, from vouching for the Islamic credentials of those seeking official employment to centres for the distribution of rationed food during the war with Iraq.

It was a combination of all these features that gave the politics of the first decade of the Islamic republic much of its particular character. In spite of the role of Khomeini and, at another level, the IRP as arbiters, the presence of so many different centres of power encouraged a fierce rivalry which made co-ordination difficult. It was also natural that this rivalry should be largely couched in a religious rhetoric which was the only way to win arguments in arenas dominated by the *Faqih* and the Council of Guardians. But this did little to conceal the more conventional contests for position and for influence over policy that animated the mullah politicians just as much as anybody else.

The problems that such a pluralism posed for political management have already been described in Chapter 5. It only remains to look in somewhat greater depth at the politico-religious implications of the Ayatullah Khomeini's attempt to solve some of these problems just before his death. This began with his rejoinder to what seems to have been no more than a routine restatement by President Khamanei of the then prevailing orthodoxy: that in an Islamic state both executive and legislature were subordinate to a superior religious law.[29] In what was certainly a new interpretation of his own views, Khomeini wrote back: 'it appears that you [Khamanei] don't recognize government as a supreme regency bestowed by God on the Holy Prophet and that it is among the most important of divine laws and has priority over all other peripheral divine laws'. And he went on to argue that hundreds of government functions would be inoperative if Khamanei's argument were correct and that 'the government is empowered to unilaterally revoke any *Sharia* agreement which it has concluded with the people when these agreements are contrary to the interests of the country or of Islam'.[30]

Khomeini's intervention was widely regarded as the prelude to an attack on the authority of the Council of Guardians. It also raised a host of unanswered questions about his new position regarding the role of the *Faqih*. Was he saying that the *Faqih* can overrule the *Sharia* in the interests of the community? Or was he making the larger claim that an Islamic government is automatically right simply because it is an Islamic government? In the event, any debate that might have taken place over these issues was then dramatically curtailed, first by Khomeini's own death, then by the appointment of a successor so lacking in authority that he was in no position to take a stance on anything of religious importance. As a result the new government of President Rafsanjani was forced to assert itself and to move against rival power centres by more piecemeal methods of attack. These included a successful push to drive its clerical opponents from the council of experts, the body entrusted to choose any future *Faqih*, and a greater use of non-clerical experts in government. Nevertheless, the questions raised by the Ayatullah Khomeini were so central to the practice of an Islamic government that they will have to be faced, sooner or later, by his successors or by anyone contemplating the establishment of a similar regime.

Religious politics in the Arab countries

The Islamic revolution had an enormous impact in the Arab countries, both on the local Shi'i populations as well as on many sections of the Sunni Muslim community, particularly those living under dictatorial or western-allied regimes – including those under Israeli occupation in the West Bank and Gaza. Nevertheless, it is also important to note that the Iranian revolution came at the end of over a decade of increasing religiosity and of religio-political activity which most commentators ascribe to the impact of the cataclysmic defeat by the Israelis in the war of 1967 coupled with the rising financial power and prestige of religiously conservative states like that of Saudi Arabia. Secular and Arab nationalist regimes and ideologies were now very much on the defensive. Meanwhile, many different political actors were re-discovering the vitality and mobilizing power of an Islamic vocabulary, particularly when it incorporated other powerful themes such as nationalism and social justice.[31] It was not just that religion itself seemed untainted by the defeat of Nasserism and similar projects but it also provided a better language for addressing the grievances that arose from the violation of self-respect and human dignity.[32] The fact that the mosque provided one of the few spaces that an authoritarian state found difficult to control only made its use as a instrument for proselytization and recruitment all the more important.

In seeking to analyse the phenomenon of a revived political Islam in the Arab countries I will begin by describing some of the most influential Sunni movements before turning to the role played by predominantly Shi'i organizations in Lebanon and Iraq.

Far and away the most significant Sunni movement, both in terms of continuous impact and in terms of the organizational and ideological model it provided, was the Muslim Brothers. This was started by an Egyptian teacher, Hasan al-Banna, in Ismailiyya in 1928 and then moved to Cairo in 1932. To begin with it was just one among a large number of tiny Islamic associations engaged in charity and mutual support; al-Banna himself had previously belonged to a number with names like The Society for Moral

Behaviour and The Society for the Prevention of the Forbidden.[33] However, the Brotherhood rapidly grew far beyond the others in membership and scope, and it is important to ask why. One factor is certainly the organizational skill of its charismatic leader. This allowed him to create a loose structure by which an endless multiplication of self-sustaining local neighbourhood groups could be linked and directed at the national level through the activities of a high-profile leadership with access to the newspapers and other forms of direct communication. Second, al-Banna developed what Ayubi calls a distinctive concept of the 'comprehensiveness of Islam' in which the construction of mosques, schools and clinics provided the framework in which an urban Muslim could live much of his life without reference to the western and secular influences around him.[34]

Given these various strengths, the Muslim Brothers were able to recruit at a rapid rate in the particular atmosphere of the 1930s and were soon large enough to come into competition with the other major forces in the political arena. This had a number of important consequences. First, it forced the Brothers to adapt their message to attract persons like workers or government employees who had previously belonged to the Wafd or one of the other more radical nationalist groups. Second, Hasan al-Banna and his lieutenants were alternatively wooed and attacked by the other politicians, and in such a way that it became necessary to try to define their political role more precisely. While al-Banna himself seems to have been content to act as the religious conscience of the nation, for example, by writing letters to the king giving his views on matters of national importance, others began to prepare the movement for a more active role, either by trying to seek power directly through turning it into a conventional political party or, when they felt that the organization and its assets were in danger of direct attack by its opponents, forming a 'secret apparatus' which began a series of pre-emptive assassinations against what it took to be its most dangerous enemies.[35] Al-Banna's own role in these latter developments has been endlessly debated.[36] But it is more important to observe that the logic of large religious movements inevitably drives them to face choices of this type and that, in almost every case, there will be internal forces driving them in a number of different possible directions.

The subsequent history of the Muslim Brothers after the Second World War provides much evidence for this observation. While during the late 1940s it acted more and more like the other major political parties – and losing Hasan al-Banna himself to assassination in 1949 – it then became so close to the new revolutionary government of Nasser's Free Officers that one of its most important new recruits, Sayyid Qutb, was appointed secretary general of the regime's Liberation Rally in 1953.[37] But relations soon deteriorated and in 1954 the organization was proscribed, while Qutb and most of the rest of the leadership were arrested after an unsuccessful assassination attempt on Nasser himself. Qutb then used his ten years in prison to produce a powerful reworking of Islamic history which he used to support his argument that Egypt was not an Islamic country but in a state of *jahiliya* (religious ignorance) and that Muslims could not lead a properly religious life without a root and branch overthrow of the existing political order.[38] This argument became widely known after Qutb's execution in 1965 and provided the inspiration for many of the small extremist religious groups that were formed in the 1970s.

The Muslim Brotherhood was allowed by President Sadat to re-establish itself in the early 1970s and was soon playing a role as complex as that in the 1940s. While the bulk of its members contented themselves with building up new clusters of mosques, schools and clinics, others took advantage of Sadat's economic liberalization to start various types of Islamic companies and financial institutions, while others again broke away to participate in a shifting set of religio-political organizations which went under the general title of *Al-Jama'at al-Islamiyya* (The Islamic Groups), with a particular stronghold in the universities, where they were given initial encouragement by the regime as staunch opponents of the Nasserites and other oppositional forces. It was members of some of these groups that sought the overthrow of the Sadat government. However, they were too impatient and too small in number to manage more than isolated attacks on public buildings and Coptic churches, as well as a few assassinations. Their one major success was to kill the president himself at an Army Day parade in October 1981. Thereafter the new president, Husni Mubarak, pursued a dual policy towards the religious movements, encouraging the Muslim Brothers to take part in the political process of parliament and elections (although never as an official party) while seeking to isolate the smaller, more radical, groups through confrontation and imprisonment. In these circumstances, the mainstream of the Muslim Brothers returned to a strategy of pressing for the piecemeal introduction of parts of the *Sharia* while building up the institutions of an alternative Islamic economic and social structure, against the day when they could obtain real political power.

Groups calling themselves Muslim Brothers were founded in Syria and Palestine in the 1940s, in Jordan in 1953 and Sudan in 1954. As a rule they adopted the same organizational style: networks of local, usually mosque-related, groupings with a national leadership to provide cohesion and ideological uniformity. This had the advantage of being able to make use of the pre-existing Islamic charities and welfare associations to be found in almost every town. It also had the additional advantage of encouraging the type of loose structure that allowed most parts of the organization to maintain themselves should the parent organization find itself proscribed. Furthermore, as in Egypt, the local groupings could be used as a basis for the establishment of a system of secret cells should it become necessary to operate underground. Nevertheless, in spite of all these obvious similarities, what is even more remarkable is the extraordinary differences in the experience of these various movements, faced as they inevitably were with quite dissimilar Arab political environments. I will look at three of these briefly by way of making the same point.

In its early days the Syrian Muslim Brothers corresponded most closely to the Egyptians in terms of organization and political practice. They too made use of the presence of other Islamic groupings; they too quickly attracted recruits by providing a wider range of economic, social and cultural activities than any of their predecessors.[39] But, unlike their Egyptian counterpart, they were quick to organize themselves to participate in Syria's various general elections, obtaining 3 seats in parliament in 1949, 5 in 1954 and 10 in 1961 – when they obviously profited from the fact that they had been banned by President Nasser during the short-lived United Arab Republic.[40]

The Syrian Muslim Brothers played only a minor role in the turbulent politics of the 1960s but then emerged as the Ba'th party's most implacable opponents in the next decade. Although never numbering more than 5,000–7,000, they were successful in obtaining the tacit support of a sizeable proportion of the Sunni urban population who were resentful at being ruled by what they saw as a secular, socialist, rural and, above all, Alawi regime.[41] To do this, they took initial advantage of the fact that members of various Muslim groups to which they were allied had received weapons training from allies within the PLO in the late 1960s to launch hit-and-run attacks on Alawi and Ba'thi targets. But what transformed their movement into something much more potent was the growing resentment at some of the Asad administration's policies – notably economic mismanagement and the invasion of Lebanon in 1976 on the side of the Christians against the Muslims and their Palestinian allies – and then the impact of the Iranian revolution, which seemed to demonstrate that even the most powerful regimes could be overthrown by mass popular action. This gave the Brothers the opportunity to take the lead in a widespread campaign of civil disobedience in Aleppo in the early months of 1980. However, once it had been put down by the security forces along with smaller manifestations of opposition in Damascus and elsewhere, they were unable to generate the mass support they needed to keep their campaign going. The situation became still more difficult in July 1980 when membership of the organization was made punishable by death. As a result, they had to face a final armed confrontation in Hama early in 1982 on their own. And in spite of determined resistance by their armed followers they were finally overwhelmed in the midst of great destruction and loss of life. Thereafter, the leadership of the movement, now mostly in exile, began to fragment, while the Ba'thi regime took major steps to re-establish its authority in the cities and, in particular, over the country's mosques by means of a wholesale recruitment of loyal prayer leaders.[42]

The situation in Sudan was quite different again. There the Muslim Brothers had to operate in an arena dominated by two large sectarian Islamic groupings, the Ansar and the Khatmiyya, both with their associated parties, which dominated the communalistic politics of the country during periods between military regimes. Hence there was little scope for the Brothers' more ideological appeal, and it took several decades before they were able to make their presence felt. When they did it was as much the result of skilful leadership as anything else; after a split in the mid-1970s, the faction led by Hassan al-Turabi (now reorganized as the National Islamic Front – NIF) was able to take advantage of Nimeiri's policy of reconciliation with the opposition to participate closely with the regime, to obtain important posts in the administrative and educational systems for some of its members and then to win a substantial number of seats in the 1980 parliamentary elections.[43] It was then able to take further advantage of Nimeiri's decision to introduce parts of the *Sharia* in 1983 to increase its influence still further. This not only allowed the NIF to pose as the main implementers of the holy law but also to profit from the inevitable rise in tension between Muslims and those non-Muslim Christians and animists who were now unwillingly subject to its provisions. As a further bonus, the application of *Sharia* principles outlawing interest to the Sudanese banking sector paved the way for the tremendous expansion of Islamic banking that provided the Front with a major source of funds.

The growing power of the NIF is well illustrated by the way in which its leaders were able to negotiate the rapidly changing political situation after 1983. Their unsuccessful coup attempt against Nimeiri in January 1985 meant that they were out of his government when it was overthrown some months later. This in turn allowed them to participate in the subsequent general election in March 1986, when they and their supporters obtained enough seats, and a sufficiently powerful position in the new coalition government, to be able to block any move towards withdrawing the *Sharia* or adopting a more conciliatory attitude to the anti-government revolt that had been restarted in the south.[44] Finally, they were able to play a powerful behind-the-scenes role in the new military government that came to power in July 1989. In all this they made maximum use of the growing polarization in Sudanese politics between Muslims and non-Muslims seeking to present everything in terms of a simple contradiction: Islamic (meaning the *Sharia*)/non-Islamic (meaning secular Sudanese or Christians).[45] In such an equation the NIF was clearly to be seen as the protector of the *Sharia* and the main opponent of any policy that might be interpreted as the granting of concessions by Muslims to non-Muslims. By the end of 1990 the use of this strategy had given the NIF sufficient influence to persuade the military president, General Bashir, to announce the introduction in March 1991 of a new version of the *Sharia* as it related to religiously defined criminal offences but not the establishment of an Islamic state, for which it had been pressing hard.

A final example of Brotherhood activity comes from the area of Israel/Palestine/Jordan. As far as the Gaza Strip was concerned, which came under Egyptian administration in 1949, the organization did not survive the general crackdown on the movement by the Nasser regime in 1954.[46] However, it managed something of a revival in the new situation produced by the Israeli occupation in 1967 when it was able to make use of growing Palestinian nationalist sentiment and a proliferation of small Islamic groups to recruit members under the general umbrella of the Islamic Congress. In spite of its uneasy relationship with the PLO, it soon managed to gain control over most of the religious institutions in the Strip. Once the Intifada had got under way, however, its stress on the overwhelming importance of a religious revival and its strategy of avoiding direct confrontation with the Israelis encouraged some of its followers to form the more activist HAMAS – Harakat al-Muqawama al-Islamiya (Islamic Resistance Movement) – which sought to direct much of the popular resistance like strikes and demonstrations during 1988. This at once brought it into opposition both with the Israelis (who banned it) and with the Palestine Liberation Organization and the local Unified National Command, and it was only after the intervention of Yasser Arafat and the leaders of the Muslim Brothers in Egypt that it agreed to co-ordinate its activities with the PLO and to acknowledge its leadership of the national struggle.[47]

The history of the Muslim Brothers on the West Bank was different again. During the Jordanian regime the organization benefited from the fact that the Brothers were allowed to operate openly in Jordan itself, in recognition of the support they had given to the Hashemite regime against its leftist and Arab nationalist opponents. But after 1967 it was forced to adopt a much more clandestine form of organization, while maintaining its links with the movement in Amman. Like its counterpart in Gaza, it also used its growing strength from the later 1970s onwards to challenge the hold of the PLO and its associated groups over major West Bank institutions like the universities, the unions and the popular committees.[48] However, it was rarely able to obtain the same position of influence as in Gaza, and remained open to the criticism that it was splitting the nationalist movement and thus doing Israel's work for it. The same constraints continued to obtain after the outbreak of the Intifada; following a period of challenge to the Unified National Command in 1988 the movement agreed to co-ordinate its activities with the leaders of the uprising in the interests of unity.

Apart from the Muslim Brothers and its more radical offshoots, other Sunni Islamic movements began to appear in the late 1970s, many of them stimulated directly by the impact of the revolution in Iran. To speak very generally, these were of two types. The first, to be found in countries like Tunisia and Algeria, were mass movements organized very much along the lines of the Muslim Brothers, with the avowed aim of obtaining power through parliamentary means. The second were smaller, more militant, groups dedicated to the establishment of an Islamic state, often by violent means. I will discuss examples of each of these in turn.

Tunisia's major Islamic organization, the Mouvement de la Tendance Islamique (MTI), was the creation of a group of men who were radicalized by the 1978 general strike and then by the Iranian revolution, which convinced them that religion should play a more active role in political life. Their response was to found an Islamic Association of Tunisia which built up support for itself in schools and in mosques, where the prayer leaders were not directly associated with the government and the official religious establishment.[49] The nature of its political message is well captured by a statement by its leader, Rashid al-Gannushi: 'It is not enough to pray five times a day and fast in order to be worthy of Islam. Islam is activism . . . it is on the side of the poor and the oppressed.'[50]

The leadership changed its name to the MTI in 1981 when President Bourguiba announced his programme of political liberalization, in an unsuccessful attempt to obtain permission to operate openly as a regular party. Thereafter, it sought to extend its influence in two ways. One was to set up a network of welfare programmes, free legal assistance and medical care. The second was to co-operate with other oppositional forces in support of various human rights and social issues. It was this latter activity that differentiated it most strongly from the contemporary Egyptian Muslim Brothers, whom Gannushi accused of being simply concerned to exercise tutelage over society without trying to change it.[51] In spite of the fact that its leaders were in and out of prison, and its newspaper and publishing organization subject to regular harassment, the MTI continued to seek recognition as a political party. But this was again refused by the new regime of President Ben Ali just before the April 1989 general election, presumably on the grounds that it might obtain enough support to pose a serious challenge to the government. Two years later, however, the leadership of the movement was completely split by the Gulf War of January 1991 and was forced to announce that the MTI itself was no longer a cohesive force.

The second type of Sunni politico-religious organization consisted of groups calling for the overthrow of an existing regime and the immediate establishment of an Islamic state. The majority of these were small, clandestine and ready to use force. They took their cue from the ideology of the Iranian revolutionaries, stressed the importance of Sunni/Shi'i co-operation and sometimes received financial and other support from Teheran. Their names – Jihad (Holy War), Tawhid (oneness/unification) – often expressed the same connection. Given their militant activism and the impatience of their followers, they were involved in frequent clashes with the regimes they opposed and in many cases the sense of personal comradeship among their members was formed in prison. Such groups existed in Egypt, Tunisia, Morocco, Lebanon, Jordan and among the Palestinians in the West Bank and Gaza.[52]

The context in which militant Shi'i groups tended to operate was quite different again. Historically, the Shi'i communities had been forced to the margins of the Arab world by a long series of Sunni ruling dynasties, and still tended to live in poor, mountainous or desert areas with access to few resources and the poorest land. Their members were thus particularly responsive to 20th-century movements of communal self-assertion, whether these were expressed in religious or class terms. Another feature of Shi'i life was the role of their clergy and the influence on it of study in the holy cities of Iraq and Iran. It was there, for instance, that some of them became acquainted with the ideas of men like the Ayatullah Khomeini or Muhammad Baqr al-Sadr of Najaf, whose thinking had a very obvious political component which combined a stress on clerical activism with an obvious engagement with the powerful vocabularies of Marxism and secularism with which they competed for followers. In these circumstances, the Iranian revolution was bound to have a particularly potent effect, both on communal organizations seeking greater equality for the Shi'is and on the more ideologically motivated movements committed to the overthrow of existing regimes and the immediate establishment of an Islamic state.

Examples of two quite different types of Shi'i communal movements stimulated by the events in Iran can be found in Saudi Arabia and Lebanon. In the former, some of the 400,000 or so Shi'is living in the country's eastern province were emboldened to hold their celebrations of Ashura in public in 1979, despite an official prohibition. The police then opened fire and some 17 persons were killed. As often happens in such cases, the Saudi government then succeeded in calming the situation by making an obviously communally related response which involved pouring money and public-works projects into the area.[53]

The Lebanese context was quite different. There the collapse of the central government during the civil war and the disruptions caused by the frequent Israeli incursions into the south released the Shi'i population from the constraints of institutionalized politics and allowed the development of new forms of political organizations with different projects for the reconstruction of state and society.[54] One was Harakat Amal, created in the late 1970s, which combined a militia with an appeal to Shi'i solidarity that found an echo throughout much of the community.[55] This at once made it an important political actor in the various attempts to create a new Lebanese political order. However, the fact that it was poorly led by a basically secular leadership meant that its members could be quite easily detached by other groups, notably the clerically led, pro-Iranian, movement Hizballah that was created in 1982. Like any Lebanese organization that hoped for political influence at this time, it had to be based on a militia. But where it differed from Amal was that its declared mission was not to improve the relative position of the Shi'is as a community but to establish an Islamic republic. As an avowedly revolutionary party with many enemies, its organizational structure remained secret, as did its close relationship with the shadowy Jihad group that was responsible for many of the kidnappings of foreigners in Beirut in the mid-1980s. But it is known that it was forced to become a more centralized and accountable movement by the Iranians who provided it with weapons, funds and support against the Syrian army in Beirut.[56]

The last Shi'i movement to be examined is one that developed out of the particular politics of contemporary Iraq. This was the Islamic Dawa party, which was founded in the 1950s and continued to represent Shi'i religious interests in the face of the secularizing tendencies of successive regimes. Such tendencies were particularly apparent after 1968 when the new Ba'thi administration tightened its grip on religious activity and sought closer control over the institutional life of the holy cities of Najaf and Kerbala. This triggered sporadic resistance which reached a peak during widespread demonstrations during Ashura in February 1977. As in Saudi Arabia two years later, the regime's initial

response was to try to win over the Shi'is as a community by
opening up the Ba'th party and the administration to greater
Shi'i representation.[57] However, this policy was soon overtaken
by the excitement engendered by the Iranian revolution, which
encouraged the leaders of the Dawa to reorganize their movement in preparation for increasing confrontation with what they
identified as a secular, un-Godly, ruling group. One element of
their policy was the *fatwa* issued by Muhammad Baqr al-Sadr
in June 1979 forbidding Muslims to join the Ba'th party and
calling for total support for the Iranian revolution. A second
was a campaign of demonstrations and attempted assassinations.
The regime's response was swift and brutal; Baqr al-Sadr himself
was executed, membership in the Dawa was made punishable by
death and by the time Iraq invaded Iran in September 1980 the
movement had been so completely crushed that it was only able to
continue a shadowy existence outside the country in Teheran and
Kuwait.[58] The opportunity was also taken to reduce the power
of the Shi'i clergy still further, while seeking to win over the bulk
of the population with programmes of economic development and
even wider access to posts in the party and administration.[59] This
seems to have been enough to secure the loyalty of the majority of
Shi'is during the long war with Iran but not during the breakdown
of central government control that followed the end of the Gulf
War in February/March 1991.

The Christians between communalism and nationalism

Arab Christians were affected by many of the same processes
as Arab Muslims, most notably the shock of the 1967 war and
the atmosphere of heightened religiosity that it engendered. But,
as with the Muslims, their response was highly contextual and
depended very much on their place within each country's national
movement and their relations with their non-Christian neighbours.
I will illustrate these points with brief reference to three areas in
which the Christian population constitutes a small minority: Egypt,
Sudan and Israel-Palestine.

Since 1923 successive Egyptian regimes have attempted, with
great success, to demonstrate that the small Coptic minority –
no more than 6–7 per cent of the total population – has been
an integral part of the national community. This was more easily

accomplished in the days of the Wafd Party, which served as an important vehicle for Christian politicians. But, with the abolition of the old parties in 1953, the most salient representatives of the community became the clergy, and it was they, under the energetic leadership of Pope Shenuda III who was elected patriarch in 1971, who encouraged a process of Coptic self-assertion which began in the early Sadat period.

This took the form of communal mobilization focused on the churches, and the creation of many new benevolent and community associations.[60] It was fuelled by a general unease that some of Sadat's policies were leading to a more pointed definition of Egypt as a Muslim state, suggested, *inter alia*, by the participation of the Muslim Brothers in the discussions on the 1971 constitution. And it was not long before it encountered opposition from some of the more radical Islamic groups which began with a dispute over an attempt to convert a philanthropic association into a church at Kanqa near Cairo in 1972 and climaxed in a series of explosions and attacks on Christian property in Cairo and Upper Egypt in 1980.[61] President Sadat's response was to order the arrest of hundreds of both Christian and Muslim activists in the summer of 1981. The process of communalism continued under President Mubarak, with attempts to draw as many Copts as possible into church-led institutions. But its leaders also made more efforts to temper its implicit separatism with a stress on the importance of religious culture in Egyptian history and the role of Copts as saints and heroes.[62]

The Christian populations in Sudan were too divided to act as a basis for the same type of communal response when they felt that their status as Sudanese citizens was under attack. Hence opposition both to what was seen as Muslim domination of the state and, after 1983, to the attempts to impose sections of the *Sharia* on non-Muslims has taken various forms. These range from protests by the northern churches to the role played by Christian leaders in the rebellion in the south.[63]

A third context was provided by the situation of Christian Palestinians under Israeli occupation. Lacking a state of their own, or even the possibility of creating national institutions, the maintenance of unity had to be the work of individuals and groups on the ground, assisted by the leadership of the PLO from outside. Given these constraints it was probably inevitable that the main activity should be in the cultural field, the one area not subject to direct Israeli control.[64] And it was here that strenuous efforts were made to popularize particular readings of Palestinianism and Palestinian history in which religion was seen as cultural tradition rather than a mark of identity.[65] All this proved of great importance during the Intifada, which gave greater salience to groups like the Muslim Brothers – and then Hamas – that sought to reinterpret everything in religious terms. The Intifada also made it easier to counter Israeli attempts to split the Christian churches in Jerusalem by putting pressure on the Orthodox Church, in particular, to take a public stand against military policies in the West Bank and Gaza.[66]

A final note concerns the intensification of the confessional system in Lebanon, where religion became more and more important as a source of identity as the civil war progressed. The war had many causes but certainly one of the most important was the policies taken by influential Christian leaders to protect the privileged position allotted to the Maronites within the Lebanese state. These included the development of parallel institutions such as militias that could be used if the state's own police and army could no longer cope with the pressures for reform coming from the alliance of leftist and radical Muslim groups with Palestinian military support.[67] It also included largely successful efforts to mobilize their own community as well as to disrupt the ideological drive of the opposition by deliberately sectarianizing the conflict once it had begun. Given the importance attached to religious identity in Lebanon it was a relatively easy matter to shell predominantly Muslim districts in Beirut and elsewhere and so turn the fighting into a basically Christian/Muslim conflict.

Religion and politics in a Jewish state

Ever since 1948 there has been an almost universal consensus among Israeli Jews that Israel should be a Jewish state. This found expression in 1949 in a series of compromises between Ben-Gurion's government and the newly created National Religious Party (NRP), which won 16 seats in the first general elections. They included agreement not to draw up a permanent constitution – something that the NRP insisted would have to be based on the *Halacha* or religious law – and the establishment of a ministry of religious affairs with formal authorization over many aspects of

Jewish life, for example, marriage. It was on this basis that the NRP came to play a central role as the mediator between the state and the majority of the religious Israelis. Other religious parties such as Aghudat Yisrael (Jewish Association), which represented a section of the ultra-orthodox community, also obtained Knesset seats but rarely sought cabinet office in the Labour-dominated coalitions of the 1950s and 1960s.

The overwhelming victory over the Arab armies in 1967 and the occupation of the West Bank (known historically as Judea and Samaria) called all these arrangements into question. The war was given a religious, sometimes a messianic, interpretation. It raised the possibility of new definitions of what it was to be an Israeli and a Jew. And it encouraged expressions of a very much more intense form of territorial and ethnic nationalism in which the religious obligation to settle and to annex the West Bank – and even to purge it of its non-Jewish population – was given increasing prominence. Hence, although the share of the vote going to the purely religious parties remained more or less the same in all subsequent general elections, the way was open for activists to develop new forms of politics based on new combinations of religion, communalism, ethnicity and more extreme forms of Jewish nationalism.[68]

The first organization to respond to the new environment was the NRP, which, even before 1967, had contained a group advocating the more active use of religious tradition to inform a much wider range of social and political issues. One immediate result was a strong focus on questions like West Bank settlement where religious and political factors were closely mixed. This in turn led to the creation by NRP members of the Gush Emunim (Block of the Faithful) movement in 1974 with an activist programme that combined pressure for new settlements with the creation of a powerful lobby for annexation of the West Bank as against any territorial compromise with the Palestinians or the Jordanians.[69] To back this up, its members established a series of Jewish colonies close to major Palestinian population centres, such as at Kiryat Araba just outside Hebron. Later, when the leaders of the Gush became disappointed with the support they were receiving from the Likud government after 1977, they sought other ways of pursuing their major aim which was now to secure the inclusion of the West Bank within the boundaries of effective Israeli control. So successful were they that, although the number of Gush Emunim settlers numbered no more than 5,000 in the late 1980s, they were widely credited with creating a powerful constituency for holding on to the occupied territories.[70] In addition, their representatives had been given an official role by the government in the promotion of further Jewish settlement on the West Bank.[71]

Gush Emunim was followed by the creation of other parties and movements with new politico-religious projects. One of the first of these was Kach, the party founded by Meir Kahane, which obtained one seat in the 1984 election on a platform which included the need to purge the Holy Land of the presence of gentiles such as Palestinians. Kahane's message also included an unusually strong attack on those Jews he described as 'Hellenists', in other words, assimilationists. Such views aroused widespread opposition and eventually led to his party's disqualification from the Knesset on the grounds of racialism and undermining the democratic character of the state.[72]

Other new parties were then formed to represent different sections of the orthodox and ultra-orthodox communities. Perhaps in competition, members of Aghudat Yisrael began to play a more active role in politics after their spiritual leader, the Lubavitcher Rabbi, began to order his supporters – many of whom had previously abstained – to vote in elections. Such parties had only to gain a handful of seats to be considered as potential coalition partners during the complex negotiations that preceded the formation of the national unity governments of 1984 and 1988. And this, in turn, allowed them to obtain ministerial posts as well as the promises of funds and of the implementation of measures that concerned them deeply, for example, the restriction of movement on the Sabbath. By the end of the 1980s they had all managed to build up extensive networks of schools and clinics and subsidized houses for their followers. This also allowed them to derive maximum benefit from Prime Minister Begin's 1978 concession to allow the wholesale exemption of pupils in *yeshivas* (religious schools) from military service. The result, as Margalit argues, was a further increase in electoral support which gave Aghudat Yisrael 5 seats in the 1988 election, Shas (founded by the chief Sephardic rabbi in 1984) another 5 and Degel Hatorah (a party that had broken from Aghudat Yisrael that same year)2.[73]

Notes

1 The question is posed in Sami Zubaida, 'Reading history backwards', *MEREPORT*, 160 (Sept./Oct., 1989), pp. 39–41. For a fuller discussion see his *Islam, The People and the State* (London and New York: Routledge, 1989), pp. 152–5.
2 Ibid., p. 39.
3 For example, arguments of Hasan al-Banna in Charles Wendell (ed. and trans.), *Five Tracts of Hasan Al-Banna' (1906–1949)* (Berkeley: University of California Press, 1978), pp. 40–65).
4 V. S. Naipaul, 'The shadow of the guru', *New York Review of Books*, 20 Nov. 1990, p. 69.
5 Roger Savory, 'Ex Oriente Nebula: An inquiry into the nature of Khomeini's ideology', in Peter J. Chelkowski and Robert J. Pranger (eds), *Ideology and Power in the Middle East* (Durham, NC, and London: Duke University Press, 1988), p. 340.
6 For example, ibid., p. 341.
7 I have drawn from ideas to be found in Talal Asad, *The Idea of an Anthropology of Islam* (Washington, DC: Center for Contemporary Arab Studies, Georgetown University, Occasional Papers, March 1986), pp. 14–15.
8 For example, Richard T. Antoun and Mary Elaine Hegland (eds), *Religious Resurgence: Contemporary Cases in Islam, Christianity, and Judaism* (Syracuse: Syracuse University Press, 1987), p. 259.
9 Zubaida, *Islam, The People and the State*, pp. 152–4.
10 Ibid., p. 153.
11 I have borrowed these ideas from Dr Huri Islamoglu-Inan. See also Roderic H. Davison, *Reform in the Ottoman Empire 1856–1876* (Princeton, NJ: Princeton University Press, 1963), pp. 251–6.
12 For example, Nazih N. Ayubi, *Political Islam: Religion and Politics in the Arab World* (London and New York: Routledge, 1991), p. 131.
13 For example, J. Schacht, 'The schools of law and later developments of Jurisprudence', in Majid Khadduri and Herbert J. Leibesny (eds), *Law in the Middle East*, 1, *Origin and Development of Islamic Law* (Washington, DC: Middle East Institute, 1955).
14 Asad, *The Idea of an Anthropology of Islam*, p. 13.
15 Fred Halliday, 'The Iranian revolution and religious populism', *Journal of International Relations*, 36/2 (Fall/Winter, 1982/83), p. 197.
16 Shaul Bakhash, *Reign of the Ayatollahs* (London: I. B. Tauris, 1985), p. 73.
17 Ibid., p. 74.
18 This is the personal suggestion of a member of the revolutionary council at the time.
19 Bakhash, *Reign of the Ayatollahs*, pp. 84–5.
20 Chibli Wajdi Mallat, *The Renaissance of Islamic Law: Constitution, Economics and Banking in the Thought of Muhammad Baqer As Sadr* (Ph. D., London University, Sept. 1989), pp. 131, 146.
21 Bakhash, *Reign of the Ayatollahs*, pp. 99–110 and Ch. 6.
22 SWB, 2nd series, ME/8491 (13 Feb. 1987), A/3.

194   *II: Contemporary politics*

23 Bakhash, *Reign of the Ayatollahs*, pp. 227, 241.
24 For example, Zubaida, *Islam, The People and the State*, pp. 173–4.
25 Ibid., p. 174.
26 *The Independent* (London), 31 Dec. 1990.
27 Bakhash, *Reign of the Ayatollahs*, pp. 241–2.
28 Zubaida, *Islam, The People and the State*, pp. 174–7; Mallat, *Renaissance of Islamic Law*, p. 54.
29 Ibid., p. 110.
30 Ibid., p. 111.
31 Albert Hourani, 'Conclusion', in James P. Piscatori (ed.), *Islam in the Political Process* (Cambridge: Cambridge University Press, 1983), pp. 228–9.
32 This is another idea of Dr Huri Islamoglu-Inan.
33 R. P. Mitchell, *The Society of Muslim Brothers* (Oxford: Oxford University Press, 1969), p. 2.
34 Ayubi, *Political Islam*, p. 131.
35 Mitchell, *Society of Muslim Brothers*, pp. 30–2.
36 For example, ibid., pp. 54–7, 62, 73, 88.
37 Ayubi, *Political Islam*, p. 138.
38 For example, Zubaida, *Islam, The People and the State*, pp. 51–3.
39 Ayubi, *Political Islam*, p. 87.
40 Raymond A. Hinnebusch, *Authoritarian Power and State Formation in Ba'thist Syria: Army, Party, and Peasant* (Boulder, Colorado: Westview Press, 1990), p. 287.
41 Ibid., pp. 282–5, 292–7; Hanna Batatu, 'Syria's Muslim Brethren', in Fred Halliday and Hamza Alavi (eds), *State and Ideology in the Middle East and Pakistan* (Basingstoke and London: Macmillan, 1988), pp. 127–30.
42 See, for example, *Al-Nazeer*, 61 (Oct., 1983). *Al-Nazeer* was an organ of the Islamic opposition.
43 Alexander S. Cudsi, 'Islam and politics in Sudan', in Piscatori (ed.), *Islam in the Political Process*, pp. 48–53.
44 Ayubi, *Political Islam*, pp. 108–12.
45 This is the view of Idriss al-Hassan as reported by Ghassan Salamé in 'Note de lecture: La religion dans la société Arabe', *Maghreb/Machrek*, 129 (July/Aug./Sept., 1990), pp. 146–7.
46 Mohammad K. Shadid, 'The Muslim Brotherhood movement in the West Bank and Gaza', *Third World Quarterly*, 10/2 (April, 1988), pp. 659–62.
47 Ibid., pp. 679–80; Ze'ev Schiff and Ehud Ya'ari, *Intifada: The Palestine Uprising – Israel's Third Front* (New York: Simon & Schuster, 1989), pp. 234–5.
48 Shadid, 'Muslim Brotherhood', pp. 662, 679–80.
49 Ayubi, *Political Islam*, pp. 114–115; Ben Wilkinson, 'Who will succeed Bourguiba?', *The Middle East* (London), 130 (Oct., 1985), pp. 42–3.
50 Linda G. Jones, 'Portrait of Rashid al-Gannoushi', *MEREPORT* (July/Aug., 1988), p. 20.
51 Ayubi, *Political Islam*, p. 115.

52 For example, Jamal Benomar, 'The Islamic movement and religious discourse in Morocco'; Marion Boulby, 'The Islamic challenge: Tunisia since independence'; Saad Eddin Ibrahim, 'Egypt's Islamic activism in the 1980s'; Marius Deeb, 'Shia movements in Lebanon: Their formation, ideology, social basis, and links with Iran and Syria'; all in *Third World Quarterly*, 10/2 (April, 1988). And Thomas Mayer, 'Pro-Iranian fundamentalism in Gaza', in Emmanuel Sivan and Menachem Friedman (eds), *Religious Radicalism and Politics in the Middle East* (Albany, NY: State University of New York Press, 1990), pp. 146–9.

53 Joseph P. Kechechian, 'Islamic revivalism and change in Saudi Arabia', *The Muslim World*, LXXX/1 (Jan., 1990), pp. 4–5.

54 Michael Humphrey, 'Islam, state and society: the Lebanese case', p. 2.

55 Augustus Richard Norton, *Amal and the Shi'a – A Struggle for the Soul of Lebanon* (Austin, Texas: University of Texas Press, 1987). AMAL is an acronym for Afwaj al-muqawama al-Lubnaniya.

56 Martin Kramer, 'The moral logic of Hizballah', *Occasional Paper*: Dayan Center for Middle Eastern and African Studies, Tel Aviv 1987, pp. 2–3.

57 Ofra Bengio, 'Shi'is and politics in Ba'thi Iraq', *Middle Eastern Studies*, 21/1 (Jan., 1981), pp. 2–4.

58 Amatzia Baram, 'The radical Shi'ite opposition movements in Iraq', in Sivan and Friedman (eds), *Religious Radicalism*, pp. 96–7.

59 Bengio, 'Shi'is and politics', pp. 9–11.

60 Hamied Ansari, 'Sectarian conflict in Egypt and the political expediency of religion', *Middle East Journal*, 38/3 (Summer, 1984), pp. 398–400.

61 Ibid., pp. 408–15.

62 For example, William Suliman Kilada, 'Christian–Muslim relations in Egypt', in Kail C. Ellis (ed.), *The Vatican, Islam and the Middle East* (Syracuse, NY: Syracuse University Press, 1987), pp. 258–9.

63 Abdullah Ahmed An-Naim, 'Christian–Muslim relations in the Sudan: Peaceful coexistence at risk', in ibid., pp. 267, 269, 273.

64 Glenn Bowman, 'Nationalising the sacred: Transformations in Christian Palestinian identities in the Israeli-Occupied Territories', *Review of Middle East Studies*, V (1992).

65 Idem.

66 Daoud Kuttab, 'Christians, Israel and the intifada', *Middle East International*, 353 (7 July 1989), pp. 18–19.

67 Kamal S. Salibi, *Crossroads to Civil War: Lebanon 1958–1976* (London: Ithaca Press, 1976), pp. 43–6; Frank Stoakes, 'The supervigilantes: The Lebanese Kataeb party as builder, surrogate and defender of the state', *Middle Eastern Studies*, 11/3 (Oct., 1975), pp. 219–24, 230–1.

68 Itzhak Galnoor, 'The 1984 elections in Israel: Political results and open questions', *Middle East Review*, XVIII/4 (Summer, 1986), p. 54.

69 David J. Schnall, 'Religion and political dissent in Israel: the case of Gush Emunim', in Antoun and Hegland (eds), *Religious Resurgence*, p. 171.

8 The military in state and society

Theoretical approaches to the study of the military's political role

Most studies of the political role of Middle Eastern armies have been written from one of two perspectives: either an attempt to explain the occurrence of military 'coups'; or a discussion of the larger question of the place of the army within the whole process of state or nation building. This is perhaps understandable given the recent history of the region but it has yielded little insight. By and large, writers on Middle Eastern coups have tended to base their explanations on the simple premise that an army's only way to exercise political power is by means of the overthrow of a civilian regime. They have also been prone to attach too much importance to specifically local factors, such as the allegedly militaristic nature of Islam or of Arab culture, as reasons for military intervention. However, officers in barracks can be just as influential as officers in government. And coups and military regimes are such a common feature of the post-colonial world that their occurrence must be due in large part to universal, rather than simply Middle Eastern, factors. Notions such as the one that seeks to define the nation-building role of the officer corps as that of the 'middle class in uniform' have proved equally unhelpful. Armies have their own institutional imperatives which mean that their technological, educational or administrative resources are not just available to the rest of society in whatever way they happen to be needed. Just as important, the relationship between the military as an organization and, say, the civilian bureaucracy or the capitalist industrial class is far more complex than most analyses allow.

Given the unsatisfactory nature of such simplistic approaches, it is more helpful to examine the role of the army within a much larger frame of reference; one that seeks to identify its place within both state and society. Following the work of Maurice Janowitz, Robin Luckham and others, this involves concentration on three specific features.[1] The first is the notion of an army as a special type of organization, with its own particular form of hierarchy, its own well-defined boundaries and its own type of professionalism – one that it may well feel that it shares with other military organizations and other countries. Typically, the military will want complete control over the way it recruits, trains and then promotes its own officers. And it will try to protect itself from influences that threaten its institutional integrity, and thus its effectiveness; for example, the accelerated promotion of politically favoured officers or the politicization of its other ranks. All such institutional necessities can certainly be observed in a Middle Eastern context. But, unfortunately, with the exception of two books on the Turkish army and a few on the Israeli, there has been little research allowed on the way they actually work out in practice.[2] To make matters more complicated, the region contains a wide variety of different types of military organization, from the professional armies of Egypt or Tunisia to the tribal forces in the Arabian peninsula, not to speak of the attempts to create popular revolutionary armies in Libya, Iran and South Yemen, or the guerrilla army of the Palestinians.

A second area of examination involves the international sphere. Most Third World armies were originally modelled on the European types of organization required to fight colonial wars using European weapons and tactics. Later, new types of dependencies were created by the gifts or purchases of complex modern weapons systems that largely dictate their own type of organizational structure and tactics and that need skills, spare parts and general technical support only found abroad. In these circumstances, local staff officers have usually to take what armaments others choose to give them, while their only chance of obtaining a better offer is either to obtain strong diplomatic support from their own government or to build up a special relationship with their suppliers in Washington, Moscow or Europe. Efforts to establish a domestic arms industry are usually subject to the same constraints. In a Middle Eastern context, only the Israeli army has managed to free itself to any degree from such dependencies by means of the quality of its technical know-how and its close ties, first with the French, then with the Americans. Nevertheless, their weakness has not prevented either the Turks or many of the Arab armies from deliberately imitating certain international military practices, for example, the enormous emphasis placed on sending officers on training courses abroad.

The third, and final, feature that requires examination is the relationship of an army to the state of which it forms a part. This is another extremely complex subject. One useful place to begin is with the observation that both the military and the civilian sections of the government will try to ensure that their relations are mediated only by a few persons at the highest level, usually the president and the minister of defence who is often the commander of the army as well. This has the advantage of preserving their institutional integrity from interference by the other. Typically the army will want to maintain maximum control over its own internal affairs while the civilians will try to prevent the military from seeking political allies outside the cabinet. Beyond this, both sides will seek to influence a whole variety of working practices governing their relationship, for example, the methods by which budgets are drawn up, resources allocated and roles established. As a rule, in most systems, the final results are a matter of hard bargaining in which their relative strengths can be judged by their success in getting their way in a number of key areas, for example, over the military's share of the annual budget or the size of the defence industry or the often vexed question of whether the army should share internal security duties with armed paramilitary forces over which it has no control. In addition, the military may feel that it has a legitimate concern with shaping developments in the wider environment such as the educational system, the economy and the relations between people of different classes or sects. A good example of a typical view concerning this last point can be found in a phrase on the tomb of Egypt's Unknown Soldier: 'None shall fix the rank of religion on this dear symbol: he is no more than an Egyptian soldier.'[3]

What determines their relative strengths? At this level a whole host of other factors come into play, including the prestige of the army, its ability to overawe or simply to bypass a civilian cabinet, the cohesiveness of its senior officers and, perhaps most important of all, the degree to which the country is perceived to be in pressing military danger. Viewed from these perspectives, the position of an army within a state and the larger society is unlikely ever to be a fixed or a stable one and will, necessarily, change over time.

Chiefs of staff will continually struggle for scarce resources or to be allowed to define their own role in the maintenance of national security. Politicians, whether civilians or retired officers, will seek to keep military activity under some sort of control. Both sides will manipulate public opinion, look for allies, try to win over or divide key opponents. Rules establishing their relationship will be agreed to, challenged and then broken. Temporary balances will be reached, only to come apart. This is the essence of civil–military relations in the Middle East, and I will now go on to say something about it in detail within several different types of institutional and historical context.

The growth of large armies within relatively strong Arab states: the cases of Egypt, Syria and Iraq

The modern Egyptian, Syrian and Iraqi armies were all created, completely anew, by the British and the French colonial powers after the disbandment of previous military formations. They were kept small, unless needed in an external role (for example, in Iraq at the time of the Turkish threat in the mid-1920s); given only simple weapons; and usually required to co-exist with a paramilitary police. Real growth only began soon after independence, and led to a considerable expansion in the number of young officers accepted for training. As in the colonial period, an army's main role was one of maintaining internal security, for which it generally managed to obtain control over all other armed units. As in the colonial period, too, there was a continued emphasis on the necessity for officers to obey their civilian masters and to keep out of politics. But this was now much more difficult to maintain as armies found themselves closely involved in highly politicized activities such as putting down strikes, and as their officers became the target of recruitment by small, radical, nationalist groups which sought to increase their strength with military support.

The first coups, in Iraq in 1936, in Syria in 1949 and in Egypt in 1952, can be explained in terms of a combination of institutional and political factors. In the case of Iraq, the army was large enough and had obtained sufficient prestige from its role in putting down internal rebellion for its commander-in-chief, General Bakr Sidqi, to be quite easily persuaded to throw his weight on the side of certain reform-minded politicians.[4] In Syria, just over a decade later, the main incentive for another commander-in-chief, General Husni Zaim, to take over was to defend the army's honour in the midst of an acrid dispute between the military and civilian politicians over responsibility for its poor showing in the Palestine war. But, in both cases, there was little unity among senior officers about what to do with the power they had seized, leading to serious internal disputes, marked by, among other things, the killing of Generals Bakr and Zaim only a few months after their respective coups, followed by a period of great political instability in which the Iraqi and Syrian armies were able to dominate civilian cabinets without being strong enough to replace them.

Zaim's overthrow by a colonel later in 1949 can be said to mark a new era of military intervention in which coups were led by young officers who had first to get rid of their own generals before going on to establish a new regime. Such men had often become radical nationalists while at the Military Academy. They were also well placed to organize coups as, in most military structures, colonels are the most senior men with direct command over troops in barracks. Colonel Nasser's well-planned takeover of the key installations in Cairo in July 1952 is a perfect example of this new type of intervention. Nevertheless, even with complete control over the army and the civil administration, the establishment of a military regime was severely hampered by disagreements among the Free Officers themselves, while the problem of creating a new balance between the army and the military-dominated cabinet was only solved by giving the commander-in-chief, Field-Marshal Abd al-Hakim Amr, an increasingly free rein to run his domain in any way he chose. Elsewhere, coups by officers below the rank of general re-commenced in Iraq in 1958 and in Syria in the early 1960s. There, too, each new ruler found it extremely difficult to institutionalize his relationship with the army in a satisfactory way, given the fact that the officer corps was so highly politicized. As a result, military commanders were too closely involved in domestic affairs to be able to run their institutions as efficient fighting machines, and this was certainly one of the many reasons for their poor showing in the 1967 war with Israel.

The 1967 defeat, followed so closely by the establishment of new military-led regimes in Iraq in 1968 and Syria in 1970, as well as the succession of President Sadat in Egypt, paved the way for yet another shift in the balance between the army and the state. Three features of the new situation were of particular importance.

First, the three armies were enlarged, re-equipped with more sophisticated Russian weapons, given better educated recruits and, in general, turned into more professional organizations whose main purpose was stated, very clearly, as that of defending the country against its external enemies. The first fruits of this new policy can be seen in the improved performance of all three formations in the next war against Israel, in 1973. Second, various types of other, paramilitary, organization were developed to take over the major responsibility for internal security. In Egypt this was the Central Security Police, in Syria the Defence Companies commanded by the president's brother, Rifat al-Asad. Third, the three regimes were much more successful in establishing their control over the military, sometimes by old and tried methods such as Sadat's repeated changes of minister of defence and chief of staff, sometimes by new ones like the use of the Iraqi Ba'th party organization as a kind of watchdog over the army, using a local version of the political commissars to be found in China or the Soviet Union.[5]

Table 8.1 The armed forces in relation to population and national income in Egypt, Iraq and Syria, 1989

	Armed forces	Population (million)	Defence expenditure ($bn)	GDP ($bn)
Egypt	450,000	54.774	6.81	102.01
Iraq	1,000,000	19.086	12.87 (1988)	46.09 (1988)
Syria	400,000	12.983	2.49	20.26

Source: International Institute for Strategic Studies, *The Military Balance 1990–1991* (London; Brassey's, 1990).

Even if rendered coup-proof, the Syrian, Egyptian and Iraqi armies were too large and too important not to occupy a salient position within state and society (see Table 8.1). There are no accurate figures but it would seem that, by the early to mid-1980s the Syrian armed forces, heavily committed in Lebanon and facing possible war with Israel, had grown to some 400,000 men. This represented some 5 per cent of the total population and over 20 per cent of the country's labour force.[6] At the same time, military expenditures took up at least 30 per cent of the annual budget and were the equivalent of 15 to 16 per cent of the national product. The long war with Iran meant that the Iraqi armed forces had grown even larger, with perhaps one million men in the mid-1980s. In these circumstances, the salience of the army as an institution was bound to have a significant impact on national policies of all kinds. A good example of this is the way in which the Syrian and Iraqi armies were encouraged to use their own resources to develop the factories and the repair shops needed to maintain their huge arsenals of modern weapons and, where possible, to reduce their dependence on imports by making as much of their equipment as they could themselves. This was accompanied by a tendency to move into certain areas of non-military activity, pioneered in Syria by the military-run contracting firm Sharikat al-Iskan al-Askari, which, by the mid-1980s, is said to have become the country's leading business enterprise.[7] A similar role was played by the powerful ministry of military industry in Iraq.[8]

Developments in Egypt followed a somewhat different trajectory. There, President Sadat took advantage of the peace agreement with Israel to make drastic reductions in the size of the army and to redefine its role now that it was no longer expected to have to confront its long-time Israeli enemy. Both initiatives had a deleterious effect on army morale and were blamed, by some, for the fact that the president was finally assassinated by disgruntled soldiers. In contrast, the new president, Husni Mubarak, who was much more of a military man than his predecessor, sought to reverse the process, building up the size of the army again, replacing its aging Russian equipment with new weapons from the United States and providing its officers with numerous extra privileges. In this he was greatly assisted by his minister of defence and general commander of the armed forces, General Abu Ghazzaleh. However, within a few years Abu Ghazzaleh had expanded the role of the military into so many new areas of Egyptian life that obvious tensions developed between him and the president, causing many commentators to compare their uneasy relationship to the one that had developed between President Nasser and Field Marshal Amr in the mid-1960s.[9] Such comparisons tend to blur important distinctions between different historical contexts. But, in this case, it does have the advantage of raising a number of questions about a situation in which an army is able to obtain more or less what it wants in the way of autonomy and access to national resources; but only at the expense of increasing friction with different civilian groups and the risk of a sharp decrease in military cohesion and operational effectiveness. I will now examine the politics of this process in somewhat greater detail.

The expansion of the role of the Egyptian army after 1981 affected three major areas. The first was that of internal security, where it was able to establish its control over the major paramilitary force, the Central Security Police, after troops had had to be used to end several days of rioting involving many of its Cairo units in February 1986. As Field Marshal Abu Ghazzaleh was to define the new relationship later the same year: 'The role of the police and the army are complementary and cannot be separated. To both of them falls a unique task: to guarantee the security of Egypt both internally and externally.'[10] The army's domestic presence was also maintained through the continued use of military courts to try civilians, particularly Islamic fundamentalists, accused of plots against the state. A second area was that of military industry, where the army used its control over the National Organization for Military Production and the Arab Organization for Industry to launch an ambitious programme of manufacturing and re-building equipment, either for its own use or for export. To do this, the army was able to take advantage of the fact that Egypt had the most advanced technological facilities to be found in the Arab world, as well as long experience with the Russian weapons systems used by many of its neighbours. The third, and last, area of expansion was into public works, through the National Service Products Organization founded in 1978, and then into numerous other sectors of the economy, most notably those concerned with land reclamation and food production.

All these activities created new sets of tensions. In the case of security, for example, the expanded role of the army led to a competition between the military, on the one hand, and the police and civilian intelligence agencies, on the other, as to which was best able to apprehend plotters and to keep the peace. Meanwhile, the development of a military industrial complex outside the control of the government's general accounting organization, and run by men powerful enough to negotiate joint ventures with foreign companies and to make their own arrangements for the sale of their products to other Arab regimes, automatically brought the army into competition, and potential conflict, with a wide variety of civilian ministries involved in planning, the economy and foreign relations.

By 1986 the role of the army had grown so large and had begun to affect Egyptian life in so many ways that it could no longer hide itself from public criticism, particularly in the opposition press. It is also possible that President Mubarak was happy to use the greater freedom associated with multi-party activity to allow this to happen as part of a campaign designed to bring the situation back more under his control. The army countered with a public relations campaign in which it presented itself as an efficient, well-managed organization vitally concerned to promote the national welfare. The result was an on-going debate in which, for the first time, it was possible to discuss the proper role of the army within Egyptian society.[11] This had some advantages for Abu Ghazzaleh, allowing him to make a case for enlarging the military budget at a time when the country lacked any powerful enemy. Nevertheless, the debate did bring into the open certain difficult problems that seemed to require solutions. As far as the army itself was concerned, some of the most pressing were the accusations that its emphasis on economic activity had reduced its military efficiency, that its factories were not cost effective and that the close links between officers and civilian businessmen were a breeding ground for corruption.

It has been a central feature of this analysis that the role of the military is a continually shifting one and in constant need of adjudication and re-negotiation. A good example of this took place in Egypt with the dismissal of Abu Ghazzaleh in April 1990 after he had lost American support due to his association with an attempt to smuggle rocket parts to Egypt. The result was that President Mubarak was able to reassert greater control over the military budget and arms purchases from the United States. The move also helped to reduce friction between the army and the police and the civilian intelligence agencies. Meanwhile, it seems likely that it was welcomed by those many officers who felt that Abu Ghazzaleh's expansions of the military's role had taken it too far away from its primary concern with training and national defence.

The situation in Syria and Iraq in the 1980s was made very different by the fact that both were engaged in major military confrontations. This produced a huge increase in the size of the armed forces and in the resources they required to sustain them. It also altered the relationship between the president and his senior officers, particularly in Iraq. On the one hand, he needed efficient military commanders; on the other, he had to ensure that they

206 II: Contemporary politics

continued to obey his orders and were not moved by either great victories or great defeats to seek his replacement. This was made the more difficult by the fact that armies must retain a minimum of cohesion and are much less open to the policies of divide and rule and of personal control perfected elsewhere. President Saddam Hussain seems to have managed this difficult situation by a policy of rotating his generals rapidly from post to post so that none could build up a personal following, while paying close attention to military morale during numerous visits to front line units on the battlefield. Another change enforced by the war was a huge recruitment campaign for service in the Popular Army, some units of which were sent off to fight against the Iranians. This was bound to dilute the Ba'thi character of this paramilitary force. President Asad also had problems with the commanders of some of his own paramilitary forces as they competed with one other to dominate the streets of Damascus during the succession crisis brought on by his serious illness in the summer of 1984. Once he had exiled several of the commanders in question, including his brother Rifat, he then seems to have incorporated some of the defence companies into the regular army.[12] All this makes the situation in Syria and Iraq very much more difficult to analyse, in spite of the fact that it contained many of the ingredients that in Egypt had pushed the army into a position that necessitated huge new demands on national resources and brought it into contact with almost every area of economic and political life.

The role of the military in the smaller Arab states

None of the other Arab states has a military establishment of anything like the same size as Egypt, Syria and Iraq. Looking at the figures in Table 8.1, the only other two armies with over 100,000 men are the Moroccan, swollen since the 1970s by the need to confront the Polisario guerrillas in the Sahara, and the Algerian. Nevertheless, there are a number of countries where even a relatively small military organization has played a vital role in regime survival, for example, in Jordan, Libya and the two Yemens. And even in those cases where armies have been kept deliberately weak so as to minimize the possibility of direct military intervention, it has still remained possible for ambitious officers to make political capital out of control over what still remained

Table 8.2 The growth in Arab military and paramilitary forces, 1966–84

Country	Regular military			Paramilitary		
	1966	1975	1984	1966	1975	1984
Egypt	180,000	298,000	460,000	90,000	100,000	140,000
Iraq	80,000	101,000	640,000	10,000	19,000	650,000
Syria	60,000	137,000	362,000	8,000	9,500	38,500
Algeria	65,000	63,000	130,000	8,000	10,000	25,000
Jordan	35,000	68,000	68,000	8,500	22,000	20,000
Lebanon	10,800	15,200	20,300	2,500	5,000	7,500
Libya	5,000	25,000	73,000	n.a.	23,000	10,000
Morocco	35,000	56,000	144,000	3,000	23,000	30,000
Saudi Arabia	30,000	43,000	51,000	20,000	32,000	45,000
Sudan	12,000	38,600	58,000	3,000	5,000	7,000
N. Yemen	n.a.	20,900	36,500	n.a.	n.a.	25,000
S. Yemen	10,000	9,500	27,000	n.a.	n.a.	45,000
Tunisia	20,000	24,000	35,000	5,000	10,000	8,500

Total armed forces

	1969	1973	1979	1983/4
Bahrain	n.a.	3,000	2,000	2,700
Kuwait	10,000	14,000	10,000	12,400
Qatar	n.a.	3,000	n.a.	6,000
Oman	n.a.	9,600	13,000	19,950
UAE	n.a.	11,150	26,100	46,000

Sources: Elizabeth Picard, 'Arab military in politics: From revolutionary plot to authoritarian state', in Added Dawisha and I. William Zartmant (eds), *Beyond Coercion: The Durability of the Arab State* (London: Croom Helm, 1988), p. 119; International Institute for Strategic Studies, *The Military Balance*, 1969–84.

the most powerful armed force within their society; witness such examples as their forceful role in Sudan from General Abboud's coup of 1958 to that of General Omar Hassan al-Bashir in 1989, or the replacement of Habib Bourguiba as president of Tunisia by General Zain Ben Ali, a former director of military security, in 1987.

To speak very generally, the smaller Arab armies can be divided into a number of types. These include: the modern professional (for example, Algeria, Jordan, Morocco, Sudan, Tunisia and the former North Yemen); the modern professional that co-exists with tribal-based military organizations (Saudi Arabia and Oman); the experiment in a revolutionary people's army (Libya in the early 1980s, and the People's Democratic Republic of Yemen); the confessional (Lebanon); the largely mercenary (the UAE before the Gulf crisis); and the guerrilla (the Palestinian resistance). I now examine the political salience of a few armies from each of these types except the last two.

The two Middle Eastern regimes that rely most heavily on the support of a professional army for survival are the monarchies in Jordan and Morocco. Both have much in common. In each case their army was very largely the creation of the colonial power and continued to be commanded and largely controlled by foreign officers for the first few years after independence. Again, in each case, the process of 'nativizing' an enlarged officer corps proved difficult and led to attempted coups which were only with difficulty put down. Finally, both King Hussein of Jordan and King Hassan of Morocco came up with much the same formula for securing the loyalty of their armed forces: a combination of the monarch's day-to-day attention to the needs of the military in his role as commander-in-chief with the creation of a well-paid, prestigious career for men drawn largely from the more conservative, tribal, areas, with plenty of opportunities for going into business or government service after retirement. Once this was achieved, the monarchs possessed an efficient, reliable fighting force which performed well in battle and could also be used to maintain internal security, helped by the fact that it was allowed a large measure of control over the state's paramilitary forces as well.

As far as Jordan was concerned, the basis of the army was the British-officered Arab Legion drawn mainly from members of the smaller tribes in the south. The Legion was expanded rapidly in the late 1940s and early 1950s and experienced its first major crisis when, under newly appointed Jordanian officers, it became directly involved in the radical Palestinian and Arab nationalist politics in the period just following the combined Anglo-French and Israeli attack on the Suez Canal, when President Nasser's prestige had reached great heights. King Hussein only managed to save himself by rallying officers loyal to himself, pre-empting a possible military coup in April 1957, purging unreliable elements and then reorganizing the army on a safer basis.[13] This included reducing the importance of the better-educated, more politicized Palestinian soldiers by confining them to the technical arms, and then recruiting large numbers of men from the tribes, who were given control over the tank and infantry units that could be expected to do the bulk of any fighting. As a result the bulk of the army remained loyal to the king through all the troubled period running from the defeat by the Israelis on the West Bank during the June war of 1967 to the fierce fighting against the guerrilla forces of the Palestinian resistance in Amman and in the north in 1970/1. However, the cost of maintaining such a force has always been high, requiring large amounts of foreign aid and taking up a considerable proportion of the local budget.

The core of the modern Moroccan army, which officially came into existence in May 1956, was provided by Moroccans, mostly Berbers from the south, who had served with French and Spanish units in the colonial period. Until 1960 it relied heavily on French officers and NCOs for leadership and training. Its first chief of staff was the king's son, Prince Hassan, who devoted great attention to it both before and after he succeeded his father in 1961. This automatically involved the question of control over the army in the fierce struggle with nationalist politicians anxious to reduce the royal prerogatives. By and large the officer corps remained loyal to the king, although there were military-led attempts to assassinate him in 1971 and 1972. Since then a purged and reorganized army has been the major bulwark of the king's power, controlling internal security by providing officers for the various paramilitary police forces and playing an important role in King Hassan's forcible takeover of the Spanish Sahara.

Perhaps the best example of the second type of military organization, the one that combines tribal forces with a small professional army, is Saudi Arabia. In the first decades of the state's existence the ruling family relied exclusively on the tribes for armed men, persuading some to settle permanently in important strategic locations and calling up others whenever the occasion demanded. This proved entirely satisfactory in an era when the presence of the British at so many places round the Arabian peninsula provided the Saudis with a shield against any more modern force that might have tried to overthrow them. There was also little money for military expenses, and a justifiable fear that the existence of a professional officer corps might create a basis for political opposition. Nevertheless, there were pressures for the creation of a more permanent force, particularly after the export of the first oil, which not only provided the cash but also gave the Saudis valuable installations to defend. The result was the recruitment of a small royal guard and then of the nucleus of a professional army trained by the Americans.

A further stimulus to military expansion came in 1962 with the overthrow of Imam Ahmad's regime in North Yemen by a group of Nasserite officers, followed by a civil war in which the Saudi-backed royalists were faced by a republican regime supported by an increasingly large, and hostile, Egyptian expeditionary force which at one time numbered some 70,000 men. Nevertheless, the Saudi royal family proceeded with its usual care, aware of the importance of great caution at a time when the presence of Nasser's army so close to its border had encouraged at least two serious military plots against it. Its formula for control had the following features: the use of royal princes as senior commanders: the allocation of internal security duties to a separate national guard formed largely of loyal tribal elements; and the employment of foreign officers to provide technical advice as well as a further defence against possible coups. In addition, the family was prepared to spend huge sums of money, not just on new weapons but also on barracks, housing and military hospitals. The results seem to have been the creation of a reliable but highly privileged officer class, which, with the exception of pilots in the air force, spends little time on training or manoeuvres and cannot be expected to fight with any great effectiveness in battle. Meanwhile, much the same model was followed by Saudi Arabia's small Gulf neighbours, all of whom built small, expensively equipped, armies, trained by foreign experts and commanded by members of their own ruling families. Their weakness as an effective fighting force was cruelly exposed at the time of the Iraqi invasion of Kuwait in August 1990.

A third model, that of an experimental people's army, was attempted, briefly, in both Libya and the People's Democratic Republic of Yemen (PDRY, South Yemen). In the case of Libya, the overthrow of King Idris in 1969 was the work of a small group of young officers in the small, western-trained, professional army that was all the monarch would allow. The number of soldiers was then greatly expanded and, for over a decade, they were protected from the experiments in people's and revolutionary committees by which Colonel Qadhafi and his colleagues attempted to mobilize popular support. However, by the early 1980s, fearful of the growing dissatisfaction within the officer corps, Qadhafi began to talk about the formal abolition of the regular army and its replacement by a new popular force containing all of its citizens who were now to receive weapons training. Military power should not be left in the hands of professional armies, he said, 'lest they use it to dominate the people'.[14] However, although such training programmes were then organized for students and various groups of workers, like those in the oil sector, no attempt was made to re-organize the army itself, other than to reduce the privileges of the officers and to send members of the revolutionary guards and popular committees into the barracks to harangue them and their soldiers. This had an immediate effect on military morale and may have been one of the reasons for the various attempts on Qadhafi's life in 1984 and 1985.[15] Qadhafi's response was another series of speeches about the need to replace the regular army with 'an army of people'.[16] But, so far, nothing has been done to implement this project, no doubt because the regular army, with its huge arsenal of sophisticated Russian weapons, is an indispensible tool of regime policy both inside Libya and across the southern border in Chad.

The attempt to create a new type of revolutionary military organization was only a little more successful in the PDRY. There, soon after the retreat of the British in 1968, the National Liberation Front government instituted a series of measures designed to re-organize the army that it had inherited from the colonial period and to subject it to reliable civilian control. Political secretaries were introduced at every level of the armed forces, while conscription and promotion were managed in such a way as to reduce tribal divisions among the troops.[17] However, this was not enough to stop the army becoming involved in the internal power struggles between leaders of the Yemen Socialist Party, as was demonstrated in most spectacular fashion in bitter fighting between the military supporters of President Ali Nasser Muhammad and those of his rivals in January 1986.

The last type of Arab army, the confessional, is peculiar to Lebanon. It owed its special form of organization and its role within the political system to two main factors. One was the way in which the sectarian balance was reflected not only in the attempt to recruit roughly equal numbers of Christians and Muslims but also in the division of the army into units composed largely of one sect or another. The second was the consensus among most of the leading politicians that the army should be kept small. This was supposed to prevent the army from becoming involved in domestic politics, as well as to inhibit the country from being drawn into military conflicts with its neighbours, especially Israel. The result was that in the first years after independence in 1943 the army remained little more than a gendarmerie with limited powers to keep the peace and to ensure the proper conduct of elections. Nevertheless, just because it could act as a neutral force as long as it remained united, the army under its first commander-in-chief began to play an increasingly important role. This happened first in 1952 when Chehab refused to intervene to put down the protests against President Beshara al-Khouri's attempt to change the constitution and then acted for a few days as caretaker president himself to ease the transition to the next president, Camille Chamoun. It happened again in 1958 when Chehab again kept his troops out of the fighting between pro- and anti-Chamoun elements and was finally elected president himself.

Given the fact that Chehab, once in power, deliberately began to use the army in support of his efforts at political and administrative reform, the stage could have been set for the establishment of yet another Arab military government. This was certainly what many officers and some civilian politicians believed. However, Chehab himself then stepped back from this particular course, threatened to resign as a way of getting his way with his military supporters and then attempted to create a new relationship between the army and the state in which the former would back his efforts strongly but behind the scenes. The result was not stability, however, but a situation in which an increasing number of politicians came to fear and to resent military interference, particularly that of the army's intelligence organization, the Deuxième Bureau. This process reached its culmination in the presidential elections of 1970 when an anti-Chehabist majority elected Sulieman Franjieh with a clear mandate to reduce the ability of the army to interfere in the political process. In these circumstances the army was unable to play a positive role in the growing crisis that led up to the outbreak of the civil war in 1975, and it was left to other forces, notably the Christian and leftist militias, aided by the Palestinian guerrillas, to fight it out between themselves. General Aziz al-Ahdab's attempt at a military coup in February 1976 was the last effort by an officer to use the army as a neutral force. But the army was, by now, far too weak and divided to play such a role and, only a few days later, the mutiny by a young Muslim officer began a process of disintegration that led Christian and Muslim soldiers either to desert or to regroup in sectarian units loosely attached to the major militias.

The military and politics in Turkey, Iran and Israel

Analysis of the role of the military in Turkey, Iran and Israel presents a number of special problems. Whereas in Turkey the army has occupied a very public position in the political system, with major interventions in 1960, 1971 and 1980, in Israel its considerable influence has always been exercised behind a cover of civilian rule. As for Iran, the major problem is to define the very different position of the army under the Shah and then under the Islamic revolutionary regime after 1979.

While observers are united in acknowledging that the military has an unusually salient role in Turkey, there is no general agreement as to how this is to be explained. One factor that is often mentioned is the long continuity in the importance attached to the army, from Ottoman times and then through the creation of the republic in 1923. But just as significant would seem to be the ability of the military to control its own processes of recruitment, training and promotion, which have given it a particular ability to mould its officer cadets and to create a specific military culture representing the army's own view of its role within Turkish society. This is well illustrated in Mehmet Ali Birand's account of the way in which the army recruits young men from all over Anatolia at the age of 12 and subjects them to a long process of discipline and training clearly designed to distance them from all their civilian loyalties and attachments.[18] The result is an organization which is difficult to manipulate for political purposes from outside and which has shown a remarkable ability to maintain its cohesion and organizational integrity at times when Turkish society itself was fragmented into competing classes, ethnic and religious groups, and factions.

The first major challenge to redefine the place of the army within the state in the modern period came in 1950 with the replacement of the RPP in government by the Democratic Party led by Adnan Menderes. This at once deprived the military of its long-time political partner, as well as encouraging Menderes to try to ensure its uncertain loyalty by interfering in senior promotions. Another change came when Turkey joined NATO in 1952, an event which, although welcome to the bulk of the officer corps, forced many of them to realize just how ill trained and ill equipped they were in terms of the major European states. The resulting dissatisfactions came to a head in 1960 when the increasingly dictatorial behaviour of the Democrats sparked off a military revolt by a group of younger officers that was only just brought under control by some of the generals, who were able to direct the coup through the creation of a National Unity Committee (NUC). There was just enough unity to obtain agreement that the army should hand back power after the promulgation of a new constitution and the holding of new elections. But it took much longer to work out the terms on which the military would co-operate with civilian governments in future. This was only resolved by the creation of a new permanent body, the National Security Council, with a constitutional role that allowed it to make 'recommendations' about military matters to the cabinet, and by the tacit alliance that developed between the senior officers and Suleyman Demirel, the leader of the Justice Party, which had emerged as the electorally successful successor to the banned Democrats.[19]

The next major intervention had many of the same characteristics as the first. Once again it came at a time of growing economic difficulty, highlighted on this occasion by considerable political violence, mainly from the left. It also had all the hallmarks of having been forced on the generals by fear of yet another junior officers' coup. But on this occasion the generals were even more divided than the last and could agree on little more than the installation of a new civilian government with a mandate to introduce a few constitutional amendments restricting political freedom in a number of areas. Military division was also used by the politicians to prevent the election of the generals' own candidate as president, the former chief of staff, General Sunay. The result was to open the way for a clear return to civilian rule after the general election held in October 1973.

There is good reason to suppose that the army drew a number of lessons from the 1971–3 intervention which ensured that its next intervention, in 1980, was of quite a different character.[20] On this occasion there was clearly a great deal of prior planning mixed with a general determination to keep the army as united as possible while a new constitution and a new political structure, purged of the old politicians, was introduced.[21] But we must always be careful of accepting a military's explanation of its own motives at face value, particularly when they are accompanied by a concerted public relations campaign to present the army as a neutral arbiter and servant of the Turkish national interest, forced, unwillingly, to intervene in a situation of social chaos and total administrative breakdown.[22] While it is certainly true that the political and sectarian violence had begun to degenerate into civil war, there were also pressing military reasons for intervention as well, notably fears that the conflict would spill over into the barracks, and a concern that the economic and social environment was harmful to the military's interest in terms of recruitment, arms production and the activities of the huge Armed Forces Assistance Fund (OYAK) set up to manage military pensions in 1961.[23] There was a similar specifically military interest in getting out of the political scene as quickly as possible, as witnessed by a speech made by General Evren to some cadets at the War Academy just 12 days after the September 1980 coup:

> Whenever the army entered into politics it began to lose its discipline and, gradually, it was led into corruption. . . . Therefore I demand you once again not to take our present operation as an example to yourselves and never to get involved in politics. We had to implement this operation within a chain of command and orders to save the army from politics and to cleanse it from political dirt.[24]

The military's efforts to restructure Turkey's political system and to sanitize it from what it regarded as harmful political influences have already been discussed elsewhere (see Chapter 5). But at a more general level they raise important questions about the officers' analysis of what had gone wrong in Turkey and how it ought best to be put right. Seen from their perspective, the explanation does not begin with an examination of the problems caused by several decades of rapid economic and social change but from a sense that whatever difficulties there may have been were either not tackled properly by power-hungry and narrow-minded politicians or were deliberately exacerbated by misguided Turks under the influence of dangerous foreign ideologies. From this it followed that the way ahead was to create a structure in which new national parties led by public-spirited persons could develop constructive policies in isolation from the harmful influences of class or interest groups located in the wider society. No doubt officers in many other armies would agree. But the problem was that the political life of an industrialized, highly urbanized society cannot easily be constrained in this way and that, among many other things, the new parties were forced to link up with existing interests or face electoral extinction.

After the elections that brought Turgat Ozal's Motherland Party to power in 1983, Turkish political life began slowly to move towards a new balance between the military and the civilian. On the one hand, neither the military president, General Evren, nor the members of the National Security Council, for all their great powers, were able to find a mechanism for influencing the civilian government on a day-to-day basis once they had abandoned recourse to regular diktats. On the other, even under the new constitution, the elected prime minister had sufficient authority to begin to make his own policies and then, when confident enough, even to challenge the military on part of its own ground, for example, by seeking to influence senior promotions. Other factors strengthening the position of the civilians against the military were the stability provided by the Motherland Party government for most of the 1980s and the decision to apply for membership of the European Community in April 1987. The result was something of an implicit division of political labour, with the military nearly doubling its share of the national budget between 1980 and 1985 and playing a major role in internal security but leaving most other areas of policymaking to the civilian government.[25] This was continued after Ozal's election as Turkey's first non-military president in 1989 through his extensive use of the National Security Council (consisting of four senior ministers and the chiefs of the four main military arms – army, navy, air force and gendarmerie) as a more important advisory and policymaking body than his own cabinet. Some idea of the president's management of the council was provided by the resignation of the army commander, General Torumtay, in December 1990. General Torumtay had been Ozal's own choice when appointed in September 1987. But this was not enough to prevent what was obviously a major disagreement about the way in which decisions regarding military matters were now being made, particularly in the highly charged atmosphere following the Iraqi invasion of Kuwait.

In spite of the many similarities between Ataturk's policies in Turkey and those of Reza Shah in Iran, the role of the military developed in quite different directions in the two countries. Perhaps the most important reason for this is that, in Iran, the army always remained firmly under the control of the monarch and was never allowed to develop its own institutional identity or its own view of its place within the nation. Both shahs were obsessed with the loyalty of the officer corps, and went to great lengths to demonstrate their personal authority by preventing their generals from exercising any freedom of action and by presiding over a system of licensed corruption in which individual officers were able to make large sums of money but only at the risk of being tried and punished if the ruler should turn against them. In these circumstances, for all the size of the army and the large share of the budget devoted to it, particularly in the 1970s, it played little role in policymaking and was the simple recipient of the huge quantities of advanced American weapons it received without having any say about how they were to be used or against what potential enemy. The great advantage to the shah of this system was shown during the popular demonstrations that marked the final stages of the revolution in 1978, when there were no mutinies and the army remained entirely loyal until after he had actually left the country. But, against this, the huge power of the military could never be consistently deployed against the opposition as it relied entirely on its vacillating, moody, royal commander-in-chief for its orders.[26] As the shah's power began to crumble, the question of the future control of the military began to assume great importance, particularly for the Ayatullah Khomeini and his advisers in Paris and the American policymakers in Washington. For the Americans, fear that the army might either collapse or go over to the revolutionaries encouraged the drive to create a provisional government to replace the shah as quickly as possible. As for Khomeini, he too wanted to obtain political control of the army, although, in the end, it probably suited him just as well that it fell to pieces soon after his return to Teheran, providing a vacuum which he was quick to fill with the creation of the paramilitary revolutionary guards. This also allowed time for a thorough purge of the shah's senior officers and their replacement by men with better revolutionary credentials.[27]

It was soon after this that the Iraqis, over estimating the demoralization of the old army, chose to invade south-western Iran, forcing the new Islamic republic to rebuild its military forces in order to meet the threat. Its answer was to combine the use of regular units with revolutionary guards, lest the still distrusted army be tempted to take advantage of any victory it gained on its own to effect a counter-revolution. Both forces worked together sufficiently well to drive the invaders back across the border and then to capture significant amounts of territory in southern Iraq itself. But its longer-term military effectiveness remains a matter for conjecture. For many commentators it was the guards, with their great enthusiasm and their willingness to sacrifice themselves in huge numbers, that were the key to the Iranians' early success. But it is clear that the regular army also had an important role to play and that, within limits, it too benefited from the need to develop new and more unconventional tactics once it was no longer possible to use some of the more sophisticated weapons in the shah's huge arsenal, due to the American embargo on technical assistance and spare parts.[28] However, the sudden collapse of Iranian morale in the spring of 1988 was certainly due in large measure to the loss of large numbers of officers and NCOs in earlier attacks and the great difficulty in obtaining the new recruits needed to keep the revolutionary guards at anything like full strength.

Analysis of the role of the Israeli military in state and society presents other kinds of problems. To begin with, it is a very unusual form of organization, established in 1949 on the assumption that, as the country did not possess the resources to maintain a large standing army, what was required was 'a militia of civilians trained and equipped for combat, capable of being mobilized at short notice'.[29] The result was the creation of something that many observers have chosen to call a 'citizens' army' with its strength based largely on reserve formations. This has significance as far as civil/military relations are concerned, producing what Horowitz has characterized as a 'civilianized military in a partially militarized society'.[30] But it tends to obscure the equally important facts that, in order to have such an army, it is also necessary to have a core of long-service professionals to maintain its capability between campaigns, and that it is they who are in a position to play a major role in influencing such highly important matters as the size of the military budget and even, on occasions, the resort to war itself.[31]

Just how the military establishment exerts this influence is a complex question but there is no doubt that the key actors are the prime minister, the minister of defence and the chief of staff. For the period 1948–52, and again from 1955 and 1967, two prime ministers, David Ben-Gurion and then Levi Eshkol, served as their own ministers of defence, an arrangement that could, in principle, have given the cabinet considerable control over the military. But this was not usually the case. Ben-Gurion's strongly held belief in the overriding importance of national security led him to hide many matters from his civilian colleagues. After his retirement in 1961, his successor lacked the authority to prevent a strong chief of staff from going his own way. Hence in the crisis leading up to the June war of 1967 it was the military, not the prime minister, that began to make the important decisions, particularly after it had pressured Eshkol into surrendering the defence portfolio to General Moshe Dayan. General Dayan stayed on as minister until 1974 and was then succeeded, first by Shimon Peres and then, after 1977, by another strong general, Ezer Weizman. But certainly the minister with the greatest ability to dominate a cabinet was General Ariel Sharon, 1980–3, who used the post to become what Horowitz has called a 'super commander-in-chief'; that is, someone who was strong enough to use his control over the whole defence establishment to force major decisions involving peace and war, most notably his use of the 1982 invasion of Lebanon to try to alter the whole balance of political power between Israel and its Arab neighbours.[32]

Peri's attempt to define four different types of relationship between the prime minister, the minister of defence and the chief of staff is too rigid, and does not take account of the great importance of personality.[33] More to the point is his argument that, in many important areas of national life, the boundaries between the military and the civil have expanded to the military's advantage. This he explains in terms of a number of factors, including: the highly political role of the military as rulers of the West Bank and Gaza after its occupation in 1967; the increasing entry of senior reserve officers like Generals Rabin, Eytan and Sharon into politics; and, perhaps most important of all, the fact that relations between the civil and the military have developed more as a partnership than as a system by which the former can maintain regular control over the latter.[34] He also points to the fact that the two attempts made in 1968 and 1975 to define their respective responsibilities in terms of the constitution did not prove satisfactory.[35] And the same was also true of the third effort in this direction, the Kahan Commission of 1983, which, although effecting the removal of General Sharon for misleading the cabinet, did not introduce any new machinery for preventing similar situations in the future. Since then, the army's political role has increased once again due to its role in putting down the Palestinian uprising or Intifada that broke out in December 1987.

Nevertheless, for all the military's disquiet at having to devote so much of its energy and resources to internal security – to the possible detriment of its preparedness for a major war – most Israeli commentators, including Peri, believe that there are limits to the political involvement of the army which are unlikely to be exceeded. These are explained not so much in terms of formal structures but of shared values concerning the importance of maintaining civilian paramountcy and also of the role played by the generals-turned-politicians in keeping their former colleagues under control.[36]

Notes

1 Maurice Janowitz, *The Military in the Political Development of New Nations* (Chicago: Chicago University Press, 1964); Robin Luckham, *The Nigerian Military: A Sociological Analysis of Authority and Revolt 1960–67* (Cambridge: Cambridge University Press, 1971), Introduction.

2 For example, Mehmet Ali Birand, *Emret Kapitan*, translated as *Shirts of Steel: An Anatomy of the Turkish Army* (London: I. B. Tauris, 1991); Yoram Peri, *Between Battles and Ballots: Israeli Military in Politics* (Cambridge: Cambridge University Press, 1983).

3 William Suliman Kilada, 'Christian-Muslim relations in Egypt', in Kail C. Ellis (ed.), *The Vatican, Islam and the Middle East*, Syracuse, NY: Syracuse University Press, 1987, pp. 258–9.

4 Mohammed A. Tarbush, *The Role of the Military in Politics: A Case Study of Iraq to 1941* (London and New York: Kegan Paul International, 1985), pp. 123–33.

5 For example, Robert Springborg, *Mubarak's Egypt: Fragmentation of the Political Order* (Boulder, Colorado: Westview Press, 1989), pp. 96–7; Peter Sluglett and Marion Farouk-Sluglett, *Iraq Since 1958: From Revolution to Dictatorship* (London and New York: Kegan Paul International, 1987), p. 120.

6 Brig.-Gen. (Res.) Aharon Levran, 'Syria's military strength and capability', *Middle East Review*, XIX (Spring, 1987), p. 8.

7 Elizabeth Picard, 'Arab military in politics: From the revolutionary plot to the authoritarian state', in Adeed Dawisha and I. William Zartman (eds), *Beyond Coercion: The Durability of the Arab State* (London: Croom Helm, 1988), p. 139.

8 Peter Sluglett and Farouk-Sluglett, 'Iraq since 1986: The strengthening of Saddam', *Middle East Report*, 167 (Nov./Dec., 1990), p. 21.

9 For example, Springborg, *Mubarak's Egypt*, p. 98.

10 Quoted in *Al Yassar Al Arabi/L'Egypte Gauche* (Paris), 79 (Dec., 1986), p. 13.
11 Springborg, *Mubarak's Egypt*, pp. 118–23.
12 Alastair Drysdale, 'The succession question in Syria', *Middle East Journal*, 39/2 (Spring, 1985), p. 252.
13 P.J. Vatikiotis, *Politics and the Military in Jordan: A Study of the Arab Legion 1921–1957* (London: Cass, 1967), pp. 127–34; Uriel Dann, *King Hussein and the Challenge of Arab radicalism: Jordan 1955–1967* (Oxford: Oxford University Press, 1989), pp. 55–67.
14 Quoted from *Jamahariya Review* in 'Libya', Colin Legum, Haim Shaked and Daniel Dishon (eds), *Middle East Contemporary Survey*, VI, 1981–2 (New York and London: Holmes & Meier, 1984), p. 736.
15 Yehudit Ronen, 'Libya', in Itimar Rabinovitch and Haim Shaked (eds), *Middle East Contemporary Survey*, IX, 1984–85 (Tel Aviv: The Moshe Dayan Center for Middle Eastern and African Studies, The Shiloah Institute, Tel Aviv University, 1987), pp. 561–2.
16 Idem.
17 Helen Lackner, *P. D. R. Yemen: An Outpost of Socialism Development in Arabia* (London: Ithaca Press, 1985), p. 102.
18 Birand, *Shirts of Steel*, Ch. 1.
19 Feroz Ahmad, *The Making of Modern Turkey* (London: Harper Collins, 1991, forthcoming).
20 Mehmet Ali Birand, *The Generals' Coup in Turkey: An Inside Story of 12 September 1980* (London: Brassey's, 1987), pp. 137–8, 198–208; William Hale, 'Transition to civilian governments in Turkey: The military perspective', in Metin Heper and Ahmet Evin (eds), *State, Democracy and the Military: Turkey in the 1980s* (Berlin and New York: Walter de Gruyter, 1988), pp. 163–6.
21 For example, Feroz Ahmad, 'Military intervention and the crisis in Turkey', *MERIP*, 93 (Jan., 1981), pp. 5–6.
22 Ibid., pp. 6–7.
23 Alan Richards and John Waterbury, *A Political Economy of the Middle East: State, Class and Economic Development* (Boulder, Colorado: Westview, 1990), pp. 365–6.
24 Hale, 'Transition to civilian governments', p. 163.
25 Metin Heper, 'The state, the military, and democracy in Turkey', *Jerusalem Journal of International Relations*, 9/3 (1987), pp. 61–3; and William Hale, 'Generals and politicians in Turkey 1983–1990: The process of disengagement', mimeo (of paper prepared for Colloquium, 'Turquie 1980–1990', Institut d'Études Turques, Université des Sciences Humaines de Strasbourg, Nov., 1990). Figures from Office of the Joint Chiefs of Staff, *Milliyet* (2 May 1986).
26 Shaul Bakhash, *Reign of the Ayatollahs* (London: I. B. Tauris, 1985), pp. 16–18.
27 Sepehr Zabih, *The Iranian Military in Revolution and War* (London and New York: Routledge, 1988), Ch. 5.
28 Ibid., Ch. 9.
29 Edward Luttwak and Dan Horowitz, *The Israeli Army* (London: Allen Lane, 1975), p. 76.

30 Dan Horowitz, 'The Israeli Defence Forces: A civilianized military in a partially militarized society', in R. Kolkowicz and A. Korbanski (eds), *Soldiers, Peasants and Bureaucrats* (London: Allen & Unwin, 1982).

31 Peri, *Between Battles and Ballots*, pp. 130–1.

32 Dan Horowitz, 'Changing patterns of civil/military relations in Israel' (Lecture), Oxford, 26 Oct. 1982.

33 Peri, *Between Battles and Ballots*, Ch. 7.

34 Ibid., pp. 172–4.

35 Ibid., pp. 131–43.

36 Ibid., Ch. 5.

9 Parties and elections

Introduction

During the early part of the 20th century a variety of political organizations were created in the Middle East with the title of party, while others called themselves unions, fronts, associations or, in the case of the largest and most successful of them, a delegation (the Egyptian Wafd). They had their origins in the beginnings of the creation of a modern political field inside the Ottoman Empire and its successor states, with its associated sets of vocabularies, ideas and political practices based on notions of constitutionalism and parliamentary representation as well as on nationalism and, in some cases, revolution.[1] Such organizations took many forms and had many different types of relations with the wider society. In this chapter I will concentrate only on those parties that were structured to allow them to participate in a system of competitive elections in which the winner might, on occasions, be allowed to form a government.[2] I will also concentrate mainly on questions of organization, as these generally tend to get ignored as a result of paying an exaggerated attention to party programmes and ideology.

In the next chapter (Chapter 10) I will go on to consider the nature of those parties that were the creators, or the creation, of single-party regimes in which competition was banished as they themselves monopolized legitimate political activity. In all this I will regretfully have to exclude discussion of the Arab Communist parties, which were rarely allowed an open, legal existence and which were unable to ensure the election of any of their members to an Arab parliament before Khaled Baqdash's success in the Syrian election of 1954.

Parties and elections in the Arab states in the colonial period and after

All the Arab successor states of the Ottoman Empire, with the exception of Palestine, came to possess constitutions that specified the holding of regular elections. Not surprisingly, however, there were a variety of different interpretations as to how these elections should be carried out, as well as a process of constant change in the rules under which they were conducted, usually in the interests of bringing them more under government control. This latter process was taken furthest in Egypt, where the intense competition for political advantage between the British, the palace and the parties was enough to ensure that almost every election was fought under a different set of regulations.

In Syria and Iraq the colonial powers preferred to continue the Ottoman practice of two-tier contests in which a relatively large electorate selected a smaller number of electors who then elected the members of a parliament or national assembly. This allowed the government the possibility of considerable interference in the choices made at the second stage, and was only abolished in the new political atmosphere after the Second World War, in Syria in time for the 1947 general election and Iraq in 1952. In Lebanon and Jordan, on the other hand, the single-stage system was in use throughout the colonial period, while in Egypt there was a tendency to move backwards and forwards between the two until the late 1930s.

A second, and highly crucial, set of differences related to the question of who should be allowed to vote or to stand as a candidate for election. Given the climate of opinion after the First World War, it was difficult not to base the franchise on some notion of adult male suffrage, although efforts were often made to limit this by insisting that the voter should possess a certain amount of property as well. In Syria in the early 1920s, for example, the franchise was confined to propertied males of 25 and over, while in Iraq at the same period it was given to all male taxpayers over 21 for the first stage and 25 for the second. However, by and large, such notions proved more difficult to sustain in the post-Second World War period, particularly when there was pressure from radical parties like the Ba'th, which realized that it could only make electoral headway in areas dominated by the large landowners and their allies if as large a category of adults as possible was allowed to participate in the vote.[3]

As for Egypt, the original system of universal male suffrage at 21 was subject to radical change under Ismail Sidqi's new consti-tution and electoral law of 1930, when such stringent educational and property qualifications were introduced that, according to Vatikiotis, some 80 per cent of the population was effectively dis-enfranchised.[4] At the same time, another new regulation allowed *umdahs* (village headmen) – who were appointed by the govern-ment – to stand as candidates for parliament but not members of the liberal professions living outside Cairo – a category of persons much less subject to central control. Egypt then reverted back to its previous system with the restoration of its 1923 constitution in 1935. Not surprisingly, women were rigorously excluded from the vote in all Arab Middle Eastern states until Syria became the first country to enfranchise them in 1947, followed by Lebanon in 1952 and Iraq in 1953.

Nevertheless, even when restrictions were imposed on the franchise, the size of the electorate, and the fact that it was bound to contain a large proportion of rural and illiterate voters, created both problems and possibilities for the governments and politicians concerned. To make the obvious point first, the bulk of the electorate was inevitably to be found living outside the major cities, in conditions that made it highly subject to large landowner influence. It followed that colonial governments often devised systems that over-represented the rural vote while the new parties either co-opted as many landowners as they could or simply left them to stand as independent candidates in the elections in the hope that they could become subject to their influence once they took their seats in parliament. Other methods used to manage the rural vote involved the intervention of those government officials working out in the villages who had direct control over almost every aspect of peasant well-being. In Egypt a key figure was the *umdah* and it was a usual practice for one party to appoint its own supporters to the post when in government and to dismiss as many of its opponents' men as it could.[5]

As for the question of illiteracy, this probably made little difference to the actual conduct of polling in the days before the introduction of the secret ballot, something that did not take place in Lebanon until 1952 and Syria until 1954. But, after that, a government had either to work out a system that allowed balloting in sealed envelopes (Syria 1954) or by tokens indicating the candidates or parties (Sudan 1958), or simply to accept a situation in which an elector who was required to speak out his choice to the officials at the polling station could easily be subject to bribery or coercion by those listening close by.[6]

A final significant difference concerning the conduct of elections relates to the way in which each system sought to accommodate the presence of minorities. The importance of rules to protect such minorities was mentioned in each of the League of Nations mandates given to the British and the French and served, in some cases at least, to underpin a more general policy of divide and rule. This was particularly the case in the Lebanon, where the whole system was based on the principle of confessional representation. But it also found an important place in Jordan and Iraq, where special seats were set aside for members of officially classified minorities like Christians, Jews and, in Jordan, members of the Circassian communities. Other countries, like Syria, made special provision for the representation of tribal interests. The one country where this was not the case was Egypt, which, having gained its independence after a national rebellion, obtained a constitution that, deliberately, made no distinction between any of its citizens.

However, as we know, constitutions are not necessarily a good guide to actual political practice and, in each case, the conduct of elections was constrained not only by legislation concerning, for example, the right to form parties or the existence of official censorship but also by a whole host of manoeuvres and interventions that meant that very few of the ballots held in the Arab countries in the colonial and early post-independence period can be considered as even remotely free. Such a title can probably only be awarded to a handful of elections like the Syrian ones of 1943, 1947 and 1954, the Lebanese one of 1943, the Jordanian one of 1956, the first Iraqi one of 1954 and the few in Egypt where the Wafd's widespread popular support was allowed to be reflected in a large parliamentary majority (notably 1924, 1929, 1936 and 1950). For the rest, a list of the different types of interference and malpractice would be a long one, beginning with the use of martial law or some other type of emergency legislation to control political activity and ending with bribery, intimidation and the direct stuffing of ballot boxes.[7]

This then was the context in which would-be politicians were forced to operate. Many stood for elections as independents. Others offered their services to one or other of the parliamentary blocs formed by leading men to promote their own particular interests. Only in Egypt and Syria (and for a short period in Morocco and Sudan) did the majority of candidates at elections stand as members of a group that possessed sufficient organization and cohesion to be called a party. And, even then, only a small handful of these groups possessed a regular, dues paying, membership or branches outside the major cities.

The most important political organizations in Egypt and Syria were the two national rallies, the Wafd and the National Bloc. The former had much in common with the Indian National Congress, in that it had started as a mass anti-colonial movement with claims to be the sole representative of the national interest, before having to adapt itself in order to participate in the first contested elections beginning in 1923/4. The result was a pattern of organization in which the party was effectively controlled by its leader and his close associates in the senate and the parliament, backed up by a series of committees at the level of the provinces and the governorates which helped to co-ordinate the frequent electoral campaigns as well as to mobilize grass-roots support whenever this might be required. There was, however, no formal membership, no subscriptions and only one annual congress – held in 1935.[8] In addition, the party sometimes made serious efforts to organize particular sections of the population, notably the youth, the women and the workers. Hence there were youth sections in the local committees in the 1920s, while in 1931 a central Association of Young Wafdists was created to counter the growing influence of some of the new extra-parliamentary groups that were then being formed, notably Young Egypt (Misr al-Fatat) and the Muslim Brothers.[9]

As is the case with many similar nationalist movements, the Wafd's leadership showed an early tendency to split over matters of personality and policies, with disaffected members hiving off to form competing political organizations. This process began in 1922 with the formation of the Liberal Constitutionalist Party by a number of former Wafdists who believed in a more gradualist approach to the struggle for independence. Subsequent divisions resulted in the formation of the Saadist Party in 1938 and Makram Obeid's Independent Wafdist Bloc in 1942. Of these splinter groups, only the Saadists attempted to create an organization along similar lines to the one they had just left, with its network of local constituency committees. However, they, like the Liberal Constitutionalists before them, seem to have found it easier to gain access to rural voters, as well as to obtain much needed campaign funds, simply by giving their endorsement to the candidatures of members of large landowning families in exchange for a financial contribution.[10] When in government, such parties also had the extra option of changing the rules governing elections, or appointing new *umdahs*, in order to improve their electoral prospects.

The major Syrian nationalist organization was the National Bloc which had led the struggle for independence from the French in the 1930s. Like the Wafd, the Bloc had also taken part in the electoral politics of the period but with a somewhat weaker administrative structure consisting of an office run by a permanent secretary in Damascus supported by its two newspapers. Its main strength lay in the fact that its leaders formed a small élite, with networks of clients who were able both to raise funds and to get out the vote in the urban areas.[11] Little attempt was made to obtain support in the countryside, which continued to return landowners and tribal chiefs standing as independents. After independence the Bloc renamed itself the National Party in time for the 1947 elections. But by this time, according to Seale, it had 'lost all its cohesion' and in 1948 it suffered a major split, with disaffected members from Aleppo and the north forming the rival People's Party.[12] This too was largely a coalition of notables, and consisted of little more than its candidates for election running in terms of their own reputation and social standing.[13] In the 1954 election the People's Party obtained 30 of the 142 seats, as opposed to the National Party's 19 and the 64 gained by men running as independents.

A second feature of Syrian and Egyptian politics in the colonial and immediate post-independence periods was the appearance of new, more ideologically motivated, better organized, political structures which usually began as extra-parliamentary pressure groups before deciding to participate in the electoral system when this might advance their own interests. Organizations of this type tended to remain small. According to Jankowski, Young Egypt, which turned itself into an official party in 1936, never achieved an active membership of more than 1,000.[14] Nevertheless, it put up a number of candidates for parliament, on the grounds that election campaigns provided a good platform for disseminating its policies and drawing in new recruits. And when one of its members,

Ibrahim Shukri, was finally elected in 1950, he was able to make a considerable impact by means of his speeches and his proposals for new legislation, the more so as most of the MPs belonging to the larger groups rarely opened their mouths inside the chamber.[15]

In Syria a number of parties followed a similar course. They included: the Syrian Socialist Nationalist Party (SSNP), originally founded as a secret society in Lebanon in 1932; the Arab Socialist Party, which split off from it in 1945; and the Ba'th Party, founded in 1943. The last two joined forces in 1952 to form the Ba'th Arab Socialist Party and were sufficiently well organized to win 22 seats in the relatively open 1954 election, as opposed to the SSNP's 2.[16] Nevertheless, given the control over voting in the rural areas by the large landowners, it was inconceivable that a party of this type could come to power through the ballot box, and this became an important factor in encouraging their leaders to ally themselves with army officers in order to bring in the weight of the military on their side.

There were no large nationalist parties in Iraq, Jordan and Lebanon, and what little cohesion there was in political life was provided by the voting blocs established in the parliaments by already well-established politicians. Not surprisingly, such blocs had little life of their own; their leaders had their own independent political base, while their associates often tended to shift their allegiance from one to another in search of temporary advantage.[17] Better organized parties of a more ideological type began to appear in the 1940s and 1950s, and then only when they had made the transition from an illegal to a legally recognized organization and were ready to put up candidates for parliament. The Lebanese Kataib (Phalanges Libanaises) is one such example.[18] Founded as an extra-parliamentary paramilitary movement in the late 1930s, it was not officially registered as a political party until 1952, by which time it may have had as many as 40,000 members, with a central administration and offices throughout the country. This was followed by the establishment of Kamal Jumblatt's Popular Socialist Party, which is said to have had a membership of 18,000 in 1953.[19] Nevertheless, the role of these new organizations remained small, and in 1951 only 10 of the 77 deputies elected to the Lebanese parliament belonged to one or other of them.[20] In Iraq the largest legal party, the National Democratic Party, possessed just under 7,000 members and won only 5 seats in the 1947 election, while in Jordan the most important of the political parties that were allowed to exist between 1951 and 1957 were all branches of organizations first established elsewhere in the Arab world.[21]

Given the general conduct of political life and the inability of the major parties to deal with the pressing economic and social problems of the period, the practice of multi-party democracy had many critics and few vocal defenders in the Arab countries in the 1940s and 1950s.[22] This is one of the reasons why it was so easily swept away by the military regimes in Egypt and elsewhere and then subjected to such a sustained critique, in which it was identified as a western initiative for promoting political and social division at a time when the new states needed to concentrate all their forces on major problems like national independence, economic development, the establishment of social justice and the defence of Palestinian rights.[23] As one of the leaders of this movement, President Nasser's own personal view on this matter is of the greatest significance. As he is quoted as saying in an interview with an Indian newspaper editor in March 1957:

> Can I ask you a question: what is democracy? We were supposed to have a democratic system during the period 1923 to 1953. But what good was this democracy to our people? I will tell you. Landowners and Pashas ruled our people. They used this kind of democracy as an easy tool for the benefits of the feudal system. You have seen the feudalists gathering the peasants together and driving them to the polling booths. There the peasants would cast their votes according to the instructions of their masters. . . . I want to liberate the peasants and the workers, both socially and economically, so that they can say 'yes'. I want the peasants and the workers to be able to say 'yes' and 'no' without this in any way affecting their livelihood and their daily bread. This in my view is the basis of freedom and democracy.[24]

Party competition in the post-independence period: Morocco and Lebanon

There were only two Arab countries where the practice of multi-party competition persisted well into the post-independence period: Morocco and Lebanon. It is interesting and instructive to examine why this happened and under what conditions.

In Morocco there was a moment in the late 1950s when it looked as though the main nationalist party, the Istiqlal, would reach a position from which it could dominate the country's political life – but this was not to be. The Istiqlal had led the struggle for independence from the French and, in spite of being forced to operate underground for most of the period, it was still able to transform itself into a mass organization in the late 1940s, with strong popular support in the towns and the co-operation of the sultan, Mohamed V. The approach of independence in 1955 provided a further stimulus to expansion as a way of consolidating its position as the major national political force and of countering the recruiting drives of its rivals.[25] Such was its success that, by 1956, it may well have had some two million supporters out of a total population of ten million.[26] This provided it with the platform it needed to assert its right to a monopoly of power in what it hoped was to be a one-party state.

That the Istiqlal failed to achieve its aim can be put down to a combination of royal opposition (Mohamed V took the title of king in 1955) and its own lack of internal cohesion. As far as the king was concerned, he used his own independent power base to prevent the party from attaining a position strong enough to challenge his own authority. Only ten Istiqlalis were appointed to the first council of government of independent Morocco, and although this number was increased in some of the later cabinets – notably in 1958 – the party never achieved the monopoly in government that it demanded.[27] Meanwhile, the king took steps to ensure his own control over the army, the military and the bureaucracy, as well as over the principal sources of political patronage. He also encouraged the organization of rival organizations like the MP (Mouvement Populaire), with strong support from landowners and notables in those areas of the country like the Berber Mountains or the countryside that the Istiqlal had found difficult to penetrate. A final weapon was the king's ability to establish the rules of the political game by means of such measures as the 1958 Charter of Public Liberties, which defined the type of party that was to be allowed, and the 1962 constitution, which included a specific clause prohibiting the establishment of a single-party regime.[28]

The king's drive to protect his own position was greatly assisted by the divisions within the Istiqlal's leadership that came to a head in 1959. The reasons for this have been subject to many differing interpretations.[29] Some writers point to the importance of clashes of personality, others to the fact that the party was never more than a coalition of different interests, with an uneasy relationship with the other major components of the national movement, the trade union (the UMT), the liberation army and the palace itself. There is more agreement that the immediate cause of the split was a dispute over how the party should organize itself in preparation for the local elections that finally took place in 1960. The result was the hiving off of a dissident group under Mehdi Ben Barka and the formation of a rival organization, the UNFP (Union Nationale des Forces Populaires).

Morocco's first general election did not take place until 1963, a few years into the reign of the new king, Hassan II. This gave the king's supporters plenty of time to create a new organization, the FDIC (Front pour le Défense des Institutions Constitutionelles) consisting of many former members of the PM, which received enough assistance from the police and the central administration to win 69 seats in parliament, as opposed to the Istiqlal's 41 and the UNFP's 28. That the Istiqlal did as well as it did must be ascribed to the prestige it had gained during the national struggle as well as the fact that it was well organized in the major cities, with a dues-paying membership and a system of inspectors who maintained regular contact between party headquarters and its local branches.[30] Perhaps because of their ability to prevent the FIDC from securing an outright majority, both parties were then subject to a campaign of official harassment culminating in the arrest of most of the UNFP's leadership later the same year after the discovery of an alleged plot against the king. This was followed by a period of severe economic crisis, leading to rioting and discontent, the proclamation of a state of emergency in 1965 and abrogation of parliamentary life for five years.

King Hassan made two attempts to recreate a system of controlled multi-party activity, in 1969/70 and then again in 1977. On the first occasion, an experiment with a new parliament, elected by a combination of direct and indirect methods, came to an abrupt end as a result of the attempted military coups of 1971 and 1972. Morocco's third general election was held in 1977; 176 seats were competed for directly and another 88 chosen by electoral college. Taking the two methods together, 141 seats were obtained by candidates standing as independents, 49 by the Istiqlal, 44 by the Mouvement Populaire and 16 by a new party, the USFP (Union Socialiste des Forces Populaires), formed by members of the moderate wing of the UNFP.

A further constitutional amendment was used to prolong the life of parliament for six years until 1983. Morocco's fourth general election followed in 1984, once again under new rules. On this occasion, 204 seats were subject to direct election and another 102 to indirect. There was also a considerable amount of gerrymandering of boundaries to ensure that many mainly urban constituencies contained a large rural vote.[31] According to Sehimi, there was very little popular interest in the election and a low turn-out by Moroccan standards. He ascribes this to the fact that there was little to choose between the programmes offered by the eight parties, all of which were forced to demonstrate their allegiance to the king and his major policies if they were to be allowed to compete.[32] The largest number of seats, 83, was obtained by yet another party of palace supporters, the UC (Union Constitutionel) formed in 1983, while 47 went to the MP, 43 to the Istiqlal and 39 to the USFP. Nevertheless, the new cabinet formed in 1985 contained only members of the centre parties and no one from either of these last two groups.

The course of Moroccan politics during the 1970s and 1980s provides much further evidence in support of Waterbury's and Zartman's view that the king's aim was to create a system of organized pluralism in which he himself played the central role as arbiter between competing groups – a strategy that Waterbury characterized as 'divide and survive'.[33] But in spite of what they have written about the powers of the palace and the fragmentation of Moroccan society, the king found this no easy task. Such a system is inherently unstable and requires constant royal intervention to keep all parties in play in a situation where few will be allowed the fruits of office and the rest remain confined to more or less permanent parliamentary opposition. There was also the problem of encouraging the older parties to take part in elections against palace-backed groups which they knew in advance would receive every kind of advantage from a partisan administration. And all this in a country where there was an almost continuous expression of widespread economic and social discontent.

If it was to work at all, such a system required the existing parties to be transformed into something akin to pressure groups representing particular interests, whose cohesion derived more from their ability to obtain resources for their clients than from the maintenance of an elaborate organization which was only really needed to run candidates during Morocco's rare general elections. For the rest, the party leaders knew that they would only be allowed to exercise even these limited functions if they paid lip service to the central tenets of royal policy, like the annexation of the Spanish Sahara, while remembering to practise the type of criticism that, according to Mohamed V's 1957 guidelines, should always remain 'sincere and constructive'.[34] By agreeing to these terms such men were in a position to derive some small advantage from Morocco's periodic crises when the king needed them to deliver their well-defined constituencies in support of one or other of his programmes of economic reform.

The reasons for the comparative longevity of the Lebanese system of parliament and parties were different again. Here the parliament had an important role at the centre of the process of confessional representation and inter-confessional bargaining while, in a larger sense, some form of democracy was an essential mechanism for integrating the leaders of the major sects into the Lebanese political field and then regulating the often precarious relations between them. Party activity was only one small, but increasingly unruly, component of the whole situation. And yet, paradoxically, once it could no longer be contained within the existing set of not very well-established rules and compromises it played a significant role in the final breakdown of both government and state after 1975.

Many writers on Lebanon note the central role of parliament in the constitutions of 1926 and 1943 but then go on to explain this as the result of a deliberate attempt of men like the banker and political thinker, Michel Chiha, to provide a mechanism for confessional reconciliation.[35] In fact, it seems as if Chiha had little to do with the 1926 constitution and that much of what he wrote was a sophisticated *ex post facto* justification for mechanisms that were already in place.[36] What is more to the point is the close fit between the system of parliamentary representation devised by the French, a weak central administration and the type of economic and social structures that already existed in the area in late Ottoman times. Given France's insistence that seats in the new parliament should be allocated to members of the most numerous sects in rough proportion to their numbers within the population at large, it was inevitable that most of those elected would come from the country's leading families, whose power was based on their control over important economic and social resources. Their presence in parliament, and hence their availability for cabinet office, then offered the possibility for a further increase in power, while the fact that this possibility was open to Muslim notables as well as Christians provided an enormous encouragement to them to forget their opposition to the division of Lebanon from Syria and to participate in the new system. A final part of the argument concerns the efforts to ensure that the central administration remained weak. This had something to do with the fact that the Lebanese economy was dominated by merchant and banking interests. But it was also the result of a situation in which the ability of the notables to satisfy their political clienteles depended on their capacity to provide them, personally, with resources and services which, in a better developed administration, would have been catered for by the bureaucracy itself.

There was little scope in such a system for the organized political party. On the one hand, most economic and social interests could be represented at government level, either directly by the notable politicians or indirectly by one of the many sect-based organizations like the Maronite Church or the Maqasid Society, the leading Islamic charity. On the other, an economy based largely on agriculture and services did little to encourage the unionism or any of the other urban solidarities that might have provided scope for class-based parties. In these circumstances, the majority of the deputies elected to parliament (two-thirds in 1964) ran either as individuals or on some notable's electoral list, while the primary form of political association remained the parliamentary bloc with little or no popular appeal beyond the personal charisma of its leader.[37]

Political organizations only started to register themselves as parties for the purpose of contesting elections in the decade after independence. One of the first was the Kateab, which did so, according to Stoakes, with 'some reluctance', in 1952.[38] By this he means that it did not feel able to abandon its own military arm, which it was later to use so effectively in the limited civil war of 1958 that it was catapulted into national prominence with 9 of the 99 seats in parliament at the next elections and a regular place in the cabinet. Control over the party was exercised by its leader, Pierre Gemayal, working through a political bureau supported by a handful of specialized functionaries with a tiny permanent staff. Meanwhile, great attention was paid to the recruitment of a disciplined membership (85 per cent Christian) which reached a total of some 60,000 during the 1960s.[39] Other parties that had sufficient organization to obtain a few seats in parliament were the Progressive Socialist Party (PSP), the SSNP and the Armenian Tashnaq Party.

In Lebanon, as elsewhere, organizations calling themselves parties existed for many purposes other than electoral competition. Some represented the interests of local confessional communities, others had close links with other Arab parties or, in some cases, prominent Arab regimes like that of President Nasser. As violence became a more prominent feature of Lebanese political life after 1967, many began to organize their own militias and to develop a powerful critique of the Lebanese parliament and the Lebanese system. A good example of such a group is Ibrahim Qulailat's Independent Nasserite Movement, al-Murabitun, which combined the function of social club in some of the poorer quarters of Beirut with a growing emphasis on military recruitment.[40] In 1972 many of the more radical parties associated with Kamal Jumblatt's PSP and the Palestine Liberation Organization in Lebanon came together to form what later became known as the National Movement, with the aim of pushing for major changes in the political system. This was strongly challenged by the leaders of the Kataeb, who came to see themselves more and more as major defenders of the existing status quo. A good example of their thinking is provided by the open letter that they sent to the Lebanese president in 1973 to warn against what they saw as the danger of a Marxist attempt to impose their system on the whole country. Stoakes translates this as follows:

> We thank God that the state has decided to take firm action to meet this challenge, and we support you and we support your stand. But should the state fail in its duty or weaken or hesitate, then, Mr President, we shall meet demonstrations with bigger demonstrations, strikes with more extensive strikes, toughness, with toughness, and force with force.[41]

When the fighting began in 1975 it was the party militias that were the main protagonists, until the split in the army in early 1976 followed by the growing intervention of the various Palestinian groups and then the Syrians.

Managing elections without parties: Jordan and Kuwait

Organizations calling themselves parties have been suspect to many Arab regimes, particularly those in the Gulf and Saudi Arabia, where they have always been banned, and in Jordan, where their legal existence has been brief. As a rule they are regarded as socially divisive and as actual or potential exponents of harmful ideologies and a bridgehead for foreign political penetration. Feelings of the same kind have probably prevented rulers from forming royalist parties in their own support. Hence, in the few places where competitive elections have been permitted from time to time, candidates have been forced to stand as independents with only passing reference to the trends or groups that they might claim to represent.

Groups were first allowed to apply for licences as parties in Jordan under the Political Parties Law of 1955. Some took part in the October 1956 general election, after which the National Socialists, with 12 out of the 40 seats, were able to form a short-lived cabinet. But parties were then banned again during the political crisis of April 1957 and have remained so ever since. Candidates stood as independents in the few general elections up to 1967, after which the king thought it wiser to suspend parliamentary life almost entirely due to the problems posed by Israeli control over the Palestinian citizens of Jordan living on the occupied West Bank. Hence the Lower House did not meet at all between 1974 and 1984, on the grounds that this would contravene the resolution of the Rabat Arab summit that the PLO should be the sole representative of the Palestinian people.

Parliament was finally recalled in January 1984 to prepare for new elections on the East Bank. The introduction of a revised electoral law then took another two years and the election itself was not held until November 1989. By this time the domestic situation had been almost totally transformed, first by the outbreak of the Palestinian Intifada, then by the riots and demonstrations of April 1989 in protest against the price increases, cuts in government spending and other measures taken to deal with a severe economic crisis. A temporary government was appointed to deal with the situation and promised free elections without official interference. The following November voting took place, with 1,400 candidates contesting the 80 East Bank seats, 17 of which were reserved for Christians and 3 for members of the Circassian and Chechen communities. Women voted for the first time in a general election and there were 12 women candidates. The turn-out was about 40 per cent.[42]

Although political parties were banned from standing in the 1989 election, the authorities allowed considerable latitude to candidates who chose to advertise their connection with particular movements and trends. As a result many of them were in a position to benefit from whatever their parent group could provide in the way of funds and organization. Some candidates hired trucks to take them round their constituencies. Others had sufficient supporters at the polling station to take advantage of the fact that electors who opted to vote what was called 'illiterate' were able to shout the name of their choice loudly enough to be heard – and then later rewarded – by those listening outside. It is generally supposed that members of Jordan's well-organized Muslim Brotherhood won some 20 of the seats, with another 10 to 15 going to men associated with various leftist, reformist and liberal groups, including the co-founder of the Jordanian Communist Party and a member of the newly formed Jordanian Democratic Party, the Jordanian arm of the Democratic Front for the Liberation of Palestine.[43]

The election increased the pressure on King Hussein to define the conditions under which he would permit the proper legal existence of political parties and their right to put up candidates for parliament. His answer to this was the establishment of a 60-man royal commission in April 1990 to draw up a national charter to provide the necessary guidelines. As far as he himself was concerned, he seemed to want to ensure that such parties agreed in advance to support both the constitution and the monarchy and that there were rules to prevent them from being manipulated from outside. Members of the commission were chosen from all the existing political organizations after consultations, during which they must certainly have agreed to abide by the king's guidelines.[44] The charter itself was to be presented to a national congress in June 1991.

The idea of a national charter in which representatives of a great variety of political groups come together to establish the ground rules for a country's future political life was also put forward in Tunisia and a number of other Arab countries at about the same period. As such it has an obvious appeal to authoritarian regimes worried about the dangers of opening up their systems to multi-party competition. A modified version of the same notion was being aired in Kuwait just before its invasion by Iraq in the summer of 1990.

Kuwait's experiment in democracy had proceeded in fits and starts. Independence in 1961 was followed by the creation of a consultative assembly which, in turn, drew up the 1962 constitution with provision for an elected national assembly. The elections themselves were held in 1963, with 205 persons standing as independents and competing for 50 seats. Successful candidates included members of the ruling, al-Sabah family as well as merchants, intellectuals, Shi'is and Beduin.[45] The electorate was kept deliberately small and consisted of only 17,000 male citizens – defined as members of families that had lived in Kuwait continuously since 1920. This meant tiny constituencies in which, characteristically, a candidate would be known personally to almost all the voters and could, on occasions, invite a very high proportion of them to a large meal held in the street near his house. Further elections were held in 1967 and 1975, before the amir suddenly dissolved the national assembly in 1976 for fear that it might encourage tensions between rival Arab communities at the beginning of the Lebanese civil war. Problems had already arisen from efforts by a small opposition bloc of ten or so deputies to curb some of the powers of the al-Sabah, and there were also allegations that the family had interfered in the elections to prevent the election of some of its main critics.[46]

The amir agreed to allow new elections in 1981. Once again, government interference and the creation of yet smaller constituencies made it difficult for members of the unofficial opposition but new groups managed to obtain representation in the assembly, notably men who stressed their religious credentials as either Sunnis or Shi'is. Another election was held in 1985 and produced an assembly which contained what Peterson calls four 'unofficial groupings' of two or three deputies backed by 'readily identifiable organizations' with 'established platforms'.[47] These included Ahmad al-Khatib's Democratic Bloc, the Social Reform Society, the Social Cultural Society and the Heritage Revival Society. There were also two Arab nationalists who stressed the importance of Kuwait's role in the Arab world. This assembly, Kuwait's sixth, lasted only a year and was dissolved in 1986.

Pressures for a return to democratic life built up slowly, but by early 1990 these were strong enough to force the government to propose the establishment of a national council whose main purpose would be to discuss means of controlling parliament in such a way that the confrontations of the past between the al-Sabah ministers and the deputies could be avoided. Voting for the two-thirds of 75 seats put up for direct election was held in June. Turn-out was low compared with 1985, partly as a result of a boycott by a substantial number of former members of parliament.[48] Discussions that might have led either to further constitutional amendments or to a Kuwaiti national charter were interrupted, almost immediately, by the Iraqi invasion.

Iran before and after the Islamic revolution: one party or many?

Since 1945 Iran has gone through three cycles during which an embryonic multi-party system has given way to an abortive effort to create a one-party state. The first of these was during the period from 1941 to 1953, when the enforced abdication of Reza Shah provided an opening for a somewhat freer political life. This, in turn, encouraged the creation of many new types of association, most of which took one of two forms. The first was the coming together of groups of Majles members in so-called 'fractions' as a way of increasing their voting strength and political influence. The other consisted of groups that, in Elwell-Sutton's phrase, were 'formed from above' by some prominent personality, often with money from a wealthy capitalist.[49] The only party with a nationwide organization was the Tudeh (The Party of the Iranian Masses) which, although formed by a collection of Marxists in 1941, went to great lengths to attract a wide spectrum of popular support, including members of the clergy.[50] It benefited greatly from its association with the budding workers' movement in the towns, and was strong enough to get 8 of its 23 sponsored candidates elected in the 1943 general election. Later, however, it came under a series of such sustained attacks by successive governments in 1946, and then again in 1949 and 1953, that it was almost negated as an active political force.

The temporary success of the Tudeh encouraged other groups to try to establish national organizations of the same type. Of these, the most important was the Iran Democrat Party formed by the prime minister, Ahmad Qavam, in 1946. The new party was greatly assisted by a brief alliance with the Tudeh during its first few months, before turning against it while, at the same time, continuing to ape its characteristic structures. It too established a countrywide set of branches, together with a host of supporting organizations for women, students and workers. This gave it sufficient strength to obtain some 80 seats in the elections held in the winter of 1946/7, before it was crippled by defections and finally collapsed entirely after Qavam resigned from the government in the summer of 1947.

A final attempt to create a national political organization was made by the widely respected senior politician, Muhammad Mossadeq, based on the National Front he helped to found in 1949. This was essentially a loose association of interest groups united by their opposition both to British influence and the shah's ambitions to become more than a mere constitutional monarch. Mossadeq himself was adamant that only organizations, not individuals, be allowed to join. In his view, Iran had not reached the stage where it was ready for western-style parties but only a countrywide coalition that would allow its leaders to speak in the name of the nation.[51] Even though the Front was only able to get eight of its supporters elected in the 1950 general election, it went on to play a major role in government during the oil nationalization crisis of the early 1950s, before losing support from the clergy and other important groups and then being pushed out of office by the shah's American-aided coup of 1953.

The second cycle began with the shah's limited experiment with two-party government which began after the lifting of martial law in 1957. Members of the Majles who had been elected in conditions of tight government supervision the previous year were then invited to join one of two new groupings known as the National and the People's Party. It should be noted, however, that neither of these two groups had any organizational life of its own; they had no need for regular members, no interests to represent and little control over the electoral process, in which candidates were more likely to be selected by the shah and his secret service than by them. Furthermore, it was the shah who chose the prime minister and who also dismissed him if he proved unsatisfactory or too much his own man. Cabinets alternated between the parties until 1963, when they remained under the control of members of the National Party until 1975, at which point the shah suddenly decided to create a single national political organization known as the Rastakhiz, or Resurgence. Branches were rapidly set up throughout the country, and government officials and influential persons of all kinds were forced to join *en masse*, including almost all the members of the Majles.

The exact reasons for the shah's decision are not known. Halliday suggests that it had something to do with his desire for greater social discipline and control at a time of rapid economic dislocation at the end of the first oil boom. Evidence is provided by a somewhat chilling passage from one of the shah's speeches, in March 1975: 'We must straighten out Iran's ranks. To do so we divide them into categories: those who believe in the monarchy, the constitution, the sixth Bahman revolution, and those who don't. Those who don't are traitors and belong in prison.'[52] But it can also be seen as a deliberate piece of political and social engineering launched to counter the dangerous effects of over-centralized decision making and to bridge the huge gap that had been opened up between the shah and society. A key influence in its planning came from American-educated Iranian technocrats who followed the social mobilization approach of leading US political scientists, and were known locally as the *Massachutis* as a result of their study at the Massachusetts Institute of Technology. The role that the creation of the Rastakhiz played in both undermining the regime and paving the way for the revolution that overthrew the shah has already been underlined in Chapter 5.

The third and final cycle began in 1979. Once again a brief moment of political freedom encouraged the formation of numerous groups, parties and factions. Of these the most important was the Islamic Republic Party (IRP) founded by the Ayatullah Beheshti, an influential member of Khomeini's revolutionary council, as an instrument for clerical domination. Support came from a section of the more politicized clergy and ideological justification not only from Khomeini's own notion of the rule of the *Faqih* (see Chapter 7) but also from Beheshti's insistence that morality and good reputation were better criteria for government service than experience and expertise.[53] However, the IRP took some time to obtain the full backing of Khomeini himself, who was still looking to non-clerical technocrats like the first president, Abul Hassan Bani-Sadr, to run the administration. And it was only after the party had used its nationwide organization to win 80 or so seats (out of 270) in the 1980 elections for the Majles, and then launched into a sustained attack on Bani-Sadr himself, that the ayatullah was forced to change his mind and support a president and cabinet dominated by IRP members. Beheshti and his colleagues then used this bridgehead to establish a near monopoly of power for themselves, underpinned by a network of clerical support that extended from Teheran down to the smallest district in what was now virtually a theocracy.

But no sooner had the IRP gained its monopoly of power than it began to split and to lose cohesion. One way of looking at this would be to say that it no longer had any *raison d'être* once its goal of clerical domination had been achieved. Just as important, responsibility for government and for day-to-day decision making meant that its members inevitably found themselves on opposite sides of the new political divisions that so quickly appeared. As early as 1984 it was unable to put together an agreed list of candidates for the general election, while a number of its supporters were defeated even in cities dominated by the clergy, like Qum. The party stumbled on as an organization until 1987, when it was finally wound up by Khomeini on the advice, it would seem, of President Khamanei and the speaker of the Majles, Ali Akbar Rafsanjani, who believed that they would do better in their drive for power without it.[54]

Multi-party politics in Israel and Turkey

All writers on Israeli politics are agreed on the central role played by the major parties in the country's political life, one going so far as to say that they exercise an influence 'more pervasive than in any other state with the sole exception of the one-party state'.[55] There is also general agreement on the main reasons for this phenomenon. The first is their role in pre-state Israel, when they were major instruments in the whole process of colonization and the drive towards the establishment of a national home. In the absence of a Jewish government, leading parties like Mapai and Mapam were heavily involved in the absorption of new immigrants, as well as in providing them with education, health and welfare services and military protection through their militias. They were also the main sources for the distribution of Zionist funds from abroad, which were allocated to them according to a mechanism known as the 'key' by which they received money in proportion to the votes they obtained in the Jewish community's elections.[56] Mapai, created in 1930, became the dominant party in the pre-state period by virtue of its control over the Histadrut and of its continual electoral success.

The parties' central position was further strengthened after 1948, when the creation of a government and then their role in the absorption of the surge of new Jewish migrants gave them many new opportunities to expand their activities. Now there were not only bigger funds from abroad to allocate but also control over new institutions and the award of posts in the new Israeli administration. Once again it was Mapai, the party with the largest electoral following, that took the lead in organizing a series of coalitions which allocated governmental resources to all the major Jewish parties with the exception of Menachim Begin's Herut. The result was the creation of a system by which most of the public's demands, as well as the distribution of administrative services, were mediated by the parties.[57] Another consequence was the high degree of formal participation in party activity, with perhaps a quarter to a third of the Israeli electorate enrolled as party members.[58]

Another important influence on the development of the Israeli party system was the mechanism for conducting elections. This, in essence, was a continuation of the pre-state method, which combined proportional representation with a single Jewish national constituency to which each party presented its electoral list. The same method was used, *faute de mieux*, for the July 1948 elections to the constituent assembly, held at a time when fighting was still in progress and it was still unclear what Israel's final boundaries might be.[59] After that, in spite of the fact that Ben-Gurion and many of his colleagues were anxious to move to a multi-constituency system, such a change was always blocked by the smaller parties, which felt threatened by it. The consequences have been somewhat contradictory. On the one hand, the system has strengthened the power of the party leaders who, until the late 1970s, had total control over who should be allowed to stand as their candidates on the single national list. On the other, the fact that, under Israel's method of proportional representation, any party or list can win a Knesset seat by obtaining only 20,000 of the vote has encouraged the proliferation of splinter groups and tiny factions which has ensured that all governments have had to be coalitions.

It is conventional to divide the major parties into three groups – the left, the right and the religious – bearing in mind that left and right are only being used in terms of positions relating to defence and foreign policy. The most important parties in the first category have been Mapai and its two splinters, Achdut Ha'avoda and Rafi, which came together again in 1968 to form Labour; and Mapam, which joined Labour in the election of 1969 to form the coalition list known as Ma'arach (the Alignment). Meanwhile, the principal ones on the right have been Herut; the Liberals (a combination of the General Zionists and the Progressive), who joined Herut to form Gahal in 1965; and a number of smaller groups which also joined Gahal in 1977 to constitute the electoral bloc known as Likud. Finally, the main religious parties have been the National Religious Party, Agudat Israel and Poalei Israel, as well as some newer ones formed in the 1980s like Shas.

Parties from these three groups have dominated Israeli politics over the years, obtaining, for example, 80 per cent of the vote in 1973 and winning 100 of the 120 Knesset seats.[60] Other political organizations of importance have been the Communist Party, which split in two between 1965 and 1973 and then consolidated itself as the New Communist List (Rakah); and the Democratic Movement for Change, which gained 15 seats in the 1977 election, only to disintegrate in the early 1980s. For the rest, a whole host of groups and lists and one-man organizations have gained one or two seats in various elections but none of them has had the regular membership, the access to funds or the central administration to be called parties in the accepted sense of the term.

It has already been described (in Chapter 5) how Mapai, and then the Labour Party, came to dominate Israel's political system from 1949 to 1977. After that, with the appearance of both Likud and the Ma'arach Labour Alignment, Israeli politics were transformed into what is best described as a two-coalition system in which the bulk of the seats (99 in 1981, 85 in 1984 and 79 in 1988) were divided between them. Likud obtained a large enough majority over the Alliance in 1977 and 1981 to be able to form a government. But in 1984, at a time of great national crisis, neither was able to find enough smaller Knesset groups which would agree to serve with it and the result was the creation of a cabinet of national unity which contained ministers from both coalitions. This experiment was repeated in 1988 but came to an end in the spring of 1990 with the withdrawal of Labour and the creation of a Likud-dominated government in May.

In the Israeli context, coalitions of smaller parties that still maintain their own separate existences have several distinctive organizational features. While the parties themselves can still make an openly ideological appeal to their own members, such appeals have to be muted in terms of the coalition itself in the general interests of unity. There is also a particularly complex process required to draw up the joint electoral list in which it is necessary to ensure, first, that the leaders of the constituent parties, then their most important followers, occupy the top positions.[61] All this became even more complex in the late 1970s when both coalitions moved over to a system by which delegates to a selection conference were also allowed to play an active role in the process.

A final component of the Israeli system is the competition for the Arab vote which, although no more than 8 per cent of the total in the early 1950s, constituted the largest bloc of unattached voters. Given the power it exercised over a variety of government agencies, as well as the Israeli army during the period of military administration of the Arab areas from 1948 to 1965, Mapai (and then Labour) managed to obtain over half this vote in every election up to 1977.[62] To do this it would put up a separate list of Arab notables for its clients to support. Only in 1976, when it felt its hold over the Arabs to be slipping, did it allow Arabs to become full members. Israeli political leaders also tried to increase their domination by forbidding the formation of any purely Arab party. In these circumstances, most of the rest of the Arab population tended to vote for the communist list on the grounds that this consisted of people who were critical of the Zionist project and the only ones who would allow a joint Arab leadership to play an important role. A purely Arab organization, the Democratic Arab Party, was finally established in 1988 in time to win one seat in the 1989 election. This was the creation of an Arab member of the Knesset, Abdul Wahab Darawshe, who had resigned from the Labour Party in protest against its policy towards the Intifada. It is significant that he was only able to succeed in his project by taking advantage of the precedent that many Jewish members of the Knesset had been allowed to form their own parties before him. His move was opposed by the other parties and it was necessary for him to threaten to take them to court in order to obtain the necessary backing from the government's legal advisers.

Turkey's first contested election took place in 1950. The main contenders were the previous ruling party, the RPP (Republican People's Party), and the DP (Democrat Party) founded in 1945

by leading RPP supporters. Both presented almost identical programmes to the electorate.[63] And yet the DP was able to take
advantage of widespread hostility to the RPP, particularly in the
rural areas, to secure an overwhelming victory, with 53.35 per
cent of the vote as against 38.38 per cent for its main rival. Due
to the fact that the electoral system then in use exaggerated the
majority of the winner when it came to the award of seats, this
victory translated into 408 seats in the 450-seat grand national
assembly, as opposed to the RPP's 39.[64] The RPP was able to
regain some strength during subsequent elections but it was so
poorly supported in the countryside that it could never again
obtain more than just over a third of the total vote, and only
remained in contention as a major political force due to the military
intervention of 1960 and the fact that most of the army's leaders
wanted to see it back in power. This handicap was again in evidence
through the 1960s, when the JP (Justice Party), the successor to the
banned DP, won a popular majority at every election between 1961
and the next military intervention in 1971.

The somewhat lop-sided two-party system that emerged in the
1950s and 1960s had several key features. Both parties were
organized in a way that reflected the country's administrative
– and electoral – system, with a national leadership supported
by offices at the provincial and district level. Steps were taken
to ensure some measure of intra-party democracy – for example, the RPP instituted regular four-yearly elections for chairman in the 1940s – but the system still left the men at the
top with great powers that were rarely challenged from below.[65]
One reason for this was the way in which the parties developed,
not as the vehicles for various economic and social interests
but as clientalist networks through which government resources
could be channelled to their supporters. In these circumstances,
local organizations were generally dominated by a small group
of activists whose power came from the fact that they could
control access to the leadership higher up. Organization tended
to be loose, membership records were not well kept and the
branches only really sprang to life during national or municipal
elections.[66]

Like its predecessor, the new Turkish electoral system, based
on a complex form of proportional representation introduced in
1961, tended to discriminate against small parties.[67] The military,
as self-appointed guardians of the Ataturk tradition, also interfered

to close down any party which it believed to be either too religiously oriented or too radical. Nevertheless, two new organizations were formed in the late 1960s which made considerable inroads into the JP's support among disaffected groups on the right of the Turkish political spectrum and so gained the strength to play a significant role in the multi-party politics of the 1970s. One of these was created when Necmettin Erbakan split from the JP in 1968 to form the Islamist National Order Party and then, when this was banned, the NSP (National Salvation Party), which obtained 11.8 per cent of the vote in the 1973 general election. The other, the NAP (National Action Party), was the result of the takeover of the small Republican Peasants' Nation Party by Colonel Alparslan Turkes in the mid-1960s.

The new parties were organized on somewhat the same lines as the old. They too created strongly centralized organizations supported by branches throughout Turkey.[68] They were also just as dependent on access to government patronage, and benefited greatly from the fact that they were both required as coalition partners in the minority governments established by the RPP in 1973/4 and the JP in 1975–7. However, they had some unusual features as well. Both formed a network of alliances with associated youth groups and trade unions which shared their general ideology. Both also established branches among the Turkish workers living in West Germany and relied on them heavily for financial and other support. There was also one major difference: the NAP in particular regarded electoral politics as only one aspect of its drive for power, and paid just as much attention to the development of a military arm which it used to try to dominate the streets and to kill or drive off members of groups that it regarded as traitors to its intensely nationalistic vision of a new Turkey.

The appearance of the new parties was a symptom of an important transformation in the Turkish system as a whole. They introduced a particularly sharp ideological dimension that not only encouraged the RPP and the JP to move further to the left and right but also intensified the politicization of many Turkish institutions, including the bureaucracy, the universities and schools, the media and the police. The bureaucracy, in particular, was not well placed to withstand being staffed by partisans of the NAP and NSP.[69] All this had a powerful influence on the army commanders, who tended to see the party leaders themselves as directly responsible for much of the violence and confusion of the late 1970s. The result, as already noted in Chapters 5 and 8, was a strenuous attempt during the military intervention between 1980 and 1983 to sanitize the political system by dissolving the old parties and then encouraging the development of new ones with no connections with economic and social interest groups which would play what was thought of as a constructive rather than a divisive role in national life.[70]

The framework of the new system was supposed to be the constitution of 1982 and the electoral law and the parties law of 1983. These were clearly designed to encourage the emergence of just a few new national parties which institutionally, and in terms of leadership, would have nothing to do with the pre-1980 organizations. However, this was not to be. Although the 1983 general election was contested by three such parties, Turgut Ozal's ANAP (Motherland Party) and the Nationalist Democracy and Populist Parties, the last two were soon replaced by groups that represented an almost direct continuation with the parties of the past. These included: SODEP, the successor of the RPP (which joined with members of the Populist Party to form the SHP – Social Democratic Populist Party – in 1985); the True Path, which was the successor of the JP; and the National Endeavour and Welfare, which were the successors of the NAP and NSP respectively. The reasons for this development are various but include the fact that the old parties had developed organizational structures and links with precise constituencies strong enough to survive repeated military interventions, and that the democratically elected politicians rapidly attained a greater legitimacy than the military president who was trying to control them.[71]

The party system that had solidified by the end of the 1980s had a number of important features. At the centre stood the Motherland Party which, thanks to electoral success and the shrewd leadership of the prime minister, and then after 1989 the president, Turgat Ozal, dominated the cabinet, the government and all the major institutions of state except the army. Being a new organization this was essentially an alliance of second rank politicians who had joined it from other parties in 1983. It too had created a national organization for itself, very much in the old style, with a leadership that dominated the organization just as had happened prior to 1980. It is said, for instance, that Ozal appointed his ministers in 1983 without any reference to his party.[72] All this was in spite of the military's efforts to introduce greater intra-party democracy and participation by insisting on party primaries and regular elections for party chairman. The other parties derived benefit from their old organizational networks but suffered from the fact that they no longer had access to government patronage, as well as, in some cases, from having to share the blame, in popular eyes, for the chaos of the late 1970s. This could be seen clearly in the results of the 1987 general election, in which the Motherland Party obtained 36.29 per cent of the vote (and 292 out of the 450 seats), the SHP 24.81 per cent and the True Path 19.81 per cent. Neither the Welfare nor the National Endeavour secured the 10 per cent of the national vote required under the constitution to obtain any seats at all.

Notes

1 Sami Zubaida, *Islam, The People and the State* (London and New York: Routledge, 1989), p. 122.
2 The notion of competitive elections is central to Karl Popper's definition of democracy quoted in Chalmers Johnson, 'South Korean democratization: The role of economic development', *The Pacific Review*, 2/1 (1989), pp. 3–4.
3 Patrick Seale, *The Struggle for Syria: A Study of Post-War Arab Politics 1945–1958* (Oxford: Oxford University Press, 1965), p. 173.
4 P. J. Vatikiotis, *The Modern History of Egypt* (London: Weidenfeld & Nicolson, 1969), p. 283. For Sidqi's own account see his *Mudhakkirati* (Cairo: Dar al-Hilal Press, 1950), pp. 119–38.
5 Gabriel Baer, 'The village shaykh', in Baer, *Studies in the Social History of Modern Egypt* (Chicago and London: University of Chicago Press, 1969), p. 33.
6 Seale, *Struggle for Syria*, p. 173; Harold F. Gosnell, 'The 1958 elections in the Sudan', *Middle East Journal*, XII (Autumn, 1958), p. 411; George Grassmuck, 'The electoral process in Iraq, 1952–1958', *Middle East Journal*, XIV (Autumn, 1960), pp. 407–8.
7 For example, Philip Khoury, *Syria and the French Mandate: The Politics of Arab Nationalism 1920–1945* (London: I.B. Tauris, 1987), pp. 365–6; or Michael C. Hudson, *The Precarious Republic: Political Modernisation in Lebanon* (New York: Random House, 1968), pp. 252–3.
8 Marius Deeb, *Party Politics in Egypt: The Wafd and its Rivals 1919–1939* (London: Ithaca Press, 1979), pp. 163–72.
9 Idem.
10 Robert Springborg, *Family, Power and Politics in Egypt* (Philadelphia: University of Pennsylvania Press, 1982), p. 125; Eric Davis, *Challenging Colonialism: Bank Misr and Egyptian Industrialization 1920–1941* (Princeton, NJ: Princeton University Press, 1983), p. 140n.

11 Khoury, *Syria and the French Mandate*, pp. 266–73.
12 Seale, *The Struggle for Syria*, p. 24.
13 Ibid., pp. 28–31, 174–6.
14 James P. Jankowski, *Egypt's Young Rebels: 'Young Egypt': 1933–1952* (Stanford, CA: Hoover Inst., 1975), p. 31.
15 Ibid., p. 189.
16 Seale, *The Struggle for Syria*, pp. 177, 181.
17 Abdo I. Baaklini, *Legislative and Political Development: Lebanon 1842–1972* (Durham, NC: Duke University Press, 1976), pp. 181–2.
18 John P. Entelis, *Pluralism and Party Transformation in Lebanon: Al-Kataeb, 1936–1970* (Leiden: E. J. Brill, 1970), p. 44.
19 Hudson, *The Precarious Republic*, pp. 187–8.
20 Baaklini, *Legislative and Political Development*, p. 181.
21 Hanna Batatu, *The Old Social Classes and the Revolutionary Movements of Iraq: A Study of Iraq's Old Landed Classes and of Its Communists, Ba'thists, and Free Officers* (Princeton, NJ: Princeton University Press, 1978), p. 465n; Amnon Cohen, *Political Parties in the West Bank under the Jordanian Regime 1949–1967* (Ithaca and London: Cornell University Press, 1980), p. 25.
22 For information about the somewhat lukewarm defence of democracy by leading Egyptian thinkers in the pre-Second World War period of the 1930s, see Ami Ayalon, 'Egyptian intellectuals versus Fascism and Nazism in the 1930s', in Uriel Dann (ed.), *The Great Powers in the Middle East 1919–1939* (New York: Holmes & Meier, 1988).
23 Malcolm Kerr, 'Arab radical notions of democracy', *St Antony's Papers*, 16 (London: Chatto & Windus, 1963), pp. 9–11.
24 BBC, SWB, 194, 12 March 1957.
25 I. William Zartman, 'Political pluralism in Morocco', in I. William Zartman (ed.), *Man, State, and Society in the Contemporary Maghrib* (London: Pall Mall Press, 1973), pp. 247–8.
26 Douglas E. Ashford, *Political Change in Morocco* (Princeton, NJ: Princeton University Press, 1961), p. 246.
27 Ibid., p. 97.
28 John Waterbury, *The Commander of the Faithful: The Moroccan Political Elite: A Study of Segmented Politics* (London: Weidenfeld & Nicolson, 1970), p. 145.
29 See, for example, Ashford, *Political Change*, Ch. 8; Waterbury, *Commander of the Faithful*, Ch. 9.
30 Stuart Schaar, 'King Hassan's alternatives', in Zartman, *Man, State and Society*, p. 239.
31 Mustapha Sehimi, 'Les élections législatives au Maroc', *Maghreb/ Machreq*, 107 (Jan./Feb./March, 1985), p. 25.
32 Ibid., p. 27.
33 Waterbury, *Commander of the Faithful*, pp. 145–9; Zartman, 'Political pluralism', pp. 252–3.
34 Ashford, *Political Change*, p. 307.
35 For example, Kamal Salibi, *The Modern History of Lebanon* (London: Weidenfeld & Nicolson, 1966), p. 166.
36 Edmond Rabbath, *La formation historique du Liban politique et*

constitutionel: Essai de synthèse, 2nd ed. (Beirut: Librairie Orientale, 1986), I, pp. 393–7. The quotations from Chiha used in support of the notion of his prominent role generally come from the 1940s and 1950s; for example, Baaklini, *Legislative and Political Development*, pp. 109–12.

37 Hudson, *Precarious Republic*, p. 232.
38 Frank Stoakes, 'The supervigilantes: The Lebanese Kataeb Party as builder, surrogate and defender of the state', *Middle Eastern Studies*, 11/1 (Jan., 1975), p. 215.
39 Ibid., p. 216–17.
40 Marion Farouk-Sluglett and Peter Sluglett, 'Aspects of the changing nature of Lebanese confessional politics: Al-Murabitun, 1958–1979', *Peuples Mediterranéens*, 20 (July/Sept., 1982), pp. 67–8.
41 Stoakes, 'The supervigilantes', p. 222.
42 Valerie Yorke, *Domestic Politics and Regional Security: Jordan, Syria and Israel* (Aldershot: Gower, 1988), pp. 79–85; Lamis Andoni, 'King Hussein leads Jordan into a new era', *Middle East International*, 17 Nov. 1989, p. 3.
43 Idem.
44 Lamis Andoni, 'Preparing a national charter', *Middle East International*, 2 Feb. 1990, p 10; and 'Incorporating all trends', *Middle East International*, 13 April 1990, p. 10.
45 J. E. Peterson, *The Gulf Arab States: Steps Towards Political Participation* (New York: Praeger, 1988), pp. 39–40; Rosemary Said Zahlan, *The Making of the Modern Gulf States* (London: Unwin Hyman, 1989), pp. 37, 40–1.
46 Ibid., pp. 43–4.
47 Peterson, *Gulf Arab States*, pp. 42–6.
48 Nadim Jaber, 'Protracted internal struggle', *Middle East International*, 11 May 1990, pp. 12–13; and 'The debate continues', *Middle East International*, 22 June 1990, pp. 11–12.
49 L. P. Elwell-Sutton, 'Political parties in Iran: 1941–1948', *Middle East Journal*, III/1 (Jan., 1949), p. 49.
50 Ervand Abrahamian, *Iran Between Two Revolutions* (Princeton, NJ: Princeton University Press, 1982), pp. 281–5.
51 Ibid., pp. 251–3.
52 Fred Halliday, *Iran: Dictatorship and Development*, (London, Harmondsworth: Penguin, 1979), p. 47.
53 Shaul Bakhash, *The Reign of the Ayatollahs* (London: I. B. Tauris, 1985), pp. 105–6.
54 Ali Behrooz, 'Iran ponders the next move', *The Middle East* (Aug., 1987), pp. 6–7.
55 Benjamin Azkin, 'The role of parties in the Israeli democracy', in Gregory S. Mahler (ed.), *Readings in the Israeli Political System: Structure and Processes* (Washington, DC: University Press of America, 1982), pp. 51–2.
56 Dan Horowitz and Moshe Lissak, *Trouble in Utopia: The Overburdened Polity in Israel* (Albany, NY: State University of New York Press, 1989), p. 35.

57 Itzhak Galnoor, 'Transformations in the Israeli political system since the Yom Kippur war', in A. Arian (ed.), *The Elections in Israel – 1977* (Jerusalem: Jerusalem Academic Press, 1980), p. 134.

58 Azkin, 'Parties', p. 65.

59 Misha Louvish, 'The making of electoral reform', *The Jerusalem Post* (13 April 1977).

60 Don Peretz, *Government and Politics of Israel*, 2nd edn (Boulder, Colorado: Westview, 1983), p. 75.

61 Benjamin Azkin, 'Likud', in Howard R. Penniman (ed.), *Israel at the Polls: The Knesset Elections of 1977* (Washington, DC: American Enterprise Institute, 1979), p. 107.

62 Ian Lustick, *Arabs in the Jewish State* (Austin and London: University of Texas Press, 1980), p. 228.

63 Feroz Ahmad, *The Making of Modern Turkey* (London: Harper Collins, 1991, forthcoming).

64 Ibid. I have taken all electoral statistics from this source.

65 Ilter Turan, 'Political parties and the party system in post-1983 Turkey', in Metin Heper and Ahmet Evin (eds), *State, Democracy and the Military: Turkey in the 1980s* (Berlin and New York: Walter de Gruyter, 1988), pp. 63–6.

66 Ibid., p. 64; Binnaz Toprak, 'Politicisation of Islam in a secular state: the National Salvation Party in Turkey', in Said Amir Arjumand (ed.), *From Nationalism to Revolutionary Islam* (London: Macmillan, 1984), p. 127.

67 William Hale, 'The role of the electoral system in Turkish politics', *International Journal of Middle Eastern Studies*, 11 (1980), pp. 402–11.

68 Toprak, 'Politicisation of Islam', pp. 127–9; Jacob M. Landau, 'The Nationalist Action Party in Turkey', *Journal of Contemporary History*, 17 (1982), pp. 592–7.

69 C. H. Dodd, 'Aspects of the Turkish state: Political culture, organized interests and village communities', British Society for Middle Eastern Studies, *Bulletin*, 15/1 1 and 2 (1988), p. 80.

70 See pp. 129 and 214–5 in this book.

71 Ergun Ozbudun, 'The Turkish party system: Institutionalization, polarization and fragmentation', *Middle Eastern Studies*, 17/2 (April, 1981), p. 235; C. H. Dodd, *The Crisis of Turkish Democracy* (Beverley: Eothen Press, 1984), p. 78.

72 Feroz Ahmad, 'The transition to democracy in Turkey', *Third World Quarterly*, 7/2 (April, 1985), p. 217.

10 Single-party systems and the return to greater democracy

Introduction

The creation of single-party regimes with a monopoly of political activity was a common feature of the Third World in the post-independence period. In some cases these were the work of the organization that had led the struggle for independence, in others they were established, *de novo*, by whatever group of civilian or military leaders was able to seize power in the years that followed. The reasons for this phenomenon were also much the same. On the one hand, multi-party competition was associated with division, waste and inefficiency, and seen as a handicap to nation building and development. On the other, single parties were believed to be the best method of directing a planned economy and of supervising countrywide systems of mobilization and control.

As far as the Arab countries of the Middle East were concerned, single-party regimes were established in about a third of them from the 1950s onwards. These included: Tunisia and Algeria, where the party itself had been in the forefront of the fight against the French; Syria and Iraq, where military coups by officers associated with the Ba'th led to a vast expansion of party activity; and Egypt, Sudan and Libya, where military regimes established large mass rallies to provide themselves with civilian support. A proper examination of this phenomenon requires an analysis not only of these party organizations themselves but also of their different relationships with the administration, the military, the security forces and the leaders of each regime. In addition, there is the difficult problem of knowing what weight to attach to their ideologies. All called themselves 'socialist' at one time or another, and this needs interpretation. But what was usually of much more importance was the use of an official ideology to monopolize the legitimate political language and to try to control the contents, as well as the limits, of acceptable discourse. A final question concerns the way in which the various Middle Eastern leaders either succumbed to, or tried to benefit from, the seemingly inevitable pressures that produced a variety of different 'cults of personality'.

In this chapter I will look at these issues in terms of an analysis of three different types of party and historical situation before going on to examine those cases where attempts were made to transform single-party rule into a pluralist, and sometimes more democratic, system.

Tunisia and Algeria

Tunisia's Neo-Destour Party was founded in 1934 by Habib Bourguiba and colleagues with the intention of making it a mass, popular organization, unlike its élitist predecessor, the Destour. In this it largely succeeded. Although it functioned only intermittently as a countrywide political force, it was able to obtain sufficient support to become recognized, both by the French and the majority of Tunisians, as the leading force in the nationalist movement.[1] By 1955, the year before Tunisia obtained its independence, it possessed a political bureau, a national congress, 100 branches and a small army.[2] It was also able to survive a serious internal split when Bourguiba's leadership, and his acceptance of a Franco-Tunisian convention that left the French with a privileged economic and military position, was challenged by the party's secretary general, Salah Ben Youssef. For all these reasons, the party was able to win a decisive victory in the elections for members of the constituent assembly held just after independence in March 1956 and to be asked by the bey to form Tunisia's first national government.

Like any other nationalist leader newly in power, Bourguiba was faced with the complex task of establishing his own authority while, at the same time, supervising the new relationships between the Neo-Destour and the administration as well as between the party and the other forces in the Tunisian political arena. He took care of the first of these tasks by persuading the constituent assembly to depose the bey and then to have himself proclaimed president of the new republic. He then used his new powers not only to strengthen the party but also to ensure that its organization dovetailed with that of the administrative structures of government. This was a vital task, as there was inevitably a great deal of overlap of function when party members were also required to staff the major offices of state. Bourguiba's answer was to draw most of his cabinet ministers from the Neo-Destour's political bureau and then, in 1958, to replace the party's regional federations with party commissioners appointed to each of the 13 newly created governorates (or provinces).[3]

Nevertheless, even though this move was clearly designed to accommodate the party to the state – not the other way round – Bourguiba still believed in the importance of a strong, broadly based, national organization as an instrument of popular mobilization and as a means of monopolizing legitimate political activity. As president of the Neo-Destour he presided over a considerable surge in membership which, at one stage, may have reached 600,000 before stabilizing at some 400,000 in the 1960s – out of a total population of around 3,800,000.[4] In addition, the party dominated the five major national organizations for workers, students, women, agriculturists and businessmen and merchants, most of which it had itself created. Finally, with the banning of the Tunisian Communist Party in 1963, the Neo-Destour became the country's single, legitimate political force.

The party assumed a more active role with the introduction of new economic policies based on greater state control and the collectivization of much of Tunisia's land. In 1964 its name was officially changed to the Parti Socialiste Destourien (PSD). It was also used to invite popular participation in the planning process by organizing numerous seminars and discussions as well as by its participation in the newly established regional co-ordinating commissions that helped to make policy at the local level.[5] One result was to draw party and administration still closer together; for example, the party's co-ordinating commissions were chaired by the provincial governors. Against this, the emphasis on planning encouraged demands for its transformation into an organization more of the vanguard type, to be closely identified with new institutions like the supervised co-operatives being established throughout Tunisia under the aegis of Ahmad Ben Salah, the minister of planning and finance. Indeed, according to Entelis, the strength of these co-operatives soon 'began to rival the scope and effectiveness of the PSD itself'.[6]

Matters came to a head in 1969 when opposition to Ben Salah's policies, and the growing threat that he posed to Bourguiba's own power, led the president to take forceful steps to reassert his own authority. He dismissed Ben Salah, redefined Destourian socialism to make it compatible with a switch to a more market-oriented economic policy and then, after a brief experiment in political liberalization in the early 1970s, established such a tight control over both party and government that the PSD almost completely disappeared as a political force (see also Chapter 6). The culmination of this process took place during the party congress in 1974, when Bourguiba not only had himself proclaimed president for life but also made it quite clear that it was he who was going to appoint the members of the political bureau rather than allowing them to be elected by the central committee as agreed at the previous congress three years earlier. Thereafter he attached so little importance to the party as an autonomous structure that membership of the political bureau was made to depend not on a person working his way up the party hierarchy but simply on his being made a cabinet minister.[7]

Efforts to evaluate the role of the PSD from the mid-1970s onwards leave no doubt as to its marginal status. For Entelis, for example, it functioned simply 'to orchestrate the adulation of the leader'.[8] Given the role it still played in selecting candidates for election to the national assembly, and in helping to manage the other national organizations, this judgement is too extreme. Nevertheless, it does help to raise basic questions about the nature and trajectory of the Tunisian single-party regime. Why was the high degree of institutionalism that so many writers observed in the 1960s so easily reversed? What allowed it to succumb so quickly to the cult of Bourguiba's personality? Looking at the historical record it would seem that the party itself never possessed the organization that would allow it to protect itself from outside pressures. For all its large membership, it was only allowed a very small central bureaucracy – some 140 persons all told at the end of the 1960s.[9] Furthermore, even in its socialist period, it never seems to have screened applicants for membership or to have moved to create the two-tier structure of militants and others that even Bourguiba, at one stage, suggested.[10] The fact that it was so quickly made subordinate to the central administration only made things worse.

Opposition to the PSD's monopoly of power was manifest as early as 1976, when a group headed by Ahmad Mestiri, a former minister of the interior, issued a declaration stating that the one-party system was 'no longer adapted to the needs and aspirations of the people' and calling for an organized opposition within the Destour itself.[11] Two years later there was the challenge posed by the show of independence by the major union, the UGTT (see Chapter 2). This led, in turn, to the tentative attempts to create a system of controlled pluralism that will be the subject of the last section of this chapter.

The Algerian Front de Libération Nationale (FLN), founded in 1954, was the umbrella organization that led the country through the war of liberation and then negotiated independence from the French in 1958. But it was never a monolithic structure, and even the principle of collegiate leadership had vanished by the time it was called on to form a government in 1962. The result was a struggle for power and control over the new and fragile administrative structures, in which the Front's organization was only one actor among many. Those in direct control over its administrative apparatus, such as its secretary general, Mohammed Khider, attempted to establish a dominant role for it as a vanguard party along the lines of its Tripoli programme of May 1962, when it had declared that it was the FLN that 'decides the overall policy of the nation and inspires the activity of the government'.[12] But Khider's attempts to build up an élite organization were easily blocked by Ahmed Ben Bella, Algeria's first president, while Khider himself was dismissed in 1963. Ben Bella then took over as secretary general himself and used the long-awaited first party congress held in April 1964 to begin to transform the Front into an instrument that would support him in his contest against his political rivals. But his still half-hearted efforts did nothing to resolve the question of future relations between party and government, nor was he able to curb the activities of party militants, whose advocacy of radical socialism and of party control over the army disturbed many of the senior officers and was one of the many factors encouraging Houari Boumedienne's military coup of June 1965.[13]

President Boumedienne often referred to the importance of the FLN in his speeches but in practice he rejected any interference by the party in government and acted decisively to dismantle its central administration and to place it firmly in the hands of loyal veterans of the independence war.[14] The result was that, although the FLN retained its formal monopoly over Algerian politics, it was in no position to exercise it.[15] This left the Front, in Roberts' evaluation, with no more than a certain public relations function on behalf of the central executive and a limited role in supervising the activities of the major national organizations like the workers', students' and agriculturists' federations and in providing a forum for mediating between competing interests at the local level.[16]

Boumedienne talked from time to time of the need to revive the FLN as a major instrument of political mobilization but it was not until the mid-1970s that he began to do anything serious about it. This process began with his speech of June 1975 in which he declared that the emphasis of his regime's second decade would be on greater democracy, and led on through the drafting of the national charter in 1976 to the transfer into the Front of various substantial political figures charged with preparing a party congress, the first since 1964. Something of his intentions can be seen in the fact that the charter refers to the 'avant-garde' role of the FLN and from his renewed insistence that anyone wishing to play a political role at any level of government could only do so if he become a member.[17]

In the event, the opening of the congress was delayed until June 1979 as a result of Boumedienne's death, while the championship of the party's expanded role passed to Colonel Mohamed Salah Yahiaoui, the FLN's new co-ordinator. Yahiaoui's plans were immediately revealed by his creation of a new organizational structure very much along the lines of the Soviet Communist Party, consisting of an elected central committee which, in turn, elected a 17-man political bureau as well as 11 specialized commissions with responsibility for overseeing the major areas of government. But by this time the political situation had greatly changed. Instead of a president, like Boumedienne, who was anxious to create a vanguard party that would supervise, and then energize, the bureaucracy, there was now a new head of state, Chadli Ben Jadid, whose first priority was to establish his own authority over all the country's major institutions, including the FLN itself.[18] It was in these circumstances that he allowed some of the new structures to be put in place but only to the degree that they provided no challenge either to himself or his major supporters. An extraordinary general congress held in 1980 gave him the power to appoint members of the political bureau instead of having them elected as before. He also took over the post of secretary general, abolished the duties of the co-ordinator and reduced the number of party commissions from 11 to 5.

By the time Chadli's own counter attack was complete, all that was left of the reforms was an appointed political bureau and an emasculated central committee, both of which were little more than advisory bodies to the president with no power to act as instruments for the control of the administration.[19] As for the party, this had ended up with a somewhat enlarged role in supervising the national organizations and in managing the elections for the national assembly, for which all candidates required its specific endorsement. It was also used more extensively than in the past to exercise a general control over Algerian political life, for example, through its assertion of the rule that all government officials had to be members.[20] It was this monopoly that came under serious attack after the riots and demonstrations against government economic policy that broke out in October 1988, which will be described in the last section of this chapter.

The single-party system in Syria and Iraq

At first sight there would seem to be much in common between the systems of one-party rule established in Syria and Iraq. Both were led by men who had joined the Ba'th during the period of great ideological ferment in the Arab world in the 1950s and 1960s.[21] Both were the results of coups in which the party as a small, clandestine organization had come to power with the help of sympathizers in the army. Both were very much influenced in their initial stages by the Soviet model of the party as a revolutionary vanguard, functionally separate from the central bureaucracy, with the task of supervising the government, the military and the popular organizations like the unions. Finally, both adopted certain ideological practices aimed at strengthening the party's legitimacy and authority by magnifying its role in the past and by stressing its access to a science of politics that gave it a unique insight into the present and the future.

All this is true and important if not pushed too far. Among other things, it has the great advantage of highlighting those important areas where the Ba'thi regimes were forced to confront organizational problems very similar and those where conditions were obviously quite different. It also provides a way into a discussion of some central, and analytically more complex, issues. These include the function of an official ideology, the relationship between the party and a leader subject to a cult of personality, and the nature of the competition between parties professing the same principles and claiming an identical historical legitimacy. Having said all this, however, it is clearly important to remember the quite different political and historical circumstances that faced would-be vanguard parties in the Middle East as opposed to those in the Soviet Union, as well as the fact that the Iraqi and Syrian systems differed from one another in many significant respects.

Supporters of the Syrian Ba'th first came to power in 1963, although they were not firmly in control of the country until a second coup in 1966. During these first three years they were involved in intense discussions and political in-fighting as younger, more radical, members struggled to take over the leadership from the founders of the party, Michel Aflak, Salah al-Din Bitar and their colleagues. This was a process that also involved a sharpening of some of the major principles of traditional Ba'thi ideology in a direction that placed much greater emphasis on socialism and revolutionary social transformation.[22] It also involved the rebuilding of the party organization from the top in terms of a Leninist blueprint that included preparations for its control over both army and government.[23] Efforts in this direction were further intensified after the 1966 coup that brought in General Salah Jadid as *de facto* party secretary. However, the drive for party ascendancy was blunted by the regime's comprehensive defeat by the Israelis in the 1967 war, as well as by the fact that it could never establish its control over the parallel Ba'thi apparatus in the army dominated by General Hafiz al-Asad. And, in the end, it was the latter that triumphed over Jedid's civilian organization in a third coup in November 1970.

As many commentators have pointed out, one of the major reasons for Asad's coup was his growing dissatisfaction with the role played by the party and what he saw as its increasing isolation from almost every area of Syrian society.[24] Hence, when he came to construct his own pyramid of power under what Hinnebusch has described as his own 'authoritarian presidency', he was careful to ensure that the Ba'thi ideology was significantly watered down and that its organization played only a subordinate political role.[25] As he saw it, the party would be most useful as an instrument of mobilization and social control and as an aid to the execution of regime policies in certain well-defined areas like land reform and the management of the public sector of the economy. But he was unwilling to allow it much of a role in internal security or in keeping an eye on the loyalty of the army, where a separate Ba'thi military organization was preserved. The result was a vigorous drive to recruit new party members, particularly in the rural areas, as well as to enlarge the usual popular organizations for workers, peasants, women and young people placed under general Ba'thi control. This process was then further intensified in an effort to solidify support for the regime against its religious opponents from 1979 onwards (see Chapter 7). Various estimates of the totals involved would suggest that the number of full members increased from some 10,000 in the late 1960s to perhaps 100,000 in 1984, while the larger group of those with some association with the party had reached 250,000 at this same date.[26]

The party's rapid growth, and the fact that it was joined by a large number of opportunists or people who were recruited along regional or sectarian rather than ideological lines, was a further limitation on its ability to play a vanguard role.[27] Its position was also affected by two other developments, which will be discussed below: the attenuation of its ideology; and the ever increasing personal dominance of President Asad himself, supported by his predominantly Alawi security apparatus. All this makes it difficult to evaluate the Ba'th party's changing role within the many institutions and centres of power that constituted the Syrian political system. In Hinnebusch's analysis it remained what he calls a 'real party' and continued to perform 'crucial political functions'.[28] It still served to legitimize the regime and to provide mechanisms for élite recruitment and for the choice of President Asad's successor – even though these might eventually be disregarded in a renewed struggle for power like the one that took place in early 1984.[29] It also played a role in policy formulation and is credited by Hinnebusch with a spirited defence of the state sector and an ability to block moves towards greater economic liberalization.[30] Finally, it maintained its utility as an additional instrument of administrative control, with a network of members with sufficient commitment to the regime to keep a watch over the rest of society, to supervise organizations like the Ba'th Vanguard (membership of which is compulsory for all children between 6 and 11) and to make it difficult for all but a few officially tolerated political organizations like the Syrian Communist Party to assert themselves.

In Iraq the Ba'th obtained power in July 1968, once again with the help of a military coup in which its supporters played a leading role. To begin with its political base was so narrow that it could only maintain itself by recourse to terror, torture and harsh repression. But during the early 1970s, and particularly after it had finally solved the question of its relationship with the international oil companies in 1974, it began to institutionalize itself on the basis of a regular co-operation between President Hassan al-Bakr, who maintained the loyalty of the army, and his vice-president, Saddam Hussain, who was carefully building up a disciplined, civilian party apparatus. Unlike the Syrian party leaders, he chose to recruit new members at a slow, controlled pace with maximum emphasis on loyalty. According to some estimates it could take seven to eight years to pass through the various stages before being allowed to become a full member.[31] It was also kept a deliberately secretive organization, holding few congresses (not one between 1974 and 1982) and with rules that deliberately forbade any member from giving information about its organization, its numbers or its internal discussions.[32]

Once the party organization had become sufficiently large, Saddam Hussain used it to supervise the administration (from which it was kept deliberately independent), the military, the educational system, the popular organizations and as large a proportion of Iraqi society as a secular institution with strong ties to the dominant Sunni community could reach. There was then another period of expansion in the late 1970s when the party began to recruit extensively among members of the Shi'i community as a way of trying to maintain their loyalty at a time of increasing religious opposition to the Ba'thi regime encouraged by the Iranian revolution. By the early 1980s it was possible to write that it had some 1,500,000 associated members and that there was a party person in every government department, a party commissar in every military unit and a party cell in every school, university, neighbourhood and, in some cases, urban block.[33]

Saddam Hussain's own accession to the presidency in 1979, followed so soon by the beginning of the long war with Iran in 1980, produced changes in the role of the Iraqi party which, once again, are difficult to evaluate. From the beginning he made it clear that he was no longer interested in presenting an image of a collective leadership but one of personal power. The point was made initially by a bloody purge of opponents within the party and then reinforced by a process of orchestrated glorification that, during the early stages of the war, reached extraordinary heights. At the party's ninth regional congress in 1982, for example, it was asserted that it was he who had led the fight against Iran in 'all its military, strategic, mobilizational, political, economic and psychological aspects, in a creative, courageous and democratic manner'.[34] All this tended to dilute the salience of the Iraqi Ba'th and of its ideology, a trend that was reinforced by the conduct of the war itself, which was managed by the president himself in direct contact with the generals, without reference to the party at all.

Where all this left the party at the end of the 1980s is unclear. On the one hand, it appeared to have lost some of its role in supervising the activities of the military and the central administration.[35] On the other, in spite of its vast expansion, it continued to maintain a core of disciplined party members who could be used for a great variety of control and surveillance functions. For the rest, it remained, as it always had, simply an instrument of those in the Iraqi leadership who controlled the revolutionary command council and the party's regional command, the two most powerful bodies in the regime. It had also undergone an important change in the way in which it was presented to the general public which I would now like to discuss.

As far as ideology is concerned, both the Iraqi and the Syrian parties underwent a process of dilution in which the rhetoric was progressively emptied of almost all of its substance. To begin with, in its first years in power, and when it was still in heated competition with other ideologies like communism and Nasserism, its spokesmen were concerned to argue the Ba'thi case in a way that made sense to as wide a circle of political activists as possible. This was also a factor in the fierce war of words between the two parties in Syria and Iraq in the late 1960s and the early 1970s as to which was the single legitimate heir to the organization originally created by Aflaq and Bitar. As in the case of the similar verbal struggle between the Soviet Union and China in the 1960s, the appeal to the authority of Marxist-Leninism was constructed in such a way that there was room for only one source of ideological truth. It also followed, as Kienle argues, that the Syrian and Iraqi leaders attached great value to the mantle of true Ba'thism as an indispensable aid to constructing their respective regimes on a sound basis, as well as to recruiting from the pool of Ba'thi militants of Syrian, Iraqi, Jordanian or some other origin who were in a position to throw in their lot with one regime or the other.[36]

Later, however, all this became of less importance and Ba'thism as an ideology lost its sharpness in the same way as communism and many others. There were specifically local reasons as well. One was the fact that Ba'thism itself never consisted of more than a small number of general principles that proved incapable of meaningful theoretical elaboration. Unlike Marxism, for example, it possessed no major works of philosophy or history that could be used as the basis for such an enterprise. It was, in reality, much closer to a species of nationalism – with a typical appeal for a collective struggle towards a future goal of progress and social development – than the kind of science of society that its leaders sometimes claimed. Furthermore, for all the establishment of party institutes for training and research, there was little sign of any desire to produce a coherent body of Ba'thi doctrine. In Iraq, for instance, Saddam Hussain was regarded as the only major ideologue and in the early 1980s was already credited with having over 200 books, articles and essays to his name.[37]

The result was an official ideology which, in its Iraqi context, has been described as 'rhetorical' and 'deliberately repetitious'.[38] However, analysts who concentrate simply on its intellectual content – or lack of it – miss much of the point. As in the case of the Soviet Union before perestroika, the function of such an ideology was not as a means of intellectual enlightenment but as an instrument of political control. This operated in various ways. At one level an appeal to Ba'thism as a science was supposed to provide the leadership with the aura of people whose ability to look beneath the surface of events meant that they were never surprised, that their plans were always correct, that they were incapable of miscalculation.[39] At another, the ideology provided a set of guidelines that not only set out the party line for the membership and the people but also reinforced the leadership's monopoly of the ability to speak *ex cathedra*. In the Iraqi case again this can be seen in Saddam Hussain's emphasis on ideology as 'the only basis for the life in which the Ba'thi believes', coupled with the party's emphasis on its leader's ideological 'creativity', a trait at once estimable and yet impossible to emulate for fear that it might lead anyone but him into serious trouble.[40]

The monopoly exercised by both presidents over ideological pronouncements in the name of Ba'thism, the party and the revolution is further reinforced by the development of the cult of the personality. Just why such things emerge in some one-party states and not others is difficult to say. Looking at the communist world before perestroika there was a huge gamut of practice, from the heady adulation of a Kim Il Sung in North Korea to the attitude to much greyer political leaders like Poland's Gomulka. Clearly there is some choice involved; even in the most authoritarian state with the most cowed of populations, a leader can encourage or discourage such a development. Meanwhile, in the Middle East itself there was considerable variety in the way the official media was required to orchestrate the praise of a Nasser, a Bourguiba, an Asad or a Saddam Hussain. What would seem to be the case was that in Syria and Iraq both leaders saw positive advantage in presenting themselves as head and shoulders above their rivals, as 'indispensable' (an adjective often applied to President Hussain) and as the source of all political wisdom and authority.

Once such a cult is established, there is a tendency for the role both of the party and its ideology to diminish still further. A man who presents himself as the leader of all his people will not want to discriminate too obviously in favour of party members. He may also come to believe that his control is exercised more efficiently if there is a single chain of command that runs from the presidency through the cabinet and then the central administration, rather than a bifurcated one in which the party has to be represented at every level. As for ideology, such a leader will probably want complete freedom to define it in any way he chooses without reference to any other authority that could be used to contradict him. All these factors can be clearly seen in different degrees in the Iraqi and the Syrian cases, even though the adulation for President Asad never went anything like as far as that for President Hussain.

The rallies and unions established by the regimes in Egypt, Sudan and Libya

President Nasser's regime created a series of national rallies or unions to mobilize popular support – the Liberation Rally, the National Union and finally the Arab Socialist Union (ASU). All were conceived as mass organizations with a monopoly of legitimate political activity. The choice of name was also significant; in each case the word 'party' was deliberately avoided, for this had powerful connotations of division and lack of national purpose.[41]

The Liberation Rally was announced in 1953, soon after the formal dissolution of the pre-revolutionary parties and at a time when it was thought necessary to try to organize support for the regime in the aftermath of the serious challenge posed to it by its first president, General Naguib, and those who had used him to press for an immediate return to democratic life. This was superseded in 1956 by the National Union, in an effort to create a stronger organization to sustain Egyptian unity in the face of the tripartite British, French and Israeli attack. It was then used as the major common political organization in both Syria and Egypt during the brief period of union from 1958 to 1961.[42] Finally, the formation of the Arab Socialist Union was announced by President Nasser in October 1961 on the grounds that the National Union had been infiltrated by the type of reactionary forces that were responsible for the Syrian secession and that it had to be reorganized so that it could become a 'revolutionary instrument for the national masses'.[43] A month later, in November, he set out a four-stage process for reforming the Egyptian political system: the calling of a preparatory council to organize a congress of popular forces that was to discuss the draft of a national charter; the creation of the Arab Socialist Union; and finally the use of the new machinery to supervise the election of a 350-person national assembly.

The first two attempts at a national political organization are often dismissed as no more than rather ineffectual attempts at counter-mobilization, that is, at preventing Egyptians from joining potential opposition groups. But, as Binder notes, they set important precedents for the Arab Socialist Union that followed.[44] First, all three followed the main lines of the country's administrative structure, with committees at the four main levels, the village or urban quarter, the district, the provincial and the national. This produced predictable tensions with the ordinary state bureaucracy but also allowed the rally or union to be easily controlled by it. Second, the local-level organization was usually created by the simple expedient of either sending a leading political figure to a village to recruit members – who then elected the appropriate committee – or nominating an influential notable to undertake the same task. The result was that leadership was largely exercised by those with local economic and administrative power. It also meant, as Binder discovered, that there was a very high overlap between the members of local committees of the National Union and those of its successor.[45] Third, all three rallies and unions were organized on a mass basis, with membership open to almost the entire male population. The National Union is credited with a membership of six million while the ASU obtained some five million recruits in its first year.[46]

The basic organizational structure of the ASU was created in 14 months in 1963 and 1964, although with many lacunae and anomalies. At the top was a higher executive committee which stood in for the permanent central committee that some hoped would be created later. Next came temporary provincial committees which presided over the formation of district-level committees. At the bottom, the one innovation was the creation of so-called 'basic units' at the local level, based either on residence in a village or a quarter or on the place of work. There were nearly 7,000 of these, each run by a committee of 20 members, covering most of Egypt but not involving the army or the police.[47] This mass, pyramidal, structure contained perhaps 70 per cent of the male electorate.[48] It was hardly an autonomous organization, however, and there was a great deal of overlap between party and government, with the same man often holding posts at the national and provincial levels. There was also little attention paid to creating a regular system of membership nor any attempt to impose a party discipline except, on occasions, by the threat of expulsion. This latter sanction may have had some little power as, within a short period of time, ASU membership was a necessary requirement for anyone holding office in many official committees or who wished to be elected to any of the regional or national assemblies.[49]

What the ASU still lacked was both a clearly defined role and a coherent ideology, and this was to cause a great deal of confusion in the years that followed. Three areas in particular remained ill defined and continued to breed controversy. The first was the relationship between the party and other Egyptian institutions, notably the army, the bureaucracy and the professional syndicates. No sooner had Ali Sabri replaced the more conservative Husayn al-Shafi'i as director of the Union than he made it clear that his eventual aim was to create an instrument that could be used to dominate all but the army, and even here there were voices making the case for greater civilian control.[50] The second was the nature of the 'alliance of working forces' that President Nasser had said the ASU should represent but which continued to remain largely undefined. Matters were not made any clearer by the decree that 50 per cent of the seats put up for any election should be reserved for 'workers and peasants'. Not only did definitions of who should be categorized as a worker or peasant vary over time but it also raised the larger, and never resolved, question of whether representation in the alliance formed by the ASU should be on a class or corporate basis.[51] The last area was that of ideology and, more precisely, what was meant by socialism. Kosheri Mahfouz has identified two main streams in the debate, one that wished to place it in an Arab or local Middle Eastern context, the other that tended to identify it simply with European or Soviet practice.[52] The point was obviously of the greatest importance: by insisting on its Arab character the regime could keep its further elaboration in its own hands, while any appeal to a wider, international, meaning would open up a much more general debate over which it would have very much less control. Uncertainty on all these counts was one of the many reasons why the activities of the ASU were opposed so quickly by groups within the military and the civilian administration.

Tensions were further exacerbated by the question of whether the Union should contain a corps or vanguard of more militant and committed activists. Ahmad Hamrush argues that such a vanguard was first created by President Nasser himself, either in 1963 or 1964, as a means of surveillance and supervision.[53] It was then reorganized in 1965 to fit more tightly into the ASU's developing administrative structure. Finally, control over it passed into the hands of Ali Sabri, who used it as part of his plans to inject greater dynamism into the organization which involved, among other things, the creation of a cadre of full-time party activists and the replacement of the committees of 20 running the basic units by so-called 'leadership groups' with some of these same activists in control.

All writers are agreed that it was Egypt's comprehensive military defeat in the June war of 1967 that spelled the end of Sabri's own plans to convert the ASU into an instrument that, as he had put it in an interview in April 1967, could be used to control the public sector and the administration.[54] The organization itself soon came under fierce attack from its opponents, who were especially critical of its over-bureaucratized administration and its existence as yet another alternative centre of power. President Nasser himself tried to steer a middle path between those who wanted to cut it down to size and those who wanted to turn it into a more open, democratic organization. In his 30 March programme of 1968 he called for the

ASU to be revived and reorganized but only by means of a series of new elections for committees at all levels. This process was completed during the same year, and also included the establishment of a national congress of the ASU that in turn helped to create a central committee and then, on top of that, a higher executive committee. It is significant, however, that this drive for greater intra-party democracy was placed under the supervision of Sha'ari Goma'a, the head of Egypt's internal security service.[55] That one of the main aims was also to reduce the power of ASU militants can be seen from the concomitant abolition of the leadership groups at the local level and their replacement by the former committees of 20 which were much easier to control by village notables.

President Nasser's policy towards the ASU after 1967 is yet another example of his own highly ambiguous attitude towards the creation of a single political organization. On the one hand, he believed in the importance of rallying support for the regime and of isolating its political enemies, whether from the religious camp or from what he would have thought of as a reactionary direction. He also saw the need to match the government's growing control over the economy with a popular organization which could sustain enthusiasm for his plans for rapid social development. On the other, he was worried about initiatives that gave power to groups and organizations not directly under his own control. And, like any leader, he had to balance the interests of various different constituencies, many of which were seriously disturbed by the ASU's actual or potential power. In these circumstances, Nasser himself suggested a number of often contradictory initiatives concerning the ASU while, in practice, treating the organization as little more than an extension of the central administration, to be controlled by packing it full of his loyal allies.[56]

In the event, the 1968 reorganization did little to revivify the ASU and by the time Ali Sabri was dropped as first secretary in July 1969 it had become, in Waterbury's word, 'moribund'.[57] Nevertheless, it still retained its central position in Egyptian political life, and continued its monopoly over official activity until President Sadat's root and branch reforms of the 1970s. These will be described in the last section of this chapter.

Just as Egypt's ASU was nearing the end of its short life, its organizational structure was copied in both Sudan and Libya, where military plotters calling themselves 'Free Officers', in conscious imitation of President Nasser and his colleagues, seized power in 1969. In Libya, one of their first political initiatives took the form of the establishment of a Libyan Arab Socialist Union aimed at creating a single link between the central government and the people. It consisted of congresses and committees at three levels, the national, the governorate and the local, where basic units of the Egyptian types were established.[58] The ASU's first national congress was held in March 1972, when its president, Muammar al-Qadhafi, announced that it was to be the only organization allowed to engage in political activity in Libya. But in 1973 the members of the ruling revolutionary command council had already become dissatisfied with the inability of this new organization to obtain either the trust of the rural population or the co-operation of its élites.[59] It had also created the usual problems caused by lack of co-ordination between the party organization and the bureaucracy. In 1973 it was replaced by a new system based on the establishment of popular committees.

There was a more sustained effort to establish a political organization along Egyptian lines in the Sudan. A decision to create a Sudan Socialist Union (SSU) was announced only a month after the coup. But this was then followed by two years in which prior importance was given to setting up a number of so-called 'popular and functional organizations' for women, young people and others as well as a network of village councils – all of which were supposed to provide the basis for a programme of radical social change. But the thrust of this policy was altered in 1971 as a result of the regime's break with the Sudanese Communist Party, and there was an immediate decision to establish the SSU as a major instrument of popular support and national unity.[60] A founding congress was quickly arranged for January 1972 at which a national charter was adopted, calling for a 'single political' organization with the role of extending 'popular control over state organs'.[61] The usual pyramidal structure was then created, with organizations at all levels, from the national to the village. It is significant that while the SSU used Egyptian terminology to describe the 'basic units' at the bottom, the nomenclature used for the major institutions at the top reflected the desire for a more Leninist type of organization. Hence there was a national congress and a central committee, which in turn elected a political bureau based on nominations received from the leader of the SSU, President Nimeiri.

In January 1972 Nimeiri was able to report to the SSU's first congress that all the basic units and branch organizations were now in place. He also declared that the new organization had two and a quarter million members.[62] Not surprisingly, this suggested a much too optimistic picture. According to Niblock's extensive research conducted between 1974 and 1977, only a minority of the basic units were then politically active. He also discovered a considerable amount of confusion due to the overlap between party and government. Altogether, he concluded that such units played only a marginal role in either politicizing the people or in conveying popular concerns upwards to the political leadership.[63] More generally, analyses of the SSU assert that it had little or no autonomy and was only politically significant at the national level, where it was an arm of the regime. In these circumstances its major role was seen as that of an 'officially sanctioned arena for the political participation of various personal, political, sectarian and traditional groups'.[64]

The process of national reconciliation initiated with opponents of the regime led to a brief attempt to widen the SSU and to make it more open to a variety of social and political influences. Sadiq al-Mahdi, the leader of the Ansar, agreed to join the SSU executive in 1977 – an offer he soon withdrew – while the leaders of the Umma and the Muslim Brothers were also drawn closer to the organization.[65] This proved useful to the regime in the short term, and it was able to orchestrate the third congress in January 1980 to provide a convincing demonstration of national support for its new economic plan as well as its programme of administrative devolution by means of the establishment of regional governments. The congress was also used to elect a 300-man central committee which then elected a 17-man political bureau to manage its day-to-day business. But this was followed by a growing economic and social crisis and the beginnings of what Niblock has termed 'the disintegration of the state'.[66] Widespread rioting in January 1982 convinced President Nimeiri that the SSU was failing as an instrument of mobilizing popular support for the regime. He then dissolved the political bureau, the central committee and all the other major party institutions, replacing them with a preparatory central committee under his own direction. The national congress that was supposed to meet to ratify any proposed reorganization was postponed several times, and still had not met by the time the regime was overthrown in the coup of April 1985.

Political restructuring and the tentative return to a multi-party system

The only Arab country in which a one-party system disappeared overnight was Sudan. There the 1985 coup led to the immediate dissolution of the SSU and then, after a year of transitional military rule, to the general election of April 1986 held under the identical system to that used for the last open, competitive election in 1968 and contested by three of the same major political groups: the Umma Party led by Sadiq el-Mahdi; the Democratic Unionist Party; and the National Islamic Front dominated by the Muslim Brothers.[67] The experiment was short lived, however, and the multi-party system came to another abrupt end with General Omer El Bashir's coup of June 1989.

Elsewhere the process of transforming a single-party system into a multi-party one proved to be a lengthy and complex one, fraught with many of the difficulties later to be experienced by the states of eastern Europe after 1989. In the Middle East the first Arab country to embark on this path was Egypt in the mid-1970s, when President Sadat was faced with the problem of what to do about the Arab Socialist Union, an organization that he and his closest supporters deeply distrusted and that seemed to stand in the way of his policies of liberalization and greater economic and political freedom. In theory, he, like any other leader in the same position, was faced with three possible options: he could reform the single party and open it up to a variety of different internal trends; he could dissolve it and allow it to be replaced by a number of other political organizations; or he could retain it as the government party within a new multi-party system. In the end he opted for the third but only after a long period of discussion and debate that saw him moving from support for the establishment of a number of *minbars* (platforms) inside the ASU to allowing three of these same platforms to contest the November 1976 general election as independent parties.[68] These were the government's Arab Socialist Egypt Rally (later the Egypt Party), the Liberal Socialists on the right and the National Progressive Unionists on the left.

Descriptions of this process suggest that, for all his desire to base his regime on different principles than those of President Nasser, President Sadat showed great caution in his restructuring of Egypt's political system and, on occasions, allowed himself to be pushed along by pressures from within the élite.[69] After his purge of Ali Sabri and his associates from the leadership in 1971, his first call for a thorough overhaul of the ASU was not until 1974, and even then was only accompanied by a few very sketchy ideas about where this should lead, most notably his suggestion that it might be possible to allow several 'poles' of opinion to develop within the organization itself. He next turned the matter over to a so-called 'listening committee' to canvass opinions from the representatives of a variety of groups and interests. Various calls for the establishment of political parties were immediately met by a series of well-organized protests by leaders of workers and other organizations, who felt that their position would be at risk if the support of the ASU were removed. Further consultation was then postponed for more than another year before a majority of members of the central committee finally completed another long round of discussions with a vote to recommend the establishment of 'fixed' platforms within the ASU. This was immediately ratified by President Sadat himself in March 1976, and a few days later his supporters had moved rapidly to recruit most of the deputies to the people's assembly into a centre organization, while up to 40 or so other groups vied with each other to form different types of opposition on the left and right. These were then whittled down to three, and then ultimately to two.

Having created the rudiments of a multi-party system, it was then necessary to establish the rules governing elections and the creation of any further parties. As far as the 1976 election itself was concerned, the major decisions seem to have been taken by the regime itself, operating through its new platform/organization in the people's assembly.[70] It was decided to continue the system of 175 two-member constituencies, each one of which should contain one candidate who was officially classified as a peasant or worker. For the rest, opposition efforts to draw up rules to prevent official interference were not supported and in the end the government's centre party received an overwhelming advantage from the fact that the election was supervised by the ministry of the interior and that many of its candidates were closely associated with different levels of the administration. This was enough to give it 280 of the 350 seats, with 12 going to the Liberal Socialists, 2 to the Progressives and the rest to independents.

A new Parties Law was then introduced in 1977. Its main features were that all new parties would have to accept the principles of the constitution, the national charter of 1962 and Sadat's 'October' paper of 1974 and that none could be based on a class, sectarian or (local) geographic basis.[71] This was clearly an attempt to limit the political debate while at the same time preventing the establishment of any organization based on religion or on an appeal to the old Nasserite constituency of workers and peasants who had obtained important gains from his economic and social policies. The result was that party leaders came to represent ideological trends rather than economic and social interests. Meanwhile, important sections of the population like the workers and peasants were left without specific representation at the highest level and were thus effectively disenfranchised.

President Sadat was soon forced to backtrack in his experiment in controlled democracy as a result of growing popular opposition to many of his policies, notably his attempt to cut the level of subsidies on basic necessities and his move towards a peace treaty with Israel. Opposition groups were harassed while Sadat himself preferred to manage Egyptian public opinion through a combination of popular referenda and constant manipulation of the unions, syndicates and his new creation, the Majlis Al-Shura (consultative council), which had limited legislative powers and was half elected, half selected in 1980.[72]

The movement towards a more open political system was re-started by President Mubarak but still with a great emphasis on control. His major innovation was the 1983 amendment to the 1972 electoral law, which established a completely new system of representation designed to favour the government party but leaving some scope for a small opposition. This called for the creation of 48 large constituencies instead of the previous 175 smaller ones. Parties wishing to stand in the election would have to offer lists in all of them, thus diluting any attempt to concentrate their resources on just a few of the districts where they had most support. They were also required to obtain at least 8 per cent of the vote at the national level before they could be awarded any seats. Another important provision banned candidates from standing as independents lest this allowed people into the assembly over whom the regime would have little control. As the architect of the reformed system, the prime minister, Fuad Muhieddin, put it in private conversation, he didn't want 'new men' to stand for election because 'we don't know them'.[73]

Once the new electoral machinery was in place, it was necessary to give credence to the whole exercise by persuading opposition politicians as well as the Egyptian voters that there would be enough freedom and openness to make it worth while for them to participate. This was done quite cleverly by allowing a government candidate to be beaten in a by-election in Alexandria in November 1983 and then permitting the Neo-Wafd Party to run candidates in the May 1984 general election, even though it had not legally constituted itself as an official party. As a result some 43 per cent of the registered voters went to the polls.[74] And even though the government party, now renamed the National Democratic Party (NDP), won 73 per cent of the votes (and so 390 out of the 448 seats), the Neo-Wafd did well enough to secure the rest of the seats with 15 per cent of the vote. To do this it relied not only on the electioneering skills of its elderly leaders, who were old enough to have taken part in pre-revolutionary politics, but also on its alliance with the Muslim Brothers which brought it useful financial and organizational support. The other parties suffered greatly from their own inexperience, as well as from selective governmental interference, particularly in the rural areas.[75] Not surprisingly there were also many administrative problems connected with the fact that contested elections were still a rarity for many Egyptians, that registers had not been kept up to date and that many people were unable to find their way to their proper polling station.[76]

Egypt's next general election was held early in 1987 as the result of a successful legal challenge to the ban on independents on the grounds that it violated freedoms enshrined in the 1971 constitution. Seeing that this threatened to undermine the legality of the people's assembly which had the duty of re-electing him as president later that same year, Mubarak changed the rules to allow one independent to stand in each constituency and then called Egyptians to the polls in April. On this occasion the NDP obtained 308 seats with 70 per cent of the votes, as against the Neo-Wafd which obtained 35 seats with 11 per cent and a new alliance of three organizations, Socialist Labour, Socialist Liberals and the Muslim Brothers, which obtained 56 seats with 17 per cent. There were also four independents.[77] Once again the opposition made serious allegations concerning official interference, including the claim that three-quarters of the polling stations had no proper observers.[78] Against this it is generally assumed that, given the close ties between the administration and the NDP, the government party would have won by a substantial majority anyway and that the only choice open to voters was that of selecting which of the other parties would constitute the official opposition.[79]

Multi-party systems dominated by a government party that is seldom, if ever, defeated at the polls exist in many other parts of the non-European world, and have been subject to a number of analyses. According to Guy Hermet, the regimes in such countries do not need elections to continue in office but rely on them for a number of other functions such as mobilizing public opinion and providing themselves with extra legitimation.[80] They also provide an opportunity for the leader of the government party – in Egypt the president – to discipline his supporters by removing them from its electoral list and obviating the need for an embarrassing purge. But it has also been pointed out that, to perform these functions, such systems have to violate many of the accepted canons of democracy. If we use Hermet's indices of what constitutes the difference between a free and a controlled election, we find that in Egypt many voters were not placed on the registration lists as they were supposed to be at 18; the electorate was subject to various administrative pressures; and they could not expect the ballot to be counted and reported accurately.[81] This last feature was especially noticeable in 1987, when the opposition challenged the ministry of the interior's decision to award 78 seats to particular candidates as the result of a secret and highly complex process by which votes awarded to members of parties that did not obtain 8 per cent of the national total were reassigned to those that had.[82]

The 1990 election was the second to be held two years before its time, once again as the result of a successful legal challenge to the conduct of the one before. The result was yet another change in the electoral system, highlighted by a return to the system of two-member constituencies in use before 1984 and the final removal of all barriers to independent candidates. However, opposition efforts to obtain the lifting of the nine-year-old state of emergency, which imposed considerable constraints on their activity during any electoral campaign, were unsuccessful and led to a boycott by the Wafd and all the members of the Socialist Labour, Socialist Liberal and Muslim Brother alliance. This paved the way for another overwhelming victory by the government party, with opposition from only a few members of the Progressive Party and a variety of independents.[83]

The other two Arab regimes that attempted to open up their single-party regimes in the 1980s were the Tunisian and the

Algerian. In Tunisia the process was begun in a halting way in 1981 when candidates without PSD affiliation were allowed to stand in the elections for the national assembly. In the event, however, none of them was successful, while the government party, standing as a National Front in tandem with the newly organized labour union, the UNGTT, won 94.8 per cent of the votes and all the seats. In addition, not one of the five opposition groups obtained the 5 per cent of the vote that would have allowed it to be legally recognized as an official political party.[84]

The process was restarted after Ben Ali deposed Habib Bourguiba as president in November 1987, promising to change what he described as a 'corrupt, one-party state' into a more tolerant multi-party system.[85] A year later he called a meeting of representatives from a large number of political, social and economic organizations to discuss the guidelines necessary for such a transformation. The results were set out in a national pact signed by 16 of the groups concerned, including six recognized parties. The pact specifically underlined the right to be allowed to establish parties and the need to hold free elections and to promote 'loyal' political competition.[86] This was followed by a general election in April 1989 based on a modified form of proportional representation designed to favour the government party by awarding all the seats in each of the 25 multi-member constituencies to the organization that won the majority of the votes. The result was an overwhelming victory for the PSD, renamed the Rassemblement Constitutionel Democratique (RCD), which obtained 80 per cent of the vote and all of the 143 seats. The only significant competition came from members of the unofficial Mouvement de Tendence Islamique (MTI) who, running as independents, secured 13 per cent of the vote but no seats. Meanwhile, the combined vote of the five secular parties that had been cultivated by Ben Ali in an attempt to be able to use them as a loyal opposition came to less than 6 per cent.

Further movement towards greater political competition was then blocked, for two main reasons. First, Ben Ali refused to allow the MTI – now renamed the Harakat al-Nahda (Movement for Rebirth) – to register itself as an official political organization, on the grounds that Tunisia had no need for a religious party. Then he failed to find an electoral formula that was agreeable to the majority of the officially recognized opposition parties, all of which then boycotted the June 1990 local elections in which the RCD won 98 per cent of the seats.[87] The result was very much a stalemate:

Ben Ali was able to use the threat of electoral competition to reorganize and revive the single party but was unsuccessful in his attempt to use the formula of a national pact to provide an agreed framework for a controlled multi-party democracy. [88]

The process of political restructuring in Algeria differed in several important ways from that in Tunisia. For one thing, it was triggered off by a major series of popular demonstrations which seemed to be aimed specifically at the FLN-dominated government and its economic policies. For another, the political side of the process was always seen as complementary to the economic, and to be concerned, much more directly than in Tunisia, with the FLN's role in the management of the economy and the opposition of many of its senior figures to any attack on the state sector and its emphasis on heavy industry. Indeed, if there was a parallel with processes elsewhere it was much more with the first years of perestroika in the Soviet Union, a point that was often stressed by President Chadli and many of his senior colleagues. [89]

President Chadli's first announcement of political reforms was made only a few days after the demonstrations of October 1988. This was followed in February 1989 by the drafting of a new constitution which specifically removed all references to Algerian socialism and to the privileged position of the FLN. Next came a new parties law in July which established the rules under which new organizations could be officially recognized. As in Egypt, the law specifically banned any party based on religion or region; but also, as in Egypt, this did not prevent a number of such parties being formed, notably the Front Islamique de Salut (FIS) and the Rally for Culture and Democracy (RCD), representing Berber interests. July 1989 also saw the passage of a new electoral law based, like the one in Tunisia, on a provision that whatever party list won the majority of votes in any single constituency would obtain all the seats. Once again this was clearly designed to benefit the government party. However, when it came to the first multi-party local elections in June 1990 a similar provision was not enough to prevent the FIS from obtaining a comprehensive victory, winning 32 of the 48 provincial councils (as opposed to 14 for the FLN), 55 per cent of the local councils (against 32 per cent to the FLN) and the government of all the major cities. [90]

Meanwhile, the leadership of the FLN itself was experiencing the greatest difficulty in deciding how it should adapt itself to the new situation. President Chadli's own preferences seem originally to have been twofold. First, he wanted to accentuate the difference between party and government by, among other things, resigning as secretary general of the Front and then naming a cabinet of technocrats, many with only tenuous links with the FLN, to continue with his economic reforms. Second, he tried to get the FLN to reform itself and to open up to a variety of political tendencies under a new leader, Mohamed Mehri. However, all these moves were opposed by the forces within the organization, which were strong enough to hold on to their positions within the central committee during the FLN's December 1988 congress. Perhaps in response, Chadli began to advocate a more competitive political system in which the Front would still play a dominant role but could be challenged by other legalized political organizations, which he first called 'associations' and then parties.

This was the president's position in the summer of 1989 after the passage of the new electoral and parties law. Nevertheless, he was still slow to allow an open competition between the FLN and its opponents, and the local government elections were twice postponed, from December 1989 to the following March and then to June 1990. Meanwhile, the FLN managed to maintain a tenuous unity, even though there were major disputes between the reformers and the old guard at the December 1989 party congress.[91] Further problems followed the Front's humiliating defeat in the June 1990 local elections which exposed its continuing inability to generate mass support or to run a successful political campaign.[92] Whatever hopes it might have had continued to focus on the electoral law passed in April 1991, which was designed to provide it with as much advantage as possible in its struggle with its religious opponents.

The only single-party regimes where there was only minimal movement in the direction of political reform were those in Syria and Iraq. Leaders in both countries chose to pay only limited public attention to the local implications of perestroika in the Soviet Union or the collapse of the Communist parties throughout most of eastern Europe in 1989/90. In Syria the only concession made by President Asad was to increase to one-third the number of seats reserved for independent candidates during the May 1990 elections to the national assembly. The result was a system in which the Ba'thi-dominated National Progressive Front nominated two-thirds of the candidates in any one constituency, with independents, on a separate list, competing for the remaining seats. As the president himself noted in a speech to the Students' Union Congress, although many people in Syria were convinced that elections on a party basis were best, he believed that this was not appropriate in the country's 'current phase' and preferred to combine features of a party and an individual system.[93] Something of the same practice was adopted in Iraq, where the elections of 1980, 1984 and 1988 were contested by a combination of Ba'this and independents, with the former taking between half and three-quarters of the seats.[94]

Notes

1 Lars Rudebeck, *Party and People: A Study of Political Change in Tunisia* (Stockholm: Almqvist & Wiksell, 1967), pp. 29–32.
2 Michael C. Hudson, *Arab Politics: The Search for Legitimacy* (New Haven: Yale University Press, 1977), p. 386.
3 Rudebeck, *Party and People*, pp. 33–4.
4 Ibid., p. 33; Clement Henry Moore, *Politics in North Africa: Algeria, Morocco and Tunisia* (Boston, MA: Little, Brown, 1970), p. 319.
5 Ibid., p. 229.
6 John P. Entelis, *Comparative Politics of North Africa: Algeria, Morocco and Tunisia* (Syracuse, NY: Syracuse University Press, 1980), p. 136.
7 Asma Larif-Beatrix, 'L'évolution de l'état tunisien', *Maghreb/ Machreq*, 116 (April/May/June, 1987), p. 43.
8 Entelis, *Comparative Politics of North Africa*, p. 139.
9 Clement Henry Moore, 'Tunisia: The prospects for institutionalization', in Samuel P. Huntington and Clement Henry Moore (eds), *Authoritarian Politics in Modern Societies: The Dynamics of Established One Party Systems* (New York: Basic Books, 1970), p. 318.
10 Ibid., pp. 319–20; Elbaki Hermassi, *Leadership and National Development in North Africa: A Comparative Study* (Berkeley, CA: University of California Press, 1972), p. 165; Rudebeck, *Party and People*, pp. 143–4.
11 Entelis, *Comparative Politics of North Africa*, p. 140.
12 David and Marina Ottoway, *Algeria: The Politics of a Socialist Revolution* (Berkeley and Los Angeles: University of California Press, 1970), pp. 71–4.
13 Ibid., pp. 117, 123–4, 180.
14 Henry F. Jackson, *The FLN in Algeria: Party Development in a Revolutionary Society* (Westport, Connecticut, and London: Greenwood Press, 1977), pp. 203–4.
15 Hugh Roberts, 'The politics of Algerian socialism', in R.I. Lawless and Allan M. Findlay (eds), *North Africa: Contemporary Politics and Economic Development* (London: Croom Helm, 1984), pp. 27–8.

282 II: Contemporary politics

16 Hugh Roberts, 'The Algerian bureaucracy', in Talal Asad and Roger Owen (eds), *Sociology of 'Developing Societies': The Middle East* (London and Basingstoke: Macmillan, 1983), p. 113.
17 Entelis, *Comparative Politics of North Africa*, pp. 115–16.
18 Roberts, 'The politics of Algerian socialism', pp. 31–2.
19 Ibid., pp. 35–8.
20 Entelis, *Comparative Politics of North Africa*, pp. 115–16.
21 See, for example, President Asad's own background, in Patrick Seale, *Asad: The Struggle for the Middle East* (London: I. B. Tauris, 1988), Ch. 3; or the dates on which leading Iraqi's joined the Ba'th party, in Amatzia Baram, 'The ruling political elite in Ba'thi Iraq, 1968–1986: The changing features of a collective profile', *International Journal of Middle East Studies*, 21/4 (Nov., 1989), Appendix 3.
22 See, for example, the 'Theoretical Propositions adopted by the VIth Congress of the Party in Oct. 1963', *Nidal hizb al Ba'th al-'Arabi al-Isthiraki 'abra mu'tamaratih al-qawmiya (1947–1964)* (Beirut: Dar al-Tali'a, 1971), pp. 172ff.
23 Raymond A. Hinnebusch, *Authoritarian Power and State Formation in Ba'thist Syria: Army, Party and Peasant* (Boulder, Colorado: Westview Press, 1990), pp. 130–3.
24 For example, Seale, *Asad*, pp. 145–8; Malcolm H. Kerr, 'Hafiz Asad and the changing patterns of Syrian politics', *International Journal*, XXVIII, 4 (Autumn, 1973), pp. 697–700.
25 Hinnebusch, *Authoritarian Power*, pp. 145–7, 166–77.
26 Ibid., pp. 178–9
27 Ibid., pp. 177–85.
28 Ibid., p. 312; Yahia M. Sadowski, 'Ba'thist ethics and the spirit of state capitalism', in Peter J. Chelkowski and Robert J. Pranger (eds), *Ideology and Power in the Middle East* (Durham, NC, and London: Duke University Press, 1988), pp. 168–70.
29 Alasdair Drysdale, 'The succession question in Syria', *Middle East Journal*, 39/2 (Spring, 1985), pp. 246–57.
30 Hinnebusch, *Authoritarian Power*, pp. 316–17.
31 Christine Moss Helms, *Iraq: Eastern Front of the Arab World* (Washington, DC: The Brookings Institute, 1984), p. 87.
32 See, for example, the Ba'th Party's newspaper *al-Thawra*, 14 Feb. 1980, quoted in Ofra Bengio, 'Iraq', in Colin Legum (ed.), *Middle East Contemporary Survey*, IV, 1979–80 (London and New York: Holmes & Meier, 1981), p. 505.
33 Youssef M. Ibrahim, 'How the Baath rules Iraq: With a very tight fist', *New York Times* (11 Jan. 1981).
34 'Statement of the Iraqi Ba'th Party Ninth Regional Congress – 27 June 1982', quoted in Ofra Bengio, 'Iraq', in Legum *et al.* (eds), *Middle East Contemporary Survey*, 6, 1981–2 (London and New York: Holmes & Meier, 1983), pp. 588–90.
35 'Iraq privatises its tourist industry', *CAABU Bulletin*, 4/17 (15 Sept., 1988), p. 8.
36 Eberhard Kienle, *Ba'th v Ba'th: The Conflict Between Syria and Iraq 1968–1989* (London and New York: I.B. Tauris, 1990), pp. 38–46.

37 Helms, *Iraq*, pp. 105–6.
38 Ibid., p. 104.
39 For example, Saddam Hussain's 'Interview with Arab and foreign journalists', in *Saddam Hussein on Current Events in Iraq*, trans. (London: Longman, 1977), p. 48; or 'Arab Ba'th Social Party', *The Revolution of the New Way* by Tariq 'Aziz (n.p., n.d., printed in March 1977), pp. 30, 37.
40 'Statement of the Iraqi Ba'th Party Ninth Regional Congress', pp. 616, 618.
41 John Waterbury, *The Egypt of Nasser and Sadat: The Political Economy of Two Regimes* (Princeton, NJ: Princeton University Press, 1983), p. 313.
42 Leonard Binder, *In a Moment of Enthusiasm: Political Power and the Second Stratum in Egypt* (Chicago and London: University of Chicago Press, 1978), pp. 36, 41, 43.
43 Ibid., p. 307.
44 Ibid., pp. 36–7, 43–4.
45 Ibid., p. 315.
46 Ibid., pp. 43, 310; Raymond Baker, *Egypt's Uncertain Revolution Under Nasser and Sadat* (Cambridge, MA: Harvard University Press, 1978), p. 96.
47 Binder, *In a Moment of Enthusiasm*, p. 310; El Kosheri Mahfouz, *Socialisme et pouvoir en Egypte* (Paris: Librairie Générale de Droit et de Jurisprudence, 1972), p. 173.
48 Mark H. Cooper, *The Transformation of Egypt* (London: Croom Helm, 1982), p. 31.
49 Clement Henry Moore, *Images of Development: Egyptian Engineers in Search of Industry* (Cambridge, Mass., and London: The MIT Press, 1980), p. 58; Baker, *Egypt's Uncertain Revolution*, pp. 84–5.
50 Waterbury, *Egypt of Nasser and Sadat*, p. 323; Mahfouz, *Socialisme et pouvoir*, p. 177.
51 Waterbury, *Egypt of Nasser and Sadat*, p. 315; Cooper, *Transformation of Egypt*, p. 31.
52 Mahfouz, *Socialisme et pouvoir*, pp. 125–7.
53 Cited in Binder, *In a Moment of Enthusiasm*, pp. 332–3.
54 Mahfouz, *Socialisme et pouvoir*, p. 177.
55 Binder, *In a Moment of Enthusiasm*, p. 370.
56 Baker, *Egypt's Uncertain Revolution*, p. 108.
57 Waterbury, *Egypt of Nasser and Sadat*, p. 331.
58 Nathan Alexander, 'Libya: The continuous revolution', *Middle Eastern Studies*, 17/2 (April, 1981), pp. 214–16.
59 Omar I. Fathaly and Monte Palmer, 'Opposition to rural change in Libya', *International Journal of Middle East Studies*, 11 (1980), p. 247.
60 T. Niblock, *Class and Power in Sudan: The Dynamics of Sudanese Politics 1898–1985* (Basingstoke and London: Macmillan, 1987), pp. 256–9.
61 Peter Woodward, 'Parliaments and parties', in Muddathir Abd al-Rahim, Raphael Badal, Alan Hardallo and Peter Woodward (eds),

Sudan Since Independence: Studies in Political Development Since 1956
(Aldershot and Brookfield, Vermont: Gower, 1986), p. 61.
62 Niblock, *Class and Power*, pp. 259–60.
63 Ibid., pp. 268ff.
64 Ibid., p. 272; Peter K. Bechtold, 'The contemporary Sudan',
American-Arab Affairs, 6 (Fall, 1983), p. 93.
65 Woodward, 'Parties and parliaments', p. 62.
66 T.Niblock, 'The background to the change of government in 1984',
in Peter Woodward (ed.), *Sudan Since Nimeri* (London: Centre for
Middle Eastern Studies, School of African and Oriental Studies,
London University, 1986), pp. 38–9.
67 Details in Christian Lachon, 'Apropos élections soudanaises d'avril
1986', *L'Afrique et L'Asie Modernes* (Spring, 1987).
68 Cooper gives the most comprehensive account of this process in
Transformation of Egypt, Chs 8–11.
69 Ibid., Ch. 11; Raymond A. Hinnebusch Jr, *Egyptian Politics Under
Sadat: The Post-Populist Development of An Authoritarian-Modernizing
State* (Cambridge: Cambridge University Press, 1985), pp. 158–9;
Waterbury, *Egypt of Nasser and Sadat*, pp. 354–9, 364–6.
70 Cooper, *Transformation of Egypt*, pp. 194–8.
71 Waterbury, *Egypt of Nasser and Sadat*, p. 368.
72 Robert Bianchi, *Unruly Corporatism: Associational Life in Twentieth-
Century Egypt* (Oxford: Oxford University Press, 1989), pp. 84–6.
73 Information supplied by Ahmad Bahaeddin.
74 For full results see *Revue de la Presse égyptienne* (Cairo), 13 (July
1984), pp. 11–27.
75 Bertus Hendricks, 'Egypt's elections, Mubarak's bond', *MERIP*, 14/1
(Jan., 1985).
76 Electors who were unable to find the proper polling station included
a minister of state for foreign affairs, Butros Butros Ghali.
77 For results see *Revue de la Presse égyptienne*, 27 (1987), p. 245.
78 Bertus Hendricks, 'Egypt's new political map: Report from the
election campaign', *MERIP*, 17/4 (July–August, 1987); Adel
Darwish, 'Mubarak's electoral triumph', *The Middle East*, 151 (May,
1987), pp. 11–14.
79 For example, ibid., p. 11.
80 Guy Hermet, 'State controlled elections: A framework', in Guy
Hermet, Richard Rose and Alain Rouquié (eds), *Elections Without
Choices* (London and Basingstoke: Macmillan, 1978), pp. 3–16.
81 Ibid., p. 3.
82 Enid Hill, 'Political issues and justifiable questions: Adjudicating the
constitutionality of laws in Egypt', mimeo (paper presented to panel
on 'Law and Society', Middle East Studies Association, San Antonio,
November 1990, pp. 12–19).
83 Max Rodenbeck, 'Egypt: disdain and apathy', *Middle East International*, 7 December 1990, pp. 15–16.
84 John R. Nellis, 'A comparative assessment of the development
performances of Algeria and Tunisia', *Middle East Journal*, 37/3
(1983), p. 375.

85 Fred Halliday, 'Tunisia's uncertain future', *Middle East Report*, 163 (March/April, 1990), p. 25.

86 Lisa Anderson, 'The Tunisian National Pact of 1988', *Government and Opposition*, 26/2 (Spring, 1991), pp. 244–60.

87 'Tunisia: Sharp contrast', *Middle East International*, 378 (22 June 1990), p. 10.

88 Idem.

89 But the similarity is also rejected by some, for example, Mahfoud Bennoune, 'Algeria's facade of democracy', *Middle East Report*, 163 (March–April, 1990), p. 13.

90 Arun Kapil, 'Algeria's elections show Islamist strength', *Middle East Report*, 166 (Sept.–Oct., 1990), p. 31.

91 Bennoune, 'Algeria's facade of democracy', pp. 12–13.

92 Kapil, 'Algeria's elections', pp. 34–5.

93 Reuters, RTU242 4 XEL 316, 'Syria-Elections', Damascus, 16 May 1990.

94 Ofra Bengio, 'Iraq', in Itimar Rabinovitch and Haim Shaked (eds), *Middle East Contemporary Survey*, IX (Tel Aviv: The Moshe Dayan Centre for Middle Eastern and African Studies, Tel Aviv University, 1989), p. 464.

Epilogue: Towards the 21st century

The Gulf War of February and March 1991 proved a major test of many of the arguments put forward in this book: the durability of regimes; the importance of state nationalism as opposed to region-wide Arab or religious solidarity; the viability of civilian control over the military; and, perhaps most important of all, the strength of the whole post-colonial order in the Middle East. By and large, its outcome was a vindication of most of these hypotheses. The war was launched by the United States and its Arab allies to defeat an explicit Iraqi challenge to existing boundaries and regimes. In the short run, at least, it caused serious divisions inside Arab nationalist and Islamic groups. Existing patterns of political control over the military were confirmed: in Iraq, where Saddam Hussain continued to ignore the advice of his senior commanders; in Turkey; and in Saudi Arabia and the Gulf, where the appeal for American assistance was seen by the ruling families as a necessary consequence of the impossibility – for both technical and political reasons – of creating professional armies large enough to defend themselves.

And yet, in the slightly longer run, the impact of the war was bound to affect the existing *status quo* in a variety of ways. This can be seen most clearly in terms of the political future of the two states most immediately involved, Iraq and Kuwait. As far as Iraq is concerned the war, and its aftermath, posed an enormous challenge not only to Saddam Hussain's system of control but also to its sovereign integrity as a result of the growing pressure for Kurdish autonomy in the north. As for Kuwait, the legitimacy of family rule was seriously called into question as a result of its failure, first to ward off the Iraqi threat, and then to rebuild the shattered political and social structure along lines satisfactory to the majority of its citizens.

What happens in Iraq and Kuwait will be closely watched in neighbouring states. Behind Iraq stands Syria, with its similar system of political control now so firmly entrenched as to make it almost impossible for its architect – President Hafiz al-Asad – to alter without seriously undermining his own power. And behind Kuwait stand all the other family states whose rulers' skills of leadership and government were put to an almost equally searching test. They too face the problem of maintaining their own unity while addressing the difficult task of working out whether they can allow even the smallest increase in popular participation without creating a major challenge to their own authority. It has been a major argument of this book that the transition to constitutional rule is virtually impossible: families base their right to rule on their ability to take care of the key issues of internal security, foreign policy and defence, and if these are removed it is difficult to see what lesser role they can be expected to perform.

The Gulf War also had an immediate impact on the balance of power in the eastern part of the region. For the time being, at least, the strength of Iraq was severely weakened. Meanwhile, Turkey was added to the list of non-Arab actors – notably Israel and Iran – whose alliances or relations with Arab states formed an essential ingredient in the existing order. This will have an important impact on attempts to deal with many of the most sensitive local issues: the GCC's states' effort to secure their own defence; the reconstruction of Lebanon; and the future of those two stateless peoples, the Kurds and the Palestinians. The result will be enough to ensure that this part of the Middle East will exist in a condition of considerable international tension for many years to come.

In North Africa, the Gulf War produced a series of more mixed effects. As far as the regimes themselves were concerned, the majority derived some benefit from it in the short run. In Egypt, the financial compensations it received from the members of the American-led coalition emboldened its government to sign an agreement with the IMF and World Bank designed to take advantage of these favourable circumstances to obtain a huge reduction in the debts owed to its major creditors grouped together in the so-called 'Club of Paris'. To do this it had to agree to implement a series of price rises and cuts in subsidies designed to reduce the budget deficit, as well as to a longer-term programme of economic restructuring involving the removal of price distortions and the wholesale reorganization of the public sector. In Tunisia, Algeria and Morocco, the immediate advantage came from the disarray of the Islamic religious opposition, caught as it was between loyalty to Saudi Arabia, which provided it with finance and other support, and its fear of a further extension of American and western influence. Among other things, this allowed the Algerian regime, and the still FLN-dominated national assembly, more leeway when it came to drafting the electoral law that would govern the future general election. Meanwhile, the only North African regime that was seriously weakened by the war was that of Sudan, which lost much international support as a result of its overt pro-Iraqi stand.

The splits in many North African oppositions posed a severe check to those who had hoped for either a united Arab or a united religious response to the crisis. Indeed, there were some who made the point that the forces of Islamic renewal received a major blow to their claims to represent a homogeneous, region-wide, movement. But this is too simple a claim. While the leaderships of the various movements were certainly deeply divided, there is much evidence that the majority of their followers were deeply affected by Saddam Hussain's various Arabist appeals and deeply opposed to a war led by the United States to regain Kuwait. And it follows that, even if Arab unity remained a distant aspiration, popular feelings of Arabism and the need for Arab solidarity were as alive as they ever were – perhaps even more so to judge from the hundreds of thousands of anti-war demonstrators in Algeria and Morocco, the two Arab countries that were, geographically, furthest away from the centre of the Gulf crisis. However, as always, such popular sentiments required political guidance and leadership if they were to make a coherent impact across state boundaries.

The division between North Africa and the eastern end of the Middle East provides a useful clue to future developments. In North Africa, with the possible exception of Libya, the major problems are seen to be domestic and internal to each state, and to demand a satisfactory process of economic and political reform. This at once places the region in something of the same condition as eastern Europe, with many of the same difficulties involved in trying to alter deeply entrenched systems of economic management containing all the vested interests and monopolies that have grown up since independence. They also share the question of how best to accommodate the growing power of the

European Community. All this raises a more fundamental issue as well: can such states combine whatever advances they have already made towards industrialization and welfarism with membership in an international order which requires that they abandon many of their basic policies of protection and control? A final and essential preoccupation will be with the practicalities of organizing elections and parliamentary procedures in such a way as to combine regime control with the demands for greater freedom and governmental accountability.

In the east, however, the unsettled relations between states, both Arab and non-Arab, will continue to play an enormous role in domestic politics. In some cases, as in the West Bank and Lebanon, basic questions of sovereignty still remain to be settled. In others, like Jordan, Iraq and Kuwait, their boundaries have still not solidified sufficiently for regimes to be completely confident that they will remain sovereign over all their present territory in the years to come. Partly because of this, a general movement in the direction of economic and political reform in the Arab states of this part of the Middle East will take longer to gain momentum. Such a movement will also continue to be constrained by the presence of large oil revenues that reduce the economic pressures for immediate change.

Viewed from this perspective, the most important Arab country in terms of the regional impact of its policies will be Egypt, with its central position between the eastern part of the region and North Africa. It was an Egyptian regime that was the first to attempt to create a one-party state devoted to rapid economic and social change, and then the first to embark on the difficult path of major political and economic reform. In both cases the lessons of these experiments proved extremely influential – as well as threatening – for its Arab neighbours. Egypt's foreign policy will also be of great importance as it resumes leadership of the Arab League and uses its considerable diplomatic expertise to try to create new frameworks for Arab co-operation and interaction while remaining closely linked to Israel and the United States. Should all this fail, should the regime be overthrown by an Islamic or a political radical movement, this too will have major repercussions throughout the rest of the region.

Turning to the major non-Arab states of the Middle East, the political future of two of them – Israel and Iran – will remain greatly influenced by the demands of their own very special social and religious experiments as Jewish and Islamic states respectively. As before, this will have a considerable impact on political rhetoric and political practice, on definitions of citizenship and on attempts to create new agendas. It will also act as a brake on programmes to reduce the power of the public sector over the economy, which will continue to be defended in terms of those ideological necessities that lie right at the heart of each national project. Against this, Turkey's economic and political future will depend more and more on its links with the European Community, whether or not it obtains full membership. Such links should be enough to ensure that present political and economic practices continue to operate in the same general way.

Finally, it has been a major theme of this book that Middle Eastern politics are much less unpredictable than is often supposed and that this stems from the fact that the structures that support them have a stability and a logic that permit systematic analysis. The proof of such an assertion must lie not only in whether or not such an approach is a guide to the present but whether it also stands the test of time.

Select bibliography

Chapter 1 The end of empires: the emergence of the modern Middle Eastern states

Albert Hourani, *A History of the Arab Peoples* (London: Faber, 1991; Cambridge, MA: Belknap/Harvard, 1991).

Philip S. Khoury, *Syria and the French Mandate: The Politics of Arab Nationalism 1920–1945* (Princeton, NJ: Princeton University Press, 1987; London: I.B. Tauris, 1987).

Elizabeth Monroe, *Britain's Moment in the Middle East 1914–1956* (London: Chatto & Windus, 1963).

Clement Henry Moore, *The Politics of North Africa: Algeria, Morocco and Tunisia* (Boston, MA: Little, Brown, 1970).

M.E. Yapp, *The Near East Since the First World War* (London and New York: Longman, 1991).

Sami Zubaida, *Islam, the People and the State* (London and New York: Routledge, 1989).

Chapter 2 The growth of state power in the Arab world: the single-party regimes

Adeed Dawisha and I. William Zartman (eds), *Beyond Coercion: The Durability of the Arab State* (London: Croom Helm, 1988).

Bruno Etienne, *L'Algérie: Cultures et révolution* (Paris: Editions du Seuil, 1977).

Raymond A. Hinnebusch, *Authoritarian Power and State Transformation in Ba'thist Syria: Army, Party and Peasant* (Boulder, CO: Westview Press, 1990).

Michael C. Hudson, *Arab Politics: The Search for Legitimacy* (New Haven, CN, and London: Yale University Press, 1977).

Samir Al-Khalil, *The Republic of Fear: The Politics of Modern Iraq* (London: Radius, 1989).

Joel S. Migdal, *Weak States and Strong Societies: State-Society Relations and State Capabilities in the Third World* (Princeton, NJ: Princeton University Press, 1988).

C.H. Moore, 'Authoritarian politics in unincorporated society', *Comparative Politics*, 4/2 (Jan., 1974).

Peter Sluglett and Marion Farouk-Sluglett, *Iraq Since 1958: From Revolution to Dictatorship* (London and New York: Kegan Paul International, 1987).

John Waterbury, *The Egypt of Nasser and Sadat: The Political Economy of Two Regimes* (Princeton, NJ: Princeton University Press, 1983).

Chapter 3 The growth of state power in the Arab world under family rule, and the Libyan alternative

Nathan Alexander, 'Libya: The continuous revolution', *Middle Eastern Studies*, XVII/2 (April, 1981).

John Davies, *Libyan Politics: Tribe and Revolution* (London: I.B. Tauris, 1987).

Giacomo Luciani (ed.), *The Arab State* (London: Routledge, 1990).

G.S. Samore, *Royal Family Politics in Saudi Arabia (1953–1982)*, Harvard University PhD, 1984 (University Microfilms).

John Waterbury, *The Commander of the Faithful: The Moroccan Political Elite: A Study of Segmented Politics* (London: Weidenfeld & Nicholson, 1970).

Valerie Yorke, *Domestic Politics and Regional Security: Jordan, Syria and Israel* (Aldershot: Gower, 1988).

Rosemary Said Zahlan, *The Making of the Modern Gulf States* (London: Unwin Hyman, 1989).

Chapter 4 Arab nationalism, Arab unity and the practice of intra-Arab state relations

Benedict Anderson, *Imagined Communities: Reflections on the Origin and Spread of Nationalism* (London: Verso, 1983).

Amatzia Baram, *Culture, History and Ideology in the Formation of Ba'thist Iraq, 1968–89* (Basingstoke and London: Macmillan/ St Antony's, 1991).

Georges Corm, *Fragmentation of the Middle East: The Last Thirty Years* (London: Hutchinson Education, 1988).

C. Ernest Dawn, *From Ottomanism to Arabism. Essays on the Origins of Arab Nationalism* (Urbana, II: University of Illinois Press, 1973).

Ernest Gellner, *Nations and Nationalism* (Oxford: Basil Blackwell, 1983).

Sylvia G. Haim (ed.), *Arab Nationalism: An Anthology* (Los Angeles, CA: University of California Press, 1962).

Ahmed M. Gomaa, *The Foundations of the League of Arab States: Wartime Diplomacy and Inter-Arab Politics 1941 to 1945* (London and New York: Longman, 1977).

Malcolm Kerr, *The Arab Cold War: A Study of Ideology in Politics* (Oxford: Oxford University Press, 1965).

Baghat Korany and Ali E. Hilal Dessouki, *The Foreign Policy of the Arab States* (Boulder, CO, and London: Westview Press; Cairo: The American University of Cairo Press, 1984).

Yehoshua Porath, *In Search for Arab Unity, 1930–1945* (London: Frank Cass, 1986).

Chapter 5 State and politics in Israel, Iran and Turkey from the Second World War

Ervand Abrahamian, *Iraq Between Two Revolutions* (Princeton, NJ: Princeton University Press, 1982).

Fahkreddin Azimi, *Iran: The Crisis of Democracy* (London: I.B. Tauris, 1989).

Feroz Ahmad, *The Making of Modern Turkey* (London: HarperCollins, 1991).

Metin Heper and Ahmet Evin, *State, Democracy and the Military: Turkey in the 1980s* (Berlin and New York: Walter de Gruyter, 1988).

Dan Horowitz and Moshe Lissak, *Origins of the Israeli Polity: Palestine Under the Mandate* (Chicago, Il, and London: Chicago University Press, 1978).

Caglar Keyder, *State and Class: A Study of Capitalist Development* (London and New York: Verso, 1987).

Don Peretz, *The Government and Politics of Israel*, 2nd edn (Boulder, CO: Westview Press, 1983).

Chapter 6 The politics of economic restructuring

Tusun Aricanli and Dani Rodrick (eds), *The Political Economy of Turkey: Adjustment and Sustainability* (London: Macmillan, 1990).

R. Bianchi, *Unruly Corporatism: Associational Life in Twentieth-Century Egypt* (Oxford: Oxford University Press, 1989).

Patrick Clawson, 'Islamic Iran's economic policies and prospects', *Middle East Journal*, 42/3 (Summer, 1988).

S. El Naggar (ed.), *Privatization and Structural Adjustment in the Arab Countries* (Washington, DC: International Monetary Fund, 1989).

Mustafa Kamel Al Sayyid, 'Privatization: The Egyptian debate', *Cairo Papers in Social Science* (The American University in Cairo), 13/4 (Winter, 1990).

Michael Shalev, *Labour and the Political Economy of Israel* (Oxford: Oxford University Press, 1991).

Rosemary Thorp and Lawrence Whitehead (eds), *Latin American Debt and the Adjustment Crisis* (London: Macmillan/St Antony's, 1987).

Chapter 7 The politics of religion

Ervand Abrahamian, 'Khomeini: Fundamentalist or populist?', *New Left Review,* 186 (March/April, 1991).

Richard T. Antoun and Mary Hegland (eds), *Religious Resurgence: Contemporary Cases in Islam, Christianity and Judaism* (Syracuse, NY: Syracuse University Press, 1987).

Nazih Ayubi, *Political Islam: Religion and Politics in the Arab World* (London and New York: Routledge, 1991).

R.P. Mitchell, *The Society of the Muslim Brothers* (Oxford: Oxford University Press, 1969).

Henry Munson, Jr, *Islam and Revolution in the Middle East* (New Haven, CN, and London: Yale University Press, 1988).

James P. Piscatori (ed.), *Islam in the Political Process* (Cambridge: Cambridge University Press, 1983).

Emmanuel Sivan, *Radical Islam: Medieval Theology and Modern Politics* (New Haven, CN: Yale University Press, 1985).

Emmanuel Sivan and Menachem Friedman (eds), *Religious Radicalism and Politics in the Middle East* (Albany, NY: State University of New York Press, 1990).

Sami Zubaida, 'An Islamic state? The case of Iran', *Middle East Report,* 153 (July/Aug., 1988).

Chapter 8 The military in state and society

William Hale, 'Military rule and political change in Turkey', in A. Gokalp (ed.), *La Turquie en transition* (Paris: Maisonneuve et Larose, 1986).

Mehmet Ali Birand, *The Generals' Coup in Turkey: An Inside Story of 12 September 1980* (London: Brassey's, 1987).

Robin Luckham, *The Nigerian Military: A Sociological Analysis of Authority and Revolt 1960–67* (Cambridge: Cambridge University Press, 1971).

Yoram Peri, *Between Battles and Ballots: Israeli Military in Politics* (Cambridge: Cambridge University Press, 1983).

Elizabeth Picard, 'Arab military in politics: from the revolutionary plot to the authoritarian state', in Dawisha and Zartman (eds), *Beyond Coercion.*

Robert Springborg, *Mubarak's Egypt: Fragmentation of the Political Order* (Boulder, CO, and London: Kegan Paul International, 1987).

P.J. Vatikiotis, *Politics and the Military in Jordan: A Study of the Arab Legion 1921–1957* (London: Frank Cass, 1967).

Sepehr Zabih, *The Iranian Military in Revolution and War* (London and New York: Routledge, 1988).

Chapter 9 Parties and elections

Feroz Ahmad, 'The transition to democracy in Turkey', *Third World Quarterly*, VIII/2 (April, 1985).

Asher Arian and Michael Shamir (eds), *The Elections in Israel – 1984* (New Brunswick, NJ: Transaction Books, 1986); and *The Elections in Israel – 1988* (Boulder, CO: Westview Press, 1990).

Abdo I. Baaklini, *Legislative and Political Development: Lebanon 1842–1972* (Durham, NC: Duke University Press, 1976).

Izthak Galnoor, 'The 1984 elections in Israel: Political results and open questions', *Middle East Review*, XVIII (1986).

J.E. Peterson, *The Arab Gulf States: Steps Towards Political Participation* (New York: Praeger, 1988).

I. William Zartman, 'Political pluralism in Morocco', in I. William Zartman (ed.), *Man, State and Society in the Contemporary Maghrib* (London: Pall Mall Press, 1973).

Chapter 10 Single-party systems and the return to greater democracy

C.M. Helms, *Iraq: Eastern Flank of the Arab World* (Washington, DC: The Brookings Institution, 1984).

Guy Hermet, Richard Rose and Alain Rouquié, *Elections Without Choices* (Basingstoke and London: Macmillan, 1978).

Clement Henry Moore, *Tunisia Since Independence: The Dynamics of One Party Government* (Berkeley, CA: University of California Press, 1965).

T. Niblock, *Class and Power in Sudan: The Dynamics of Sudanese Politics 1898–1985* (Basingstoke and London: Macmillan, 1987).

Hugh Roberts, 'The politics of Algerian Socialism', in R.I. Lawless and Allan M. Findley (eds), *North Africa: Contemporary Politics and Economic Development* (London: Croom Helm, 1984).

Index

Note: Numbers in italics refer to figures or tables where these are separate from the textual reference.